Suicide

of related interest

Music Therapy Research and Practice in Medicine
From Out of the Silence
David Aldridge
ISBN 1 85302 296 9

The Social Symbolism of Grief and Mourning
Roger Grainger
ISBN 1 85302 480 5

Suicide

The Tragedy of Hopelessness

David Aldridge

Jessica Kingsley Publishers
London and Philadelphia

First published in the United Kingdom in 1998 by
Jessica Kingsley Publishers Ltd,
116 Pentonville Road,
London N1 9JB, England
and
325 Chestnut Street
Philadelphia, PA 19106, USA.

www.jkp.com

Second impression 1999

Library of Congress Cataloging in Publication Data
A CIP catalog record for this book is available from the Library of Congress

British Library Cataloguing in Publication Data
Aldridge, David
Suicide: the tragedy of hopelessness
1. Suicide
I. Title
616.8'58445

ISBN 1 85302 444 9

Printed and Bound in Great Britain by
Athenaeum Press, Gateshead, Tyne and Wear

Contents

List of figures

List of tables

This book is dedicated to Emily

Acknowledgements

My special thanks go to Jacqueline Gannoway for being my friend and colleague. I would also like to thank Rudi Dallos for the academic and personal support, and inspiration, that he gave me during this research and without whom the work would never have been completed. This research was supported by the Open University, Milton Keynes and provided the basis for my doctoral thesis.

Note: All names of patients and their families have been changed.

CHAPTER ONE

The Tragedy of Hopelessness

The grim bottom line therefore is that suicide, in a double sense, will prove to be the death of the future. (Diekstra 1996, p.21)

...we can no longer, as social workers or social scientists, claim to make authoritative judgements about individual or social problems based upon scientific objectivity any more than we can seek certainty in tradition. Instead, we are in a world which is more relativist, more modest in its knowledge claims and hopefully more sensitive to cultural difference as the eurocentric base of modernity becomes clearer to us. (Leonard 1996, p.23)

One morning my daughter rang from abroad. She asked me to telephone her back and, like most fathers with grown up daughters, I knew from the sound of her voice that something wasn't quite right. She needed money. Those readers who are parents will recognise the plot so far. So, hearing her concern, I called her back. She needed money to buy flowers for her friend's funeral. One of her best friends, Ruth, had committed suicide. A week before they had been out shopping together and gone out to lunch. Ruth gave no obvious clues as to what she was about to do, nor that she was in any way disturbed. The death of a close friend was difficult enough to cope with, but how was my daughter to reconcile to herself the feelings following the manner of her friend's death. This book then, like the conversation between daughter and father, isn't about money or flowers, its about relationships and understanding despair. Its a father's attempt to explain to his daughter what happened and an acknowledgement that no matter how hard we try as parents to prepare our children for the world, there are some matters left undone.

Within the heart of our late-twentieth-century industrial societies we are experiencing the phenomenon of young people killing themselves. And not only that, at the opposite end of the age spectrum, old people too are choosing death before life in ever-increasing numbers. In the following pages I hope to try and make sense of this age-old phenomenon such that we can perhaps understand how, as the architects of well-being, we can close the doors of despair. For those working with the suicidal, I hope that the voices of the people with whom I have worked will resonate and bring a patient's understanding to the process of suffering. In many of the chapters I will be using material from clinical practice in varying therapeutic settings and from letters that women have written to me.

My interest in the problem of suicide was raised to another level after working the Samaritan night shift one summer in the 1980s. Although there were the usual desperate telephone callers abandoned alone to their own terrors of the night, there had been no alarms where anyone had been actively suicidal. Yet, as morning dawned, a colleague came to relieve me from my vigil with the news that the local emergency ward had admitted six people who had attempted suicide in the night. Clearly, what we were striving to provide as a service wasn't meeting the needs of those who were indeed desperate. Driving home, I saw an advertisement for our crisis service that pictured the harrowed face of a middle-aged woman. How did this relate to the young men and women lying in the hospital ward? Would they identify themselves with this image? So began a study of what factors were involved with suicidal behaviour and what could be done to alleviate the problem.

Like all academics, I was trained to distance myself from events and with such distance and thoroughness of investigation I hoped to learn the mysteries of human behaviour. However, in this task I must admit to having failed hopelessly for the presence of suicide and attempted suicide in our modern cultures cannot be left as an exercise of academic description alone. With each step of the way to understanding, and with each person with whom I spoke, I can reflect upon a personal anger that within so-called welfare communities, in the midst of nominative Christian cultures, we are witnessing the estrangement of those who are in despair. Before people kill themselves, or attempt to kill themselves, many of them have had a recent contact with a helping agency. Two-thirds of those that contact their general practitioner have received medication, which about half use to poison themselves (Stenager and Jensen 1994). Furthermore, within our helping endeavours, whether they be medicine, psychiatry or social work, there seems to be little understanding that it is the way that people live their lives together, and the meaning of those lives, that is of ultimate value. How we choose as a community to treat the sick, the poor, the old and the lonely contributes significantly to the distress of individuals. If that understanding exists, we still treat individuals rather than looking at the circumstances within which they live their lives.

A consequence of maintaining distance from people who are distressed is that we no longer identify with them. What if, for one moment, we look at the life of a distressed person sitting before us and actually understand the difficulties they face. A person isolated, dependent upon medication, abandoned by their family with little to eat and no roof over their head. Then we too would despair. It is at this crux of sympathetic engagement where, realising our own helplessness, we begin to label the other as being incompetent, beyond help or damaged. Too do otherwise challenges us to face up to the reality of own hopelessness and our own existential poverty. None of us in the healing trades likes to admit that we have limitations and that there are personal and social problems for which we can find no immediate remedies. Thus we transfer our own doubt onto those in our communities that are the weakest. That is the one explanation that I can find for the continuing way in which suicidal behaviour is ignored in its magnitude of occurrence in modern society and for the way in which practitioners treat their patients. A further explanation lies at the heart of medical science. Those practising medicine seek their success in cures. Death is the ultimate failure for curative strategies. Diseases have clear causes that can be identified. Suicidal behaviour challenges such an approach. Causes are multivarious and the causal trains complex. The treatment of those who are suicidal rarely brings simple successes that can be laid at the feet of the heroic therapist or the brilliant doctor. Furthermore, embedded in the logic of medical science, and in the heartland of statistics, is the notion that tomorrow will be the same as today. The future is predicated on the present. Yet most of us know that this is a philosophical stance that is seldom true. Indeed, many of our patients or clients hope for the opposite, that somehow tomorrow will be different. For patients in pain, the next pain-free day is a sign of change. Therapy is all about a changed future. It is when patients are forced to accept that the future will indeed be no different, that there is no escape from the past, that there are only curtailed promises from a statistical fate, that they then lose hope and become suicidal. Within medical science we have a flight from the realities of life by denying death and have tried to build security upon the false premises of statistics. Small wonder that there is a high rate of suicide among medical practitioners (Sonneck and Wagner 1996).

I am not going to abandon the individual in this book. As you will read in Chapter Six onwards, it is individual voices that tell their own stories. But these stories, the narratives of misfortune and grief, are told in the drama of a social world. Such a perspective is indeed complex, but so is the world of daily life and complexity must be grasped. Thus this book will wander between psychology, social psychology and sociology, gleaning understandings that fit. My intention is not to throw out what we know already, rather to build upon what is already known – sometimes re-interpreting what others have said – to propose a way of understanding that retains the complex drama of human life rather than the reduced facts of an academic treatise. At the heart of the work are the stories that people tell. Not only that, it's the way that they tell them and to whom they are told. In some ways this reflects a revolution in a corner of modern psychology. Our grasp of people's lives, if we are to help them, has to be made through the plots and players that are involved in daily living.

Stars that fade

As an introduction, I want to present three short case studies from popular culture that illustrate the process of becoming suicidal. As we will see in these stories, suicide is an event that occurs, but unlike many of the medical and epidemiological understandings that concentrate on isolated events, such an event is one in a series. It is not simply one event in a cross-section of similar events illustrating a statistically significant trend. Such an event is a culmination of similar events, the apotheosis of episodes of humiliation and hopelessness where, eventually, the story-line, for the individual, comes to a close. And that is where the plot becomes even more complex. The thread of each human story is interwoven as a personal narrative within the cloth of social life. Those who are left behind must also deal with their own distress. Like my daughter Emily, they ask themselves: 'Could we have asked the right question? Shouldn't we have recognised the signs? Wasn't there a clue somewhere in what she said?' Or say: 'If only we had done something differently, been a little more attentive, called more often.' So, while there are individual stories, these are woven together with the stories of others.

Kurt Cobain

Kurt Cobain, the musician, was 27 years old when he died. A legend to a younger generation, his celebrity suicide reflected a generation of youth despair. After taking both Valium and heroin, he locked himself in his garage and shot himself in the head with his shotgun. He had pioneered an alternative style of rock music, like others before him, that itself had been accommodated into the pop music world. As a singer and songwriter in the rock band Nirvana, he had attained a worldly success. He reflects an alarming trend; young men aged 15 to 29 years are a group at risk within New World and Old World communities.

Kurt Cobain's life was not always successful. He was described as a difficult child and teenager with problems that seemed to have been exacerbated by his parent's divorce when he was 8 years old. While rock music played an important part in his life, the abuse of various substances also assumed an influence on what he was to achieve. Within his tumultuous marriage, to another pop star, drug abuse was to play a significant role such that their child was taken from them briefly. He also suffered from chronic stomach pain and a severe depression that proved recalcitrant to treatment. Open talk of suicidal preoccupations and a previous attempt to kill himself, reported in the newspapers as an accident, are all clues as to a worsening situation. Furthermore, he had access to firearms (Jobes *et al.* 1996).

As we will see later, there are typical factors here for a completed suicide: his youth and gender, the abuse of drugs, continuing recalcitrant suffering, a history of delinquency and the availability of the means to kill himself. But this is only one picture of suicide. All suicides are not alike and the description of his life is taken from a particular perspective that highlights his deviancy as well as his genius. How such lives are interpreted will be a feature of this book. Who is telling the story, and to what end, is important.

Marilyn Monroe

Marilyn Monroe, the film star, also died in the pitiable circumstances of a questionable suicide. Anthony Summers (1992), in his book *Goddess*, brings together the varying strands of a life both glamorous and tragic. As in the above example, Marilyn Monroe lived a life that abused drugs and belonged to a milieu where drug abuse was common. If not openly accepted, there was a tacit acceptance of recreational drug use and the use of prescribed medications for personal problems and for sleeplessness. Combine this drug misuse into the cocktail of alcohol abuse and the scene is set for a tragedy. Throughout her life she had made several suicide attempts and talked openly of wanting to die. In her teenage years, when disappointed or depressed, she had taken overdoses of barbiturates. However, despite such abuse, she managed to remain alive and seemingly fit. Throughout her life she relied upon regular contact with her psychiatrist, to bring her back from the pit of despair, and her physician. As in the previous example, there is a continuing presence of illness and treatment. In the final days she became increasingly isolated, rejected by a lover and the fabric of her career was in tatters. Outwardly it seems she took an overdose of the barbiturate medication that until then she had managed to abuse and survive.

What we also see in the case of Marilyn Monroe is that understanding the cause of her death, and the reasons why she died, brings a complex story of events into play. Her suicidal behaviour was indicated in her early years. Apparently, she had made three attempts before she was twenty-one years old. We will read later that repetition of suicide attempts is a precursor to completed suicide. To prevent completed suicide then we need to prevent repeated attempts at suicide, and to prevent repetition we need to know how best to intervene at the first attempt. These matters will be addressed in the second half of the book from Chapter Seven onwards. What is also clear from her death is that the judgement about the nature of her dying is controversial, as we shall see later in this chapter.

Kenneth Williams

The open verdict returned by the coroner on the death of the British actor Kenneth Williams illustrates this point of controversy. While no one would want to overturn such a verdict, as his biographer also suggests, if we read his diaries we see that throughout his lifetime there was an underlying suicidal intent (Davies 1994). He died in 1988 at the age of 62 years. Four years previously he acknowledges, just before Christmas, that he is conscious of death all the time (p.708). He has been unemployed and depressed before and this depression, for him, seems to centre around the beginning of the new year, but its nature appears to be changing. Even the possibility of work has lost its attraction. By the winter of the following year he is still conscious of death and aware that fewer friends are calling to ask how he is. As he says, he is suicidally depressed. By the beginning of the new year he mentions this state of mind to his physician and gastroenterologist, who are treating him for what turns out to be a stomach ulcer. It is this intractable pain, and feelings of exhaustion, that brings him to the point where he feels there is no point in going on (p.801). Yet, what is also apparent from the diaries is that his aged mother, for whom he feels responsible, is becoming increasing feeble. While undoubtedly sincere in his caring for her, he is locked into the dilemma of becoming increasing annoyed with her. And he has the means to kill himself. He has a cache ready for when the moment comes, as he mentions two years earlier.

As we will read later, there are features here that are common with people that have committed suicide. He has the means, the intent is evident, his pain is persistent, and his social world is becoming impoverished. He is lonely and hopeless. It is this hopelessness in the face of life's difficulties that we see in all three examples and that will recur as a continuing theme. Similarly, it is apparent that all three had life-long friends and intimates that were dedicated to them. Yet, in the final moments, this friendship is ignored. Somehow they have become isolated from their immediate social contacts.

What we have to be aware of is that in dealing with the taboo of suicide, we seek to describe a world of personal deviance in the person that has died. Suicide is indeed a multi-dimensional malaise (Leenaars 1996; Levy, Jurkovic and Spirito 1995) and some of these dimensions are relational and social. Blaming individuals ignores the context in which they live and it is all too easy to shuffle out of our own responsibilities. On the other hand, I am aware that what I will be saying in this book can be seen as blaming those with whom the person lives. This is not intended. I am merely trying to shift away from the individualisation of deviance, the stigmatising of the other, to a position where we assume our communal responsibilities one for another. Blaming each other for a lack of understanding will not bring us any further, just as blaming the suicidal person for his predicament does not help him. A willingness to co-operate in bringing varying perspectives together may benefit our mutual understanding and, thereby, our mutual therapeutic endeavours.

While I have used stars from the world of entertainment as examples here, the rest of the book will deal with us lesser mortals, like my daughter's friend, stars from another firmament.

The bigger picture

Since the early 1960s there has been a massive increase in the numbers of people who intentionally overdose or deliberately injure themselves, which has led some commentators to suggest that it is unlikely that the problem of suicidal behaviour will diminish significantly in the near future (Hawton and Catalan 1982). As such, suicidal behaviour is a major health care issue (Mccrea 1996). An aim of the World Health Organisation is that by the year 2000 there will be a sustained and continuing reduction of the current rising trends in suicide and attempted suicide (Schmidtke *et al.* 1996). It this rising trend that is cause for concern (Diekstra 1989; Diekstra 1996). Increasing numbers of young men are committing suicide (Diekstra 1993) and, although the reasons are unclear, the factors known to be associated with this rise are a change in attitude towards the morality of suicide (Kelleher, Daly and Kelleher 1992), psychosocial stress (McClure 1994), unemployment, family breakdown, drug abuse, AIDS (Hawton 1992) and the availability of methods for completing suicide (Carlsten, Allebeck and Brandt 1996; Hawton 1992; Ohberg *et al.* 1996; Retterstol 1993).

Present generations of adolescents and adults world-wide are at greater risk of becoming suicidal than previous generations. On the basis of international collected data and a review of the extensive literature, Diekstra (and Garnefski 1995) concludes that a true increase in suicide mortality and morbidity has occurred over the larger part of this century among the White urban adolescent and young adult populations of North America and Europe. He recognises as possible causal mechanisms: the corresponding increase in the prevalence of depressive disorders, an increase in the prevalence of substance abuse where abusers are becoming younger, the dramatic lowering of the age of puberty, an increase in the number of social stressors and their consequences and changes in attitudes towards suicidal behaviors and the related increased availability of suicidal models.

In addition, relatively more women in some areas are taking their lives (Bille-Brahe 1993) and this is a change in the pattern for suicidal behaviour as previously more men than women completed suicide and more women than men attempted suicide. Pritchard (1996b) argues that suicide in China occurs more in rural than urban areas and more females than males kill themselves. This contrasts with Western industrialised societies and is a strong argument for the role of cultural factors influencing suicidal behaviour (Zhang 1996). While the target is to reduce suicidal behaviour by the year 2000, there are precious few years left to bring about any significant changes. From looking at the possible causal factors in this paragraph alone, we may be left wondering where to begin.

A geographical perspective of suicide rates in England and Wales found that males experience a higher risk in agricultural regions and densely populated urban areas while females experience a high risk mainly in the latter (Saunderson and Langford 1996). The highest risk areas were those of the large urban centres to which people have migrated and where there are socially isolated lifestyles of loneliness and anonymity. Saunderson and Langford conclude that unemployment and isolation interact and that it is in specific districts within inner cities that suicide rates are high. Alienated, jobless young people without homes and futures are at risk. Tackling youth unemployment seems to be one reasonable starting point and that must be a political decision. As long as we consider suicide to be a personal problem of individual psychopathology then we will make no inroads on the problem.

From a world-wide perspective, it is not only the young that are causing concern but also the rise in elderly female suicides (Mireault and De Man 1996; Pritchard 1996a). When we consider suicide in the elderly, we cannot isolate such a debate from the increasing calls for euthanasia and physician-assisted suicide. Declining social services, the restriction of community care budgets and the increasing isolation of the elderly are all part of a modern milieu that offers little comfort and support. Couple this with a strenuous debate about how death can be assisted and we have the foundation for despair and hopelessness. Medical practitioners are being challenged to face death and the problems of dying. Rather than face up to this challenge to their own competence, they seek to control death by assisting it. This is simply avoidance. Assisted suicide is failed palliative care. To my mind, it is not simply a statistical artefact that the region with the highest youth suicide rate in Australia is the region that has also passed the first bill to support euthanasia. As I shall continue to iterate, ideas have an ecology, they are not isolated but chained together.

In this book I shall say little further about euthanasia and assisted suicide. First, both fatal suicide and non-fatal suicide have at the heart of their definition the concept of personal agency. While I locate this personal agency within a milieu of significant others in this book, it is this concept of personal agency that separates suicide and attempted suicide from assisted suicide and euthanasia. For the latter two concepts another person is directly involved. I am aware that my own feelings are strong regarding this matter as the preceding paragraph shows. Second, my concern is that we must heed the call to protect the vulnerable in our society: the old, the poor and the sick. At a time when there is a shortage of organs for organ transplantation, a pressing need for hospital beds and the massive financial crisis facing us of caring for the elderly in the coming decade, then decisions about assisting death are open to abuse. Third, the Hippocratic oath emphasizes the ethic do not kill me and that a deadly drug should not be given. Death is irrevocable and our knowledge is limited, we cannot simply undo what has been done. However, we do live in times when the legality of such assisted suicide is being openly challenged. Doctors have been assisting their parents to die as long as medicine has been practised. What we do not need is a dogma that forbids and does violence to the compassion felt be the physicians and families of those wishing to die. A time has come for dialogue rather than dogma and the ability to discern what is needed. At the centre of all these arguments is the value and meaning of what it is to live a human life and the extent of human agency over that living.

Attempted suicide

A previous suicide attempt is considered to be a major predictive factor in a completed suicide, along with social class, unemployment previous psychiatric in-patient treatment, substance abuse and personality disorder (Hawton,

Fagg and Hawkins 1993; Suominen *et al.* 1996). It seems appropriate that we address the nature of suicide attempts as these are part of the route that some take to ending their own lives. Since attempted suicide is an important precursor of suicide, the incidence of a lowering of age for first-ever parasuicides can be expected to lower the age for suicides and thus increase the overall lifetime risk (Diekstra 1993).

The person-based suicide attempts in Europe are higher among women than men and the highest based rates are in the young (Schmidtke *et al.* 1996). More than 50 per cent of suicide attempters make more than one attempt and it is the rate of repetition that is, and has been, causing concern (Aldridge 1992; Stenager and Jensen 1994; Wells 1981). Again, we read of a connection in these accounts between destabilization, poverty and the psychosocial factors found in completed suicide (Nordentoft *et al.* 1993). What is also worrying is an echo of the problem that I mentioned at the beginning of this chapter. Up to two-thirds of suicide attempters consult a health and social welfare professional prior to suicide or a suicide attempt (Stenager and Jensen 1994). Many of these contact their general practitioner for psychological reasons. They need someone to 'talk to' (Bancroft *et al.* 1977b). What is critical, and we will see this in following chapters too, is that in the last consultation before an attempt, many have received a prescription for medication from their medical practitioner. It is this medication – opiate analgesics, anti-rheumatics, anti-depressants and anti-psychotics – that is then used in overdose to attempt suicide. Others use over-the-counter medicines to poison themselves and the ready availability of paracetemol has been criticised for its role in deliberate self-poisoning (Hawton, Fagg and Simkin 1996a; Hawton *et al.* 1996b; Mcloone and Crombie 1996; Simkin *et al.* 1995). Indeed, for both fatal and non-fatal suicide, the abuse of narcotic substances, medications or alcohol is also seen as a major contributory risk factor, particularly in young males. If we encourage a culture where it is expected that distress, much of which is relational and social in origin, can be simply tranquillised away, then we have developed the route to suicide into the highway that it has already become.

Sudden death and the categorisation of suicide

Over the past 150 years there has been an ever increasing mass of statistical data about suicidal behaviour. The usefulness of official suicide statistics has been challenged and descriptions of observable phenomena are representations of the theoretical categories of the observer and tell us little about the phenomena themselves (Atkinson 1978; Douglas 1967). Atkinson proposes that the categorisation of sudden deaths as 'suicides', 'undetermined' and 'accidental' says more about the process of categorising in the coroner's court than the validity of the categories. For example, in the event of a person dying in a car crash, it is unlikely that evidence will be gleaned about his family history, his marital relationship or his current financial status. However, if a person were to die by hanging then it would be taken as a clue to look for such relational and situational evidence. As we saw in the case of Marilyn Monroe and Kenneth Williams, sudden deaths can also be questioned either with suspicion as to the nature of the death or to the nature of the coroner's verdict.

Researchers who have reviewed suicide statistics (Jennings and Barraclough 1980; Sainsbury and Jenkins 1982) conclude that although it is likely that there are some errors in the classification of sudden death between 'suicide', 'undetermined' and 'accidental' categories, these are not sufficient to invalidate the usefulness of official statistics. What many commentators do bring attention to is the increase in the suicide rate (McClure 1984; Diekstra 1996). An increase in sudden death is a cause for concern.

Similar criticisms about categorisation can be made of the attempted suicide statistics. What is described as a suicide attempt or an accidental poisoning is dependent upon the categorisation of the medical practitioner who admits the person to hospital. Attempted suicide has become the most common reason for acute medical admissions of women to hospital and poses a major challenge to health care services (Wells 1981). In men, attempted suicide is second only to heart attacks as the most common medical reason for acute admission to hospital.

Towards an understanding; making sense of what we do

Although there has been considerable research into the problem of suicidal behaviour, there is still no adequate satisfactory theoretical understanding of why the behaviour occurs – although some have tried (Cushman and Whiting 1972; Dean and Range 1996; Leenaars 1996). There is a large body of research data about the characteristics of those who have completed suicide and those who have attempted suicide, yet this data has led to few understandings of the process of becoming suicidal and the links between social factors and suicidal behaviour. The thesis presented here is that behaviour is not 'understood' when it is isolated from social systemic contexts. Suicidal behaviour is often regarded as 'impulsive'. However, perhaps such behaviour only appears impulsive when regarded by an observer without a satisfactory theoretical understanding of such acts.

Perhaps it is time to see how persons who are suicidal make sense of what they do. Once we understand the story of a person's life then what at first appears impulsive has, indeed, a deadly and inevitable logic.

I shall be using the term 'system' throughout this book. It was Gregory Bateson's work (1973; 1978; 1979), and the family therapists that he inspired, that has been the impetus to use such descriptions. System is used here to refer to a group of related people. It has a traditional sense in that this relationship is also a political relationship, or an organisation of practice, with commonly negotiated meanings. It is a pattern of relationships. The emphasis is placed not only upon understanding elements in a system, that is the people involved, but also the relationships between those people. Systems are also located within bigger systems, like Russian dolls, one within another. Thus we have the organ systems that compose the body, and various bodies that form a family, families that form a kinship network, networks that themselves form communities and communities that form nations. While this is, of necessity, materialistic as an example, what I want to propose later is that there are such things as personal ideas that are related to a system of ideas within like-minded individuals that are related to particular cultural contexts. In this way we can speak not only of a biological or social ecology but also of an ecology of ideas as significancies and expectations. This we would call culture.

The categorisation of suicidal behaviour

Suicide is legally defined as an intentional act of self-destruction committed by someone knowing what he is doing and knowing the probable consequences of his act (Whitfield and Southern 1996). Attempted suicide is non-fatal in outcome and is also defined as an intentional act performed by an individual that without intervention by others would cause self-harm with the aim of realising changes he or she desires (Suominen *et al.* 1996)

Stengel (1958) drew a clear boundary between 'attempted' and 'completed' suicide. This distinction directed many subsequent research endeavours and promoted the notion that there were two stereotypical populations: those who 'complete' suicide and those who 'attempt' suicide. However, in reality those distinctions have become blurred by subsequent investigations. Later studies have covered a much greater and detailed range of variables and pointed to methodological inconsistencies in the Stengel evidence (Wells 1981). A common setting of both groups 'attempted' and 'completed' has been identified. This setting is characterised by high levels of geographical mobility in slum areas and indices of family disorganisation and family disruption. Finally, the two groups overlapped in that follow-up studies of attempted suicides indicated that a proportion subsequently committed suicide, and retrospective studies showed that of completed suicides, a proportion had made previous attempts. Suicide and suicide attempts are not so distinct. Attempted suicide is a strong predictor of completed suicide (Suominen *et al.* 1996). By concentrating on describing static discrete characteristics of stereotypical populations, the essential dynamic process of becoming suicidal has been missed.

The separation of 'attempted' and 'completed' suicide may be an artefact of the research methodology. As researchers, we are better off addressing the problem of how some people become suicidal, how that process escalates into completed suicide, how that process is interrupted or de-escalated or how suicidal behaviour is maintained. Rather than being concerned with personal or group characteristics, we can consider processes of interaction.

Suicidal intent

A major aspect of describing suicidal behaviour and distinguishing 'attempted' suicide from completed suicide has been the ascription of severity of suicidal intent (Arensman and Kerkhof 1996). We see from the definitions that both are intentional acts, one to destroy and the other to deliberately harm. For practitioners involved in the subsequent treatment of behaviour that is deemed to be harmful to the person, the reconstruction of events surrounding the episode has been crucial to their understanding of how life-threatening that behaviour was. However, Isometsa *et al.* (1995b) suggest that in many consultations prior to suicide, such intent is not communicated. The problem remains in our welfare cultures of medicine, psychiatry and social work that people are turning to health care professionals with a need to talk about their distress yet are not able to fully articulate that adversity.

In the literature we see how suicide is categorised by a coroner's court under certain circumstances of sudden death (Odonnell and Farmer 1995). A death may have been intentionally self-inflicted but if the strongest demands for evidential proof are not met, no suicide verdict is given. Researchers too play a part in that some define certain self-harming behaviour as 'suicidal', others as 'accidental' and others as deviance or personal neglect (i.e. smoking or the abuse of alcohol). Many researchers who describe suicidal behaviour are part of large institutions or departments which also offer 'treatment'. The inclusion of suicidal intent is invariably used in such descriptions because it has been found, by some, to be important in predicting further episodes of suicidal behaviour, including completed suicide (Pallis *et al.* 1982). In the tradition of researching suicidal behaviour, what people do is invariably linked with what to do about them. Some commentators see suicidal behaviour as impulsive (Brown *et al.* 1991; Hawton and Catalan 1982; Odonnell, Farmer and Catalan 1996). What I propose in this book is that by concentrating solely on characteristics of persons and only seeking direct causal relationships, a vital understanding of suicidal behaviour is missed. If, instead, we concentrate on a process account of how persons in an interactive milieu become distressed and suicidal, then what was previously 'impulsive' becomes understandable. Rather than saying these are the characteristics of people who commit or attempt suicide, this book will describe how, under certain relational circumstances, some persons may become 'suicidal' to achieve certain personal and social goals. The danger is that goal may become death.

There has been a debate in the literature about how true a description 'attempted' suicide is and that perhaps 'parasuicide', 'deliberate self-harm' or 'self-poisoning' might be more accurate labels (Kreitman 1977; Morgan 1979). Such labels are said to remove any motivational descriptions. However, by concentrating on reducing human behaviour to the level of observable acts, that is the laceration of skin or the ingestion of poisons, the understanding of human behaviour is substantially diminished. The whole tone of the following work concentrates on understanding the meaning of human behaviour at a number of differing levels of description, that is for the person, between persons, within the context of the family and the broader context of culture. It is this ecosystemic perspective that locates individual suffering, which indeed it is, in a broader perspective of relational difficulties and social adversity. Perhaps a time has come for practitioners from differing theoretical and training backgrounds to listen to each other and to incorporate differing opinions. By doing so, we may learn to listen to our patients.

Previous research

Atkinson (1978) makes the point that social understandings of suicidal behaviour are influenced by researchers and treatment agencies. However, what I hope to demonstrate is that those descriptions are restricted and limited. By using a limited set of descriptions (medical and psychiatric), persons are confirmed as deviant, as illegitimate in their demands, impulsive and difficult to manage. However, embedded in these individualistic descriptions are references to the way these people have lived their lives with others.

Rather than totally dismiss the previous literature about suicidal behaviour, I will attempt to tease out those characteristics that involve descriptions of other persons. For example, we know that there is cause for concern about the number of young people committing suicide (Schmidtke *et al.* 1996). As disruptions in key relationships are seen as being crucial in suicidal behaviour (Gupta, Sivakumar and Smeeton 1995; Kienhorst *et al.* 1995; Young 1994), we can begin to make tentative inferences about the social situations adolescents find themselves in, that is the school, the home, at work, at university or with friends. Levy, Jurkovic and Spirito (1995) tested such an ecologically-based model and found that hopelessness proved to be the best predictor of suicidal intent. We know from a broader literature about psychological health that poor educational achievement and unemployment are associated with diminished psychological health measures (Power and Manor 1992) and psychiatric morbidity with sociodemographic disadvantage with exposure to childhood adversity (Beautrais, Joyce and Mulder 1996).

How is it then that young people lose hope? In the next chapter we will see how hope is related to a perceived future and that in times of unemployment the identity of a young person has few possibilities to be established as being of social worth. Indeed, while suicidal behaviour is traditionally considered to be a phenomenon of the individual, economic causes like unemployment (Chuang and Huang 1996b; Dooley *et al.* 1989; Dooley, Fielding and Levi 1996; Maris 1995; Pritchard 1996a) and social causes like immigration (Trovato 1986) are often ignored, despite the classical sociological interpretation of Durkheim (1951) that we will read about in the next chapter. As Schmidtke *et al.* (1996) write, 'Compared with the general population, suicide attempters more often belong to the social categories associated with social destabilization and poverty'. If, through unemployment, we consign our young people to the category of the impoverished, then we must expect that they will choose no longer to live in a society that offers them nothing.

Living alone is also a frequent factor found among middle-aged male suicides (Heikkinen *et al.* 1995). While living alone is a category, what we need to discover is how people come to live alone. How is it that they are isolated for social contexts? For those of us with clinical experience, we also know that few individuals live totally without contact. Even the seemingly socially isolated individual has his own network of social workers and health professionals. Fullilove (1996) reminds us that when we are forced to leave home, dislocated as refugees or displaced in order to find work, then we lose those attachments to the place where we have been living as well as the network of personal relationships. This dislocation from place is another form of alienation. If we condemn our old people to lives of privation, then we must not be surprised that they no longer choose to participate in communities where they are no longer cherished.

Marital status

Those who live alone include the single, the widowed and the divorced and the rates of suicide are higher. An association has been drawn between attempted suicide and marital status, but this is not absolutely clear (Mastekaasa 1995). Rates for the elderly widowed are rising and are a cause for concern. The occurrence of attempted suicide has been consistently high in those whose relationship has been disrupted through separation. The highest rates, in Edinburgh, occurred, for both sexes, among the divorced (Holding *et al.* 1977). In Oxford particularly high rates have been found for teenage wives and single and divorced women aged 24–35 years and single men aged 30–40 years (Bancroft *et al.* 1975).

More than two-thirds of those who were married, in a study by Hawton and Catalan (1982), had marital problems. A similar proportion of those who were unmarried were having difficult relationships with a boyfriend or a girlfriend. This points to a relational context of conflict. Stemming from this conflict is a concern about children (Roberts and Hawton 1980). Parents who abuse or neglect their children, and those regarded as at special risk of doing so, have very high rates of attempted suicide. The occurrence of both suicide attempts and child abuse appear to result from marital problems and personal difficulties that persist and have taken time to develop. Such developments can be located in contexts of family or intimate relationships, as we will see in Chapters Seven to Eleven.

It is interesting to note that although traditional researchers know that marital problems exist, and that there are difficulties in 'key' relationships, they have no methodology to research the nature of those problematical relationships. It is this area of describing the nature of relationships, rather than the characteristics of persons, that this book addresses.

Attempted suicide and circumstance

The description of those who attempt suicide usually involves an account of the problems such people face in their everyday lives. Hawton and Catalan (1982) separate these problems into acute problems that occur shortly beforehand, and are considered to be precipitants, and longer-term or chronic problems in the context of which acute problems have arisen. Most authors present the behaviour in this way by placing the incident of suicidal behaviour within a context of precipitating problems, within a context of persistent problems and within a social matrix. Few relate the escalation of distress, and its associated events, in individuals to a social understanding that unfolds in time. That our lives have a narrative structure, that distress is a story that unfolds within a plot of conflict and betrayal, is rarely acknowledged within scientific research, yet it is a daily occurrence in our practice encounters.

In Chapters Four and Seven the association between life events and different forms of deviancy will be considered. Suicide attempters in previous studies (Paykel, Prusoff and Myers 1975) have been shown to have had as many as four times as many life events as their general population controls. For the purpose of this book, the description of significant life events is crucial. Those descriptions entail evidence of an interactive factor involved in suicidal behaviour. In the literature these include:

- an argument, or a major row, with a spouse (this ties in with the data about marital separation, divorce and isolation)

- having a new person in the house (again this entails a change in interpersonal relationships)

- grave illness of a family member (which raises a question about how carers are affected by the afflicted)

- serious personal physical illness (which entails, as we will see later, the occupation of a social status (Parsons 1951) within the immediate framework of significant others)

- having to appear in court for an offence (which involves a potential change in social status).

Of all the significant factors involved, the literature returns to the most significant event as being a row or quarrel within 48 hours of an episode of deliberate self-harm involving a key person (usually a close family member or boyfriend or girlfriend). It is interesting to note that few studies investigate what is a significant life event as perceived by those who are suicidal. This issue is addressed in Chapter Seven.

It is, perhaps, worthwhile mentioning here the problems associated with being ill. The occupation of the status 'sick' is not an isolated position for any person and entails a process of development within a social network. Hawton and Catalan (1982) and Morgan (1979) take care to point out the significance of poor physical health and recent general hospital admission which occurs with greater incidence than would be expected in those who deliberately harm themselves. This seems to suggest a process whereby individuals who are sick (and deemed so by their families) and try to get treatment find themselves deliberately harming themselves. As we saw with Kenneth Williams earlier, he perceived his health to be deteriorating and held out no hope for relief. In my clinical work I have come across numerous patients that have been referred to me because they have problems with chronic pain. Despite considerable interventions aimed at relieving such pain, and a history of tests and investigations to discover the causes of such pain, the pain is not relieved. Inevitably, when no organic origin for pain is discovered, or, perhaps more importantly, patients fail to respond to treatment, a psychological problem is presumed. Psychotropic medication is then prescribed or patients are referred for psychological treatment. It is at this moment that an overdose of medication occurs.

In our modern communities the referral to psychological services, or even worse, psychiatry, is stigmatising. Thus, at the moment of distress, when no organic source is found, the patient is further distressed by the supposed process of helping. When a person presents her distress as physical pain, we have to remember that this is the way that she has chosen to present her distress. While there is undoubtedly a psychological component, as there is in all human activities involving relationship, the abrupt invalidation of a physical explanation rejects the form in which the patient presents her distress to the practitioner. We may have to acknowledge in our modern societies that the only way to find solace in the face of hardship is by going to a doctor. If we systematically channel distress such that it is medicalised, then we must at least provide a service that is sufficiently sophisticated enough in its understandings of human nature to respond adequately.

What we must also understand is that when someone becomes ill, and they remain chronically so, they do so in the company of others. How a person is cared for and the range of responsibilities and obligations that they have is related to those with whom they live their daily lives. If we ask why distress is escalating, then maybe it is important to see what is happening within the context in which the individual is living her life. This shifts our understanding to a relational context or, in the terms of this book, a systems perspective. What we are forced to consider is a complex process involving life events and personal and social variables as multiple causal chains (Reich, Newsom and Zautra 1996).

What to look at?

It seems prudent then to investigate the incidence of suicidal behaviour in social contexts, first to look at the behaviour in the context of a relationship with a key other (De Moore and Robertson 1996). If conflict exists, it is difficult for that conflict to be unilateral in a relationship; the persons involved must be interactively maintaining the strife. It seems that behaviour which is problematical, like family conflict, is a process that somehow becomes exacerbated and escalates to a point where one person exhibits suicidal behaviour. This is not to ignore the social factors of unemployment. However, when young people leave home and the support of their family, then the manner and nature of that leaving and the continuing support is of consequence.

In the following pages the reader will find a number of differing descriptions of suicidal behaviour. These descriptions will be rooted firmly in particular behaviour as described in specific contexts. From these differing contextual descriptions some commonality of understanding will be teased out. Clifford Geertz (1973) calls this describing 'thick description' or a 'stratified hierarchy of meaningful structures'. Rather than reduce human behaviour to a description of specific acts, this study locates what people do within varying interactive contexts in which the meaning of behaviour is negotiated (Douglas 1967; Fernandez 1974).

However, a difficulty of synthesizing differing levels of abstraction is that inevitably some slippage occurs between descriptions. Precise definition is lost and descriptions do not always satisfy the demands of controlled sampling. A counter to this argument is that by rigidly defining populations, the very stuff of social life is lost. What is described in controlled clinical studies is groups who are distinguished by the observer, rather than processes as they occur in natural settings.

The argument presented here is that precision is not necessarily lost. The important point is that precise descriptions are made only when particular areas of importance emerge which need to be precisely defined. Rather than keep on re-defining the answers to unproductive questions, this study asks whether we can address the issue of suicidal behaviour by posing a different set of questions. Rather than supply exhaustive answers, it will seek to give some answers which themselves can be submitted for further investigation and refinement by other researchers. More important, I hope to retell clinical stories that make sense to clinicians and with which they can help their patients.

Suicidal behaviour and its meaning, in this book, will be considered as it is presented in differing social contexts as defined by those involved in those contexts. In the next chapter I will discuss varying explanations for suicide and in Chapter Three I shall look at the literature concerning family interaction and suicidal behaviour. In reviewing these explanations in Chapter Four, I can piece together an emerging theory of escalating distress and how that distress is accommodated or exacerbated. What I intend is to demonstrate that there is a common narrative element to stories of escalating distress. Maybe once we recognise this element, we can begin to improve our therapeutic initiatives.

In Chapter Six the way suicidal behaviour is presented in *The Times* newspaper will be discussed. This discussion is not intended to be an exhaustive description of media descriptions of suicidal behaviour. What it does is to present a graphic illustration of how suicidal behaviour is reported and construed in the year that the rest of the data is gathered. The news media and coroner's courts maintain a social definition of suicidal behaviour. The main conclusion is that some suicidal behaviour is deemed to be socially legitimate under certain circumstances and when a person exhibits certain characteristics. This reflects the perspective of medical research, which is also concerned with legitimating personal behaviour under certain circumstances. The gathering of this data paints a broad backcloth which contextualises the later descriptions.

Chapter Seven is concerned with women who are admitted to a psychiatric hospital after they have engaged in suicidal behaviour and who are described as being 'suicidal'. This description is one which is applied to them by the ward staff of the hospital. Rather than study the personal characteristics of these women, the emphasis is placed upon those conditions that women come to be described as suicidal. The challenge is to discover how that situation can be ameliorated. As we will see, the change lies not in the individual women alone but in the whole context of the hospital ward. What is challenging to all of us involved in the field of mental health is that women supposedly admitted to hospital for their own protection become increasingly distressed and labelled by their carers as 'bad women', forfeiting the status of being legitimately sick.

In Chapter Eight personal accounts are elicited from women who describe their episodes of attempted suicide and what has helped them to recover. It will be salutary for those of us involved in therapeutic activities to read that therapy is of little value compared to the kindness of friends.

The investigation continues in the following chapter and is concerned with how persons behave who describe themselves as suicidal, under what circumstances they do so, and with whom they are involved after admission to a hospital emergency ward.

Chapters Ten and Eleven describe suicidal behaviour in family contexts and compare descriptions with families where no suicidal behaviour is known to have occurred. The label of 'suicidal behaviour' is made by the referring agents (usually medical personnel) and by the families themselves. As I am interested in investigating the social meaning of suicidal behaviour from the perspective of those persons and their families who are deemed to be suicidal, then it is their definition that is paramount. It is the stories that people tell about themselves that I will be using to offer an explanation that we can incorporate into our thinking about suicidal behaviour in the final chapter.

CHAPTER TWO

Explanations of Suicidal Behaviour

Suicidal threats whether carried out successfully or unsuccessfully pervade our entire social structure Our study has disclosed that the threat of suicide forces persons to marry, prevents marriage dissolutions, coerces companionships between persons despite their mutual infidelity, prevents marriages, forces parents to acquiesce in their offspring's vicious habits, precludes institutionalisation, is rewarded by escape from further military induction, is used to obtain favoured treatment over siblings, is employed as a device to avoid military induction. It should be significantly stated that these by no means represent an inventory of all factual situation embracing suicidal threats. (Siegal and Fried 1955)

The behaviour of the majority of persons who commit suicidal acts suggests that the human environment is given a chance to intervene We cannot fully understand suicidal acts unless we take these reactions of individuals and groups into account. (Stengel 1962)

We might say that every human faces this dilemma: He cannot face death unless he is a whole person, yet he can become a truly whole person only by facing death. (Searles 1965)

An historical perspective

Suicide is a form of behaviour as old as man himself but the phenomenon has been described in differing ways according to the attitudes prevalent within society at various times in history. (Rosen 1971)

Self-destruction to escape the consequences of political or military defeat was considered to be an honourable act, particularly if the situation was regarded as hopeless, during biblical times. Neither the Hebrew Bible nor the New Testament prohibit suicide, nor is it described by any particular word. Such acts are reported straightforwardly and briefly: 'He went and hanged himself' it is said of Judas Iscariot (Matthew xxvii, 15).

At the same time, the population of Greeks and Romans approved of suicide as a means of maintaining one's honour to avoid capture, humiliation, shameful death and slavery. Although Christians opposed suicide among pagans, they did regard martyrdom as a blood-witness to Christ as a legitimate act. Even stoicism accepted and recommended suicide for a man under certain conditions: as an escape from evil, on his country's behalf, for the sake of his friends or if suffering from intolerable pain or incurable disease. Rosen also mentions that young girls, in antiquity, were seen as suicidal risks if prone to menstrual troubles. Suicide was tolerated throughout the Imperial period (Arnold 1911) until it became almost a social disease. The only groups that were actively dissuaded from such actions were those accused of crime, soldiers and slaves – for whom there were practical and economic causes for keeping them alive.

In the Middle Ages there was a developing recognition that mental and emotional disorder, rather than moral disorder, may lead to suicide: '...sorrow arises sometimes from previous impatience, sometimes from the fact that one's desire for some object has been delayed or frustrated, and sometimes from the abundance of melancholic humours, in which case it behoves the physician rather than the priest to prescribe a remedy' (Wenzel 1967, p.160). Other accounts involve descriptions which we may well hear today. They tell of a young girl who had borne an illegitimate child and, being abandoned by her lover, despaired and hanged herself, as well as a young man who, having gambled away his clothes, fell into melancholy and despair, went home and hanged himself. Suicide was condemned during this period by the Church, although there were exceptions made for the insane. The penalties against the body of a suicide or his kin were severe but not always imposed. Mitigating factors in such cases were the social rank of the suicide and his family and the circumstances of the act. Some suicides were considered to be more justified than others, particularly the presence of protracted pain or emotional disorders.

Outbreaks of suicide throughout history, as today, were causes for concern and throughout the 17th Century the motives ascribed to such behaviour were sickness of mind, intemperance, gluttony, duelling and foolhardiness (Hunter and MacAlpine 1963). However, by the 18th Century causal factors became related to the environment – such as air, diet, the seasonal temperature and idleness – which heralded a change from a moral to a secular view of suicidal behaviour. Not only was the climate blamed for the English Malady (Crocker 1952) but the inactivity and sedentary occupation of the 'better sort' and the humour of living in great populous and unhealthy towns. So prevalent was suicide in the 18th Century that it was considered as a problem constituting a national emergency. Such a concern is echoed today over the number of adolescent overdosers.

In early modern Geneva there was an explosion in suicides after 1750 (Watt 1996). We see a variety of causal factors playing their various parts. A greater availability of firearms appears to be a contributory factor, echoing familiar concerns today in New World countries (Adamek and Kaplan 1996a; Adamek and Kaplan 1996b; Berman and Jobes 1995; Brent and Perper 1995; Odonnell 1995; Singh and Yu 1996). Economic problems played their part as the watchmaking industry declined. While foreigners and the poor were over-represented amongst suicides, we also read of the well-to-do being also prone. Concurrently, suicide was decriminalised, the judicial authorities no longer confiscated the property of suicides and funeral rites were no longer denied.

Changing attitudes towards courtship, marriage and the family in eighteenth-century Geneva contributed to this dramatic increase in the suicide rate. Unprecedented numbers of people took their lives because of marital breakdown, unhappy love stories and deaths of family members. After 1750, marriage appeared to offer immunity to suicide for both men and women. As today, those who lived alone were at risk, particularly the widowed (Bowling and Windsor 1995; Linn and Lester 1996). Marriage appears to have protected against suicidal feelings, in that people were investing themselves emotionally in a marital relationship, yet some suicides were perceived as being motivated by relational causes: loss of a loved one, domestic disputes and romantic misadventures. As Watt (1996) writes, '...prior to 1700, not one suicide can realistically be attributed to a romantic misadventure' (p.70). Later in the century, however, suicides were beginning to be attributed to unrequited love, love affairs that went awry or marital conflict. The change to a companionate marriage, from that of a marriage of convenience, brought new expectations of personal happiness within a romantic marital relationship. With marital dissatisfaction, and failed expectations, came conflict and divorce. However, divorce itself was not seen as the cause of many suicides. Rather, a change in family expectations, accompanying the pursuit of happiness in romantic relations, emphasised an increasing individualism. Generational conflicts between adolescents and their parents made themselves apparent. Again, we see a current concern about relationships within families reflected in the past. As the family became more of a focus for emotions, grief at the loss of a family member became another attributed motivation for suicide.

Modern-day understandings of Aboriginal familial structures among North American Indians also emphasise that the Europeanised view of a private legal contract between individuals, as opposed to a public customary arrangement between kinship groups, has contributed to suicide amongst native American women (Young and French 1995). While the consequences of such a change appear in the statistics and group classifications as economic or social factors, it is the process of a failing marriage and its consequential alienation that is of importance. For a woman in such a situation it is not only being poor that is difficult enough but also the ensuing lack of support from any social network.

The description of suicides had evolved by the 19th Century as not only an emotional disorder associated with insanity but also as a disorder affecting the labouring class. Problems of social maladjustment were seen during the early Industrial Revolution and suicide became related to the problems of the labouring poor.

It is from this time onward that two diverging descriptions of suicide develop: the statistical-sociological view and the medico-psychiatric. In both views it was noticed that a number of interacting causal factors were present. Falret (Miner 1922) published, in 1822, the first study of suicide that used statistical data and offered a classification of causal factors under four headings: predisposing – heredity, temperament, climate; accidental direct – passions, domestic trouble and the like; accidental indirect – bodily pain and illness; and general – civilisation, civil disorders, religious fanaticism. Social factors were gradually cultivated and before the end of the century were recognised as insanity, alcoholism, illness, family troubles, love problems, poverty, unmarried persons, of being old and of being male.

Suicide was seen at this time as a consequence of changes in society leading to social disorganisation and alienation. This setting of individual behaviour in a context of change leading to disorganisation was a precursor or of present day descriptions. It is interesting also to note that the same behaviour was interpreted during different ages as being legitimate or illegitimate according to cultural understanding and the status of the person who was suicidal, a feature that we will see reflected later in Chapter Six.

An ecological and population explanation

Perhaps the most prevalent sociological explanation of suicidal behaviour is that proposed by Durkheim (1951). According to Durkheim, the process leading to suicide is centred on a failure to accommodate oneself to the ecological niche one occupies, either because of too great an acceptance or too little.

Although traditionally regarded as a sociological explanation of suicidal behaviour, Durkheim's explanation was fundamentally concerned with 'the nature of man' as a concrete being. This psychological standpoint enabled him to split the individual into two parts: the individual as ego or 'I' and the social as soul or 'we'. He considered 'society' to be a result of past interactions of souls that cause future interactions. Although dependent upon individuals for existence as a concrete manifestation, society transcended individuals as a whole. This means that society exists as different parts in different individuals and explanations of individual behaviour can only be explained by reference to all the different parts of society in all the different individuals. While suicide is the ultimate individual act, as Warde (1994) suggests, 'a personal exercise of will that demonstrates control over one's destiny' (p.883), that act is also patterned by social forces.

In this way, society can constrain the behaviour of individuals and, to some degree, determine the actions of individuals by a social force described as altruism. The well-being of individuals will be reflected, according to Durkheim, in the balance of such forces, individual and social. Should an imbalance exist, then the forces oppose each other and pathology is created. As the pathology of society or the individual goes up, the tendency to commit suicide will also go up. Both individual and social factors are thought to be causative but only social factors are seen as of fundamental importance in explaining suicide rates.

The relationship between individual and ecological niche is also to be found in the explanation by Henry and Short (1954), who suggest that suicide rates are higher when external restraints are weak and the individual must consequently bear the responsibility for the frustration she encounters.

A similar argument is developed by Holinger and Ofler (1981), who propose that a rapid change in the population of adolescents in the United States of America correlates with an escalation in adolescent suicide, homicide and aggregate forms of violent death. The explanation they give for this is essentially psychodynamic. With an increased population and increased competition for jobs there arises a number of adolescents who fail to find a social position – a niche – and begin to regard themselves as failures, promoting a gradual process of estrangement from society, and adolescents who attempt suicide have been through a progressive isolation from important people in their lives, leading to a dissolution of any meaningful social relationships. A process is proposed in these explanations whereby the individuals' ties with society are dissolved, particularly with those in his immediate social milieu – his niche. This may be promoted by a rapid change in social circumstance and consequent material loss.

The connection between homicide and suicide has been further investigated by Leenaars and Lester (1996). While Durkheim considered suicide and homicide to be mutually exclusive, the stream analogy of lethal violence suggests that homicide and suicide are two channels of a stream of destructiveness. Both are responses to frustration, one directed lethally against the self and the other directed outward towards another – thus reflecting the psychological perspective of Sigmund Freud that we will read about later in this chapter. Leenaars and Lester do indeed find that a large male cohort is 'a major negative life event that adds to the stream of violence for males (p.48)'. However, they do go on to caution, after Douglas (1967), that abstract social meanings do not explain specific types of social events and we should be cautious in the interpretation of such statistical studies. This is a variation of the ecological fallacy (Vanpoppel and Day 1996) where group data are treated as if they were individual data.

In investigating the ecological correlates of suicidal behaviour with particular reference to work and suicide, Shepherd and Barraclough (1980) come to some important conclusions about the process of becoming socially isolated. They develop Durkheim's hypothesis that a strong protection against suicide is to belong to a strong work-force, decentralised to avoid impersonality and to concentrate social energies but linked to ensure a large-scale division of labour and to facilitate the organisation of social living. They describe a process where 'work loss weakens the subject's social integration, deprives him of a social role all of and social status and may well increase his isolation which may drive him to suicide' (p.476). However, other authors caution us to consider that the relationship between suicide and unemployment is not that of simple direct causality (Morrell *et al.* 1993).

Trovato's (1992) study of youth suicide in Canada supports the Durkheimian hypothesis that religious detachment within the young is associated with a proneness to suicide but only partially supports the hypothesis relating to social integration. He links the abandonment of institutionalised religion to an increase in divorce rates, a decrease in family stability and, thereby, to people taking their own lives. The religious affiliation hypothesis alone, as opposed to the social integration hypothesis, has been criticised by several authors who find no links between Catholic or Protestant religions and suicide rates (Vanpoppel and Day 1996; Wasserman and Stack 1993). Indeed, in a post-modern world, the meta-narratives of science and religion have been critically questioned so that people may now no longer identify themselves with, nor allow themselves to be identified by, large social groupings. However, they do align themselves with tribal or smaller groupings of like-minded individuals. The big narratives of modernism are now being replaced by our own personal sets of meaning made locally with those whom we seek to live (Warde 1994).

Individuals are taking the definition of themselves into their own hands rather than relying upon an identity being imposed by another. Modern identities are constructed and are bound up with cultural values. The definition of health, who is to define what health is and who is to be involved in healing, is not a new activity. Such issues are raised at times of transformation when the old order is being challenged (Aldridge 1991). In postmodern society, orthodoxies are challenged, and as truth is regarded as relative with few fixed authorities to turn to, identities can be composed from a palette of cultural alternatives. Health itself is a state subject to social and individual definition. What counts as healthy is dependent upon cultural norms. Health and disease are not fixed entities but concepts used to characterise a process of adaptation to meet the changing demands of life and the changing *meanings* given to living. Negotiating what counts as healthy is a process we are all involved in, as are the forms of treatment, welfare and care which we choose to accept as adequate or satisfactory (Aldridge 1990).

Spickard (1994) reminds us that modern people do not merely accept the identities passed down by authorities. Instead, they construct their identities from various sources. Modern identity is eclectic. As in the age of Romanticism, when revolution demanded a new way of being, the primacy of the perceiver is once more being emphasised. Subjectivity becomes paramount, on the one hand reifying the individual but on the other hand running the risk that the individual will become isolated. Indeed, while post-modernism is, perhaps, itself characterised by a revolt against authority and tends towards self-referentiality, its very eclecticism, that leaves the individual valued but exhausted of significance – what Gergen (1991) refers to as 'the saturated self'. Brewster-Smith (1994) suggests that the inflated potential for selfhood, dislocated from traditional value sources, increases the potential for despair and while individuals may rise to the challenge of pluralism, there are some individuals who will seek to join groups who offer some form of reassurance in a given orthodoxy of beliefs and actions. The danger in modern Europe is that the romantic notion of individualism becomes perverted into nationalism and the dislocated individual seeking to construct his or her own identity joins a group intent on the limitation of others' freedom of self-definition, whereby he or she can maintain their own security. Consensus is fragile in a context where individual demands are reified.

What we singularly fail to see is that our current thinking about health is dominated by a medical thinking that ignores much of the reality of the persons we intend to treat and support. Few people, when they are sick, respond by seeking a health care practitioner (Andersen 1995). Perhaps even fewer consult a health care practitioner about staying healthy. What we appear to do, outside of an academic life thinking about such lofty matters, is eat, drink, amuse ourselves, love our nearest and dearest, walk the dog or chase pieces of leather across field (both dogs and football players) without thinking of medical consequences. Maybe our health care assumptions are so narrow that they have little relevance for others who do not bow down at the altars of epidemiology and empiricism. Many lay appraisals of health care activity seem be based upon holistic considerations that include feelings of mood and vitality (Andersen and Lobel 1995). As we shall see in Chapter Seven, formal therapists hardly play a role at all in the recovery of those who are suicidal. It is simple lay activities that come to the fore and how people interpret their own behaviour. Thus while we may indeed identify cohorts at risk at a macroscopic level, it is how individuals live their lives with their intimates that is a more sensible understanding of the ecology of human behaviour. While cohorts may appeal to the niceties of statistical manipulation, and have ramifications for some theorising, it is the actual social interaction of relationships that have relevance for the day-to-day world of prevention and clinical practice.

An anthropological explanation

The task of the social anthropologist is to interpret such a behavioural ecology and it is this task of observing and interpreting suicidal behaviour that will be described in this section. Each part of a custom, for the anthropologist (Leach 1976), is seen as part of a complex and it is proposed that details in isolation are as meaningless as isolated letters of the alphabet. Leach goes on to say that culture communicates and that the complex interconnectedness of cultural events itself conveys information to those who participate in events. This notion of a message implicit in the context of behaviour is also developed by Bateson (1973). As in the ecological model, it is suggested that both the individual and society must be considered (Mead 1934). However, whereas the argument in the previous section was concerned with the individual and society as separate entities, albeit at different levels of abstraction, the ecological model of anthropology proposes that we are dealing with a single interacting whole where no one element unilaterally determines the other (Geertz 1973; Leach 1976; Wilkins 1967). The central point of this section is that cultural details must always be viewed in context, that everything is meshed in with everything else. If this is so then we have a problem of analysis because any particular description will be partial. The pragmatic solution to this appears to be one of maintaining a holistic perspective whilst making particular descriptions (Varela and Johnson 1976).

Anthropologists studying behaviour also address themselves to sequences of behaviour and understanding the meaning of such behaviour. Leach (1976) argues that this symbolic meaning is condensed into concrete representations of action by ritual occasions and that these ritual occasions are concerned with movement across social boundaries from one social status to another (maiden to wife, sick to well, living to dead). The purpose of these rituals is to proclaim a change of status (Goffman 1961) and to magically bring it about. This relates to the previous ecological description where a rapid change of social status was considered to be a feature of suicidal behaviour. As we read earlier, for native American women the status change associated with marital breakdown within a Europeanised context of a former Aboriginal kinship network leads to suffering (Young and French 1995).

The change of marital status by divorce or separation is considered influential in suicidal behaviour. Similarly, we also know that the social status of chronic physical sickness, as a process of change, is implicated in suicidal behaviour. Rituals of bodily mutilation in other cultures are seen as such rites of transition where bodily mutilation marks the entry into adult society. At the level of metaphor (Fernandez 1974), these acts are described as acts of death, where one status dies and another is born. It is, perhaps, at this metaphoric level of death that suicidal behaviours are united by some common ground where one identity of self seeks death so that another can be born.

Kozak (1994) suggests that the deaths of native Americans are being medicalised. This classification of violent death emphasises an individual culpability and detracts from social problems. Social causality, like poverty and racial stigma, are ignored at the expense of personal attributes of deviance or psychopathology. What Kozak urges us to do as researchers is to think of death classifications not as events but as narrative reconstructions of death events. This returns us to the approach that I was proposing in Chapter One, where we begin to understand the events that happen to people and their loved ones as they unfold in time. It is the story that is told which we must begin to unravel and understand.

Another metaphor of death is contained in the notion of sacrifice, whereby sacrificial offerings of life are made to obtain benefits. Although the material body of the sacrificial victim may well be damaged, what matters is the act of sacrifice as such and the expression of a reciprocal relationship.

We will see in Chapter Seven that women are willing to sacrifice themselves for the benefit of their families and their loved ones.

In an anthropological description of suicidal behaviour we are concerned with changes in social status. These changes in social status are accomplished and recognised by others in particular rituals which have symbolic meaning for individuals and others as rites of transition. The rituals can be understood by describing what happens as a sequence of events in the context of culture and by considering communicative acts as metaphors. Japanese suicide cannot be understood without explaining both the person and the culture, as culture provides a resource from which the person defines herself and by which she is defined (Iga 1996). Similarly, suicidal behaviour in the women described in Chapter Seven cannot be understood without understanding the culture and rites of transition of psychiatry and the emergency hospital ward.

An ethnographical approach

Kessels (1966) and Evans (1967) suggest that changes in cultural attitudes has some correlation with the presence of suicidal behaviour and that self-poisoning and self-injury have become an acceptable means of coping with interpersonal stress. Other writers also suggest that suicidal behaviour is often a highly effective way of altering the behaviour and expectation of significant others (Bostock and Williams 1974; Sifneos 1966).

Sale *et al.* (1975) set out to investigate the presence of community attitudes towards suicidal behaviour. They adopted the hypothesis that the presence of sympathetic attitudes to suicidal behaviour could lead the prospective attempter to anticipate desired changes and thus 'select' such behaviour as a means of dealing with interpersonal conflict.

This did not prove to be the case and Sale found that in the community where there is a high rate of suicidal behaviour there is also an unfavourable attitude to suicidal behaviour. Those respondents who are unfavourable towards suicidal behaviour, or are openly hostile, believe that suicide attempts hardly ever lead to death. Ginsburg (1971) also finds that suicidal behaviour is regarded as a manifestation of mental illness and is something which 'happens' to people rather than being an intentional act. This perspective of intentionality changes when members of the community have had contact with persons exhibiting suicidal behaviour. Then the behaviour is described negatively as manipulative. Official definitions include this element of intentionality as central to defining the act of suicide, as we saw in Chapter One.

It would appear then that differing explanations can exist side by side: either suicidal behaviour is non-intentioned and is caused by social factors or suicidal behaviour is intentioned and the intent is to coerce or change the behaviour of others by illegitimate means. This second view is described as arising from contact with suicidal behaviour such that social experience informs community and personal attitudes (Jeffrey 1979).

Burvill *et al.* (1981), studying migrant groups in Australia, come to a number of interesting conclusions. First, large differences in both rates and methods of suicide are found in individual migrant groups. Second, the suicide rates are more like those of the country of origin than those of the Australian-born, no matter how long the migrants had lived in Australia – in comparison, the methods used are closer to the Australian-born the longer they have lived in Australia. Third, the change in methods is greatest in those migrant groups coming from cultures with a language and culture similar to that of Australia.

A personal motivational explanation

A number of writers have been concerned that the explanation given for suicidal behaviour by those who practice such behaviour has been neglected (Bancroft *et al.* 1979; Bancroft, Skrimshire and Simkin 1976; Hawton *et al.* 1982a; Hawton *et al.* 1982b; Parker 1981).

One of the difficulties faced by researchers trying to gain an understanding of personal motivation from patients has been that the explanations may have been concerned with maintaining some elements of social legitimacy and acceptability. Despite this consideration, the previously mentioned authors have published the work, which is summarised below.

Parker (1981; 1994; 1995) takes into consideration that marital disharmony and relationship conflicts are present in two-thirds of suicidal patients and that the behaviour is seen as an effort to re-establish a close dependent relationship with a loved one or an attempt to change that person's behaviour.

Two groups are described by Parker. One, the low suicide intent group, perceives an overdose as separate and distinct from that of suicide itself and sees an overdose as a desperate escape from tension – rather like getting drunk. The second group, described as the moderate-high intent group, perceive an overdose as a communication of needs, expression of feelings and an escape from tension – which is similar to suicide. The resolution of conflict with a key person by verbal means is seen as a sensible but personally difficult solution and one which can lead to the expression of harmful anger, resulting in tension and a denial of the problem. Although the low suicide intent group see seeking professional help as 'sensible', the moderate-high intent group view seeking help more neutrally. It is seen, in some cases, as 'blaming the other' person involved. 'Breaking off' a relationship or 'talking to the key person' is considered to be a difficult task and rated as more difficult than attempted suicide.

In Bancroft, Skrimshire and Simkins' *et al.*'s study (1976), 128 subjects were interviewed to find out their reasons for taking overdoses. Their argument, like this book, is that to provide effective and appropriate Intervention it is necessary to have an understanding from the viewpoint of the person taking the overdose and his significant others. The researchers concluded that suicidal behaviour is precipitated by an emotional crisis in a close relationship and such behaviour is best understood as an attempt to influence the other person or express anger. 'Wanting to die' may be a means of gaining social acceptability after the event and an access to sympathetic considerate treatment.

A later study (Hawton *et al.* 1982a) presents the reason given for suicidal behaviour by adolescents and by clinical assessors, again with the intention of discovering implications for treatment. It is also interesting to note that the behaviour is termed 'deliberate self-poisoning' and in itself carries its own motivational perspective of 'self deliberation'.

For adolescents, the act is interpreted by clinical observers as not being intended to result in death as, in most cases, someone else is close at hand or likely to intervene. However, few adolescents indicate that the overdose is taken in order to gain help from someone, although the clinical assessors think it is. The most frequent feelings reported at the time of the overdoses are anger and a sense of isolation and are associated with poor communication skills and a disruption in the relationship with the patients parents or with a boy or girlfriend. The feelings of anger and loneliness are also in keeping with the explanations that are given: to 'get relief', to 'escape' and 'show desperation'.

It appears that adolescents often appear to be trying to effect an immediate change in stressful circumstances, either by escaping or by evoking a response from those persons whom they are significantly involved with. The prospect of involving an outsider to resolve such difficult circumstances seems unlikely as outside help seems to be seen as inappropriate or culturally stigmatising. If the process of achieving help is one that further stigmatises, in that the adolescent is brought into the realm of psychiatric help services or confirmed as needing psychological help, then we should not be too surprised that a fragile identity will not seek further contact with agencies that are potentially damaging.

The reasons people give for taking overdoses, in the literature, are: to get relief, to escape, to show desperation and to express anger when they have become lonely or isolated within the context of a relationship with key persons. The behaviour itself is expected to bring about some change in stressful circumstances.

Motivational explanations

The following explanations have been gleaned from the literature that takes a psychological or social psychological perspective on human behaviour and range from deep individual psychological explanations to hypothetical interactive views. None is regarded as any more valid than any other; they are hypothetical constructs, but are reviewed in order to find out how we, as observers in a culture of human observation and description, describe the motives of suicidal behaviour.

A Jungian description of suicide presents a process of internal conflict which produces 'tension'. This tension leads to an equivalence of alternative paths, of which suicide is one (Jung 1957). Suicidal behaviour results from following a decision-path of linked decisions, each decision being determined by thresholds of tension or affect.

Adler (1958) considers suicidal behaviour as purposive in a process of striving for success by maintaining that the individual commits suicide to increase his gains to win over significant others, especially the most significant other. To this same end, Bateson (1973) also suggests that a runaway of such behaviour can occur up to some threshold that might be on the other side of death.

Freud (1925) considers suicide to be an introjected conflict between wanting to kill a loved-and-hated object and the guilt of this desire. Rank (1969) develops the idea of conflict as the conflict between the fear of living and the fear of dying. This results in strategies of action whereby life is bargained for non-death by the inhibition of life by an individual. This view is reflected by Skinner (1953), who suggests that organisms might deliberately expose themselves to aversive stimulation if, by doing so, they avoid even more aversive consequences.

Ross and McKay (1979) draw attention to the existential explanations made about suicidal behaviour as a means of confirming existence. Self-mutilation is described as an act that serves to reassure the individual that she is alive, that she has feelings, that she has an identity and that she is indeed distinct from her surroundings. In this way, life is confirmed by confronting death. However, Rynearson (1981) reminds us that this existential view promotes problems for the one who remains.

Miller and Bashkin (1974) and Asch (1971) suggest that suicidal behaviour is the culmination of a sequence of specific events that start with some frustrating experiences and leads to a person feeling totally rejected or abandoned, as well as overwhelmingly angry. Suicidal behaviour allows the person to discharge this rage and re-affirm himself as a person, avoiding depersonalisation. The idea of a language of suicidal behaviour (Kreitman, Smith and Eng-Seong 1969) as a 'cry for help' (Stengel 1958) functions as a means of forcing others to recognise that the individual is suffering. Other writers have suggested that this communicative action is intended to stimulate others to come to the rescue of the person who is suffering (Alderson 1974; Bostic 1973).

However, not all commentators see the action in such a benign light and regard suicidal behaviour as rather perverse strategies by which individuals manipulate others into satisfying their needs. The suggestion is that the individual will threaten to engage in suicidal behaviour if the significant others will not do as he wishes. Brenman (1952) describes this as 'emotional blackmail'. The intentionality of such behaviour has been described by differing authors as to how persons achieve particular goals, for example to obtain attention, to get access to therapy and to gain privilege (Johnson *et al.* 1975), to influence social agencies (Morgan, Barton and Pottle 1976) and even to gain access to institutions (Ross and McKay 1979).

Both the notion of existential expression and manipulation are rolled together in the explanation of suicidal behaviour as risk taking (Frankel *et al.* 1976; Sjoberg 1969). This explanation suggests that suicidal behaviour is a way of engendering a response in other people by frightening them by the very daring of the risk. In this way, the individual gambles with life but, as is seen with most people who take risks, a considerable audience can gather to observe. Such a risk taking is seen as a 'gamble with death' (Lester and Lester 1971) where the individual tries out his existence by an act, one of the consequences of which could be death. An important factor here is that a providential agent is often described as being necessary for a 'rescue' from death and, while seeming to be an individual existential view, it is linked closely to the 'cry for help' view mentioned previously as a means of communication with another person.

The explanations of the occurrence of suicidal behaviour in institutions (McNeil and Vance 1978; Rosenthal *et al.* 1972; Ross and McKay 1979) see the behaviour as a form of manipulation in that it is a means of seeking attention to a particular state of affairs. If not a 'cry for help', it is deemed to be a communication of some sort.

This communication aspect has been suggested as a form of retaliatory behaviour and provides a way of getting back at someone where a direct manner is prohibited. Not only can it be a change of 'You'll be sorry' but it can also be seen as a symbolic expression of 'Look how you have hurt me'. Again, the description is about individual behaviour but, significantly, is directed at another person. Such explanations of other related behaviour involving communicative acts and strategies is developed in the argument of 'frustration' being causative.

Bach-Y-Rita (1974), Ballinger (1971) and Lukianowicz (1972) suggest that suicidal behaviour may be a response to modify the environment that restricts and frustrates the individual. It may be an indirect way of confronting environmental sources of frustration with a demand to change when direct confrontations are prohibited. The prohibition of direct confrontation may well be isolation or loss of privileges and suicidal behaviour may elicit more humane treatment, sympathy or special consideration.

The relation between specific stressful events and suicidal behaviour was mentioned in the previous sections and it is suggested that such behaviour is a means to gain some temporary relief from such a situation of stress. This notion of escape was also discussed in the previous section about personal motivation.

George Kelly (1961) suggests that instead of making the explanations of suicidal behaviour pathological or nonsensical, we look at the act itself and see what it accomplishes for the person who performs it. He suggests that we ask 'under what conditions of outlook would anyone seek death rather than life?' This question places an emphasis on the quality of life rather than on surviving. His description emphasises the position of the observer in that, as observers, we call certain actions suicidal because we predict our own trajectory of consequences upon behaviours and have our own alternative behaviours. Kelly's (1955) theory of construing behaviour is important in that it involves the interaction of others in the validation of personal behaviour. It also stresses the prediction of the behaviour of others. Once an individual finds that he cannot accurately predict the behaviour of others and finds himself invalidated, he must constrict his own construing of the world to a manageable size. Suicidal behaviour is seen as a search for validation in a personal construing of reality. If the future is construed as chaotic, it may be better to die and validate the life as previously lived rather than live invalidly. Kelly also sees attempted suicide as a hostile act, it is a strategy by one person to get another person to behave in a way which will confirm the original person's construings. In the quote from Siegal and Fried

(1955) at the beginning of this chapter we read the same sentiments being expressed about one person unduly threatening another.

Bruno Bettelheim

Bruno Bettelheim committed suicide at the age of 86 years. David Fisher (1992) writes of an academic friendship that extended over the latter years of Bettelheim's life. During the last years Bettelheim suffered continuously from a depression, became dejected and increasing physically infirm. He could no longer concentrate adequately, nor could he generate new ideas to his own satisfaction. He lost interest in the world, became lonely and isolated, seemingly irascible, and was abandoned by his own daughter. As a leading authority on parenting, this abandonment must have been an emotional shock. From Kelly's perspective we see that he no longer confirmed the identity that he formerly presented as the mature successful academic, an authority on relationships with an active intellect. He confided freely in his friend, Fisher, about his suicidal plans and his active search for the most appropriate method. He did not say when, thus his friend and academic confidant was shocked by the news.

The date that Bettelheim chose to kill himself has a biographical relevance. On 13 March 1938 the Nazis took over Austria and on this date, 52 years later, Bettelheim was to achieve his own annihilation. He was himself incarcerated in the concentration camps Dachau and Buchenwald and the memory of those camps was to be a link to his eventual demise. As he became physically and mentally infirm he recalled some of the inmates of that time who had apparently given up on life and had become totally dependent, helpless human beings. He was adamant that he would not become so. Like many of his former compatriots, he was to survive the horrors of the camp to be accompanied by a terrible grief and the guilt of surviving. A large number of survivors were later to commit suicide (Bronisch 1996). In his own thinking, the loss of personal freedom, to act autonomously would deny his very existence until then. Despite his ability to survive the extremities of existence in the camps, the loss of hope in old age and the threat of infirmity and life in an old people's home abandoned by his loved ones was to prove a hurdle that he, like many others in increasing numbers, no longer wished to overcome. It was a potential damaged identity, albeit in his own mind, that he was not willing to validate.

Ross Lockridge

Another threatened identity that lead to suicide, at the age of 33 years, was that of the American writer Ross Lockridge Jr. Ross Lockridge wrote the prize winning novel *Raintree County*, a novel hailed as the 'Great American Novel'. Deciding at the age of seven to become a writer, after a brilliant college career, he became a well-liked teacher. Lockridge set out to write his novel and in 1948 achieved the acclaim of the American literary world and a film contract. Two months after publication, he went into his garage, fastened a pipe to the exhaust of his car, closed the garage door, turned on the engine, sat in the back seat and gassed himself.

His son, Larry Lockridge (1995) set out to discover the background to his father's death. What he found is the same jigsaw of causes that we have discovered up until now. As he writes: '…that to speak of a "cause" or "causes" is no simple matter' (p.432). Ross Lockridge suffered from depression and was hospitalised for treatment. Following the publication of his novel, he became quite grandiose and believed that he had indeed written the 'Great American Novel'. However, he also entered into a contractual dispute with his publisher about revenues. Other demands challenged the autonomy of the writer as having final say in the work. He was asked to make substantial cuts in the work that he cherished. Cutting the work and wrangling over money were material concerns that stood in stark contrast to his belief in the writer's work as a spiritual testament. Following his capitulation over the contract dispute, he entered hospital for electro-convulsive therapy. As the last straw, on the day that he killed himself, a review of his work appeared in the local press that blasted his beloved novel and which he could only have taken as a humiliation. Cause and effect became interrelated in a downward spiral from which there was no recovery. It is such sequences of events of escalating distress that we will investigate in Chapter Four.

Psychache and anguish

The anguish, suffering and mental pain that we have read about in the two previous examples should lie at the centre of any discussion about suicide (Shneidman 1993b). According to him, after a lifetime's work in studying suicide, 'suicide is caused by psychache' (Shneidman 1993a, p.147). Psychache is intrinsically psychological, resulting from 'the pain of excessively felt shame, or guilt, or humiliation, or loneliness, or fear, or angst, or dread of growing old or of doing badly, or whatever' (p.147). Each individual will have a threshold for their own distress, and it is in such terms, so Shneidman argues, that we must discuss the suffering that occurs in suicide. Such sociological, demographic variables miss the mark when the intolerable psychological pain the individual suffers is ignored (Shneidman 1993b). We will certainly find in the following chapters that the descriptions of medicine and the diagnostic categories of psychiatry are confining and sterile in terms of our understanding of the human condition that leads to escalating distress. The social and ecological understandings, while alerting us to the shamefulness of poverty that still exists within our wealthy societies, does not shed any light upon the anguish of the person who sits before us in our consulting room.

Common ground

There appears to be some common ground emerging from these apparently disparate and idiosyncratic views.

First, an element of conflict appears either intrapsychically or interpersonally with a significant other. Second, there is a suggestion that this conflict is a process which escalates over time as a sequence of events. Third, if this is so, then it appears necessary to include in any such description of suicidal behaviour the behaviour of the involved other. Finally, the process of escalating behaviours is seen as an attempt to coerce, manipulate, validate, communicate or negotiate some mutual goal whereby persons do something differently together. It is a political act with a small 'p'. In this process the original relational nexus becomes disturbed and one person becomes threatened with isolation, alienation or banishment. For example, an adolescent and his family don't see eye to eye. Eventually the arguments increase in intensity and frequency. His parents try and get him to behave and he sees that as controlling. Eventually an ultimatum is given and, in the heat of the moment, some act of rebellion precipitates his being thrown out of the house. In an effort to show contrition, when his thresholds of suffering are exceeded, and to be allowed back home, he makes what is seen as a suicide attempt. It would make sense then in any explanation to consider suicidal behaviour as a socially interactive process between, and involving, a number of persons within a particular social context. It is this perspective which will be investigated in the following chapter.

However, we cannot neglect the personal ramifications for the individual. Both Kelly and Shneidman see the problem of suicide as one of constriction in thinking, albeit when it is in a context of constricted relationship. Only one solution, death, is seen as being available to a problem as it is constituted in a narrow sense of immediate time. The individual can no longer go on being with an identity that he has achieved or can no longer maintain. The narrative stops. Hopelessness is when there is no story to go on with.

CHAPTER THREE

Family Interaction and Suicidal Behaviour

> *If the family appears as the most natural of social categories and is therefore destined to provide the model for all social bodies, this is because it functions, in habitus, as a classificatory scheme and a principle of the construction of the social world and of that particular social body, the family, a principle that is acquired within a family existing as a realized social fiction.* (Bourdieu 1996, p.21)

This chapter will describe the research that has previously investigated suicidal behaviour in the context of the family. There has been little direct research into the phenomenon compared with the research into problems of mental health and family contexts. However, some modern writers who are concerned with clinical practice have written about the family and postulated how suicidal behaviour occurs. I will be presenting both concrete descriptions and hypothetical explanations. As we saw in the previous chapter, the presence of change, conflict and a key person have been considered as important factors in the aetiology of suicidal behaviour (Aldridge 1984; Aldridge 1985).

Research and family interaction

In the 1960s, writers on adolescent suicidal behaviour (Barter 1968; Haider 1968; Tabachnick 1961) were presenting the opinion that this behaviour could not be considered fully unless it was understood within the framework of adolescent–parent relationships. Even if the nuclear family situation was not intact, the familial relationships, however strained, still continued.

Throughout the growing literature there has been a consideration of interpersonal variables as being significant in suicidal behaviour. Several authors (Henry *et al.* 1993; Kienhorst *et al.* 1995; Koopmans 1995; Lindsay 1973; Morrison and Collier 1969; Tuckman and Youngman 1964; Tuckman, Youngman and Leifer 1966; Wilde *et al.* 1992) suggest that family conflict and social disorganisation, or lack of cohesion (Payne and Range 1995), are related to attempted suicide. Social disorganisation for these authors is characterised by economic and emotional depravation, neglect, rejection and marital conflict between parents or spouses. These factors contribute to a milieu whereby individuals adapt by developing destructive or delinquent patterns of behaviour. These authors do not suggest why suicidal behaviours should be chosen, nor what particular factors stimulate one person in the family to behave in such a way and not others. Tuckman, Youngman and Leifer (1966) say it may well be that suicide is utilised when coping mechanisms have been exhausted, but they do not say whether the coping mechanisms of the family or the individual have been exhausted.

In a study by Gould *et al.* (1996) of psychosocial factors in 120 child and adolescent completed suicides, familial factors came to the fore. Suicide victims were significantly likely to come from a non-intact family of origin than a random comparison sample matched for age, ethnic and sex distribution. Communication with those parents that were available was seen as less satisfying and a failure to communicate with the father was seen as being clinically relevant for the escalation of distress. King *et al.* (1993) too found that the fathers of suicidal adolescents reported more depression and family problems than comparison families. Similarly, there was less communication between adolescents and fathers. Parents often have a history of mood disorders, trouble with the police or a family history of suicidal behaviour (Martin *et al.* 1995). Once family life is broken, and fathers fail to communicate with their children, school problems can occur. The child fails to attend school, breaks contact with his peers, becomes isolated socially and increasingly distressed with no one to confide in.

When overdose cases were assessed in a psychiatric context, and compared with community controls, a specific association was found between depression and family dysfunction in the families where an overdose had occurred (Kerfoot *et al.* 1996). Kerfoot and his colleagues suggest that in the treatment of overdose cases, the family should be involved because it is in a context of family difficulties that adolescent suicidal behaviour occurs.

In response to a growing understanding of such social disorganisation at the familial level and poor mental health, some mental health workers have attempted to investigate which factors are supportive (Bowlby 1973; Kaplan, Cassel and Gore 1977; Levy, Jurkovic and Spirito 1995; Myers, Jacobs and Pepper 1972).

Speck and Attneave (1973) described social networks that had a lasting impact on the life of the individual and maintained both her physical and psychological integrity. This group were primarily members of the nuclear family, kin, neighbours or friends – a grouping that Madanes (1981) calls a 'community of intimates'. The function of such a group is to give and receive love and affection, to be dependent and depended upon, to control others and be controlled and to provide emotional and instrumental sustenance. Spouses and members of the immediate family were found to provide the most support in times of mental or physical crises (Croog, Lipson and Levine 1972; Litwak and Szeleny 1969; Quarnatelli 1960) and, in the long term, support of men who were unemployed. Brown, Bhrolchain and Harris (1975) found that one of the most important factors that discriminated between women who developed symptoms of psychiatric illness and those who did not was the former's lack of an intimate confiding relationship with a husband or boyfriend. Individuals with confidants were best able to survive traumatic social losses such as retirement or the death of a spouse.

However, Greenblatt, Becerra and Serafetinides (1982) suggest that although intimate relationships are important for maintaining well-being and ameliorating psychological turmoil in the face of social stressors, it is the quality of these relationships that is important. It seems that should these mutually supportive relationships deteriorate, then individuals become prone to social stressors and, perhaps more importantly, these relationships can themselves promote distress (Attneave 1980). Bourdieu, too, stresses the importance of family discourse as being a set of relationships where the ordinary laws of the economy are suspended, there is a refusal to calculate and an emphasis on friendly trusting and giving (Bourdieu 1996).

This seems initially confusing in that the immediate social relationships can both buffer and promote stress. It is the patterns of such relationships which will be explored later in this chapter. What is important to reiterate here is the danger of assessing families, or communities of intimates, against a set of expert norms that further subjugates them and defines them as damaged (Soal and Kottler 1996).

Suicidal behaviour as communication

A suicide attempt has been seen as a bid by one member of a social group to communicate his distress to others intimately associated with him and that the attempt functions as part of a language. If suicidal behaviour is part of a language, it is not an individual phenomenon but a social phenomenon. This particular aspect is taken up by other authors (Rosenbaum and Richman 1970; Rosenbaum and Richman 1972; Williams and Lyons 1976), who emphasise that communication is a reciprocal process of interaction within a social context. Such a view emphasises that suicidal behaviour by one member is part of a social process and is not an initiator of a sequence of behaviour, nor is it the result of being a passive victim. In other words, the suicidal member of a social group does not communicate but participates in communication. The behaviour cannot be seen and understood as action and reaction but as part of a socially systemic transaction (Aldridge 1984; Aldridge and Rossiter 1983; Aldridge and Rossiter 1984; Watzlawick and Beavin 1967). If such behaviour is part of a familial communication, it may be possible to discover what this communication entails and to what purpose it can be attributed. Such a perspective has been outlined by some family theorists.

Hostility and death wishes

Richman and Rosenbaum (1970) investigated the handling of aggression within families where a member had attempted suicide, following the basic premise of Freud that 'no neurotic harbours thoughts of suicide which are not murderous impulses against others redirected upon himself' (Freud 1925, p.162). In their investigation they were concerned to investigate the behaviour in a family context and to discover who was the patient wishing dead, trying to kill or wanted to suffer. What the authors discovered was that aggression was a prominent feature in the behaviour of everyone involved in the situation. Within this context of familial aggression the suicidal member was described as being in a hostile alliance with one family member against another and often the spokesperson for a silent partner in a family battle. This hostility was, however, characterised in their study by the withholding of direct overt hostile confrontation and the expression of covert hostility mediated by social responsibility. For example, a family member would say 'My mother is ill and I cannot say what I want to as this would upset her'. Such a theme was found in families where suicide attempters believed that to express anger would lead others to become sick and die. The threat of death by the suicide attempter was seen as a strategy in the context of family conflict that could control or prevent change, but the prospect of death was used as a metaphor by other family members to control and prevent change (Fawcett 1969). It appears then that suicidal behaviour as communication may be a metaphor about 'dying' and 'control of change' in some families (Madanes 1981; Watzlawick, Beavin and Jackson 1967).

The use of 'death' and 'kill' were often reported in the families which Richman and Rosenbaum (1970) studied and were taken as examples of hostility by one member to another in a context of escalating conflict. Some death wishes were seen as concerns for the patient when, at times of chronic sickness or handicap, the involved parent or spouse thought it might be a good idea if the patient died to remove the burden from others. This expression of hostility is a crucial message as it entails a particular nuance, it is not a message that 'I could kill you', which is homicidal, but 'I can't kill you but we would all be better off if you were dead', which is suicidogenic.

A conclusion of the above study is that suicidal behaviour is likely to occur when there is increased stress accompanied by hostility and death wishes from the family and other significant external objects, when the other person is unable to retaliate and when external help is unavailable or withdrawn. This pattern is seen as performing a vital function for the whole family in managing and controlling change. In a perverse way, the family or group is seen as handling a difficult family problem in its own idiosyncratic style. Such family problems are explored in the next section.

Family life-cycle and transition

A number of researchers into family behaviour began to notice that problems occurred at particular times of transition in families (Fisch, Weakland and Segal 1982; Haley 1980; Hill 1964; Rapoport 1965; Richman 1978). Such transitions are everyday occurrences in all families, which result in a redefinition of family relationships: from courtship to marriage, from the initial commitment to marriage to a fuller commitment at the arrival of a first child, the surrender of the autonomy of the first child to the influence of others (peers, school, organizations), from a child-oriented marriage to a two-person marriage when the children leave home and retirement or widowhood.

All these junctures require change and it is easy to see that changes in employment or health status too can require adaptations by the family. The above theorists stress that these are normal developmental occurrences and only prove difficult when such transitions are mishandled.

Family organisation and change

Haley (1980) generalises about such transitions and their effect upon family organisation in his description of adolescent deviant behaviour. He says that 'in any organization the time of greatest change occurs when someone is entering the organization or leaving it' (p.29).

When a young person succeeds outside the house it is not merely a matter of individual success but a process of disengagement from a family, which has important ramifications for the whole organisation. This transition is handled satisfactorily in a number of ways in our culture that reflects the views of the cultural anthropologists mentioned earlier where, when there are changes in status, there are rites of transition for crossing the boundary of one state to another – that is 'in' the family to 'out' of the family, 'single at home' to 'married and away', 'schoolboy at home' to 'student away at college'.

When a person begins to act strangely and appears to fail at the stage of leaving home, Haley argues that the organisation is in trouble. In some families the parents left alone are unable to function as a dyad and threaten divorce or separation, or one member may develop pathological symptoms. Haley describes this as a process whereby the child has been a 'bridge' between the parents and to leave would mean that the family becomes unstable. All the marital themes in such a family have been communicated in terms of the child and must now be dealt with differently when the child is no longer active in the triangle mother–father–child. Should the child stay at home, the family will be stabilised, but at a price. Such stability has to be accommodated in the larger process of coherence within the social life outside of the family: school, work, outside organisations, peers. All these social situations pose normative expectations.

Richman (1978; 1979) describes such a child–parent symbiosis as pathological, whereby all members of the family system participate through the generations. When one member tries to leave then other members of the family network attempt to bring him back. However, such a process means that no new relationships are made and this, in turn, proves problematical and the family system expects a member to leave. Such an oscillation between staying and leaving appears as a number of escalating crises. These crises can stabilise a family in that the parents can continue to communicate through and about the young person with the organisation remaining the same. Even if the person is not immediately present, he can still provide a focus for the attention of his family by reminding them that he is regularly failing. In this way, not only is the individual adolescent, or young adult, frozen at a developmental stage in the life cycle, so too are the parents.

This appears as a recurrent cycle and can be schematized as follows:

- A young person prepares to leave his family and becomes successful in external relationships, which may be intimate;
- The family becomes unstable and all members manifest troublesome behaviour;
- One member may become, or appear, more extreme and the other members appear to stabilise;
- The parents, who are divided over many issues, become more divided and the young person appears to take charge and have power over the family;

- Should the parents unite, the young person may engage another member of the kinship network to give support in coalition against the parents;

- The parents become more unable to control the young person and the behaviour escalates;

- Throughout this time, family conflict and hostility is escalating;

- An outside agent is called in to restrain or treat the young person, which stabilises the situation by removing the suicidal member;

- The young person is released or discharged from a 'place of safety', begins to succeed in intimate relationships and the family conflict and instability appear again.

Haley (1980) describes this behaviour as protective. Although violent, extreme or bizarre, such suicidal behaviour is seen as stabilising an organisation. The family group is forced to organise with more stability and adapt to disruption. Parents are forced to unite to cope with a deviant member. Some theorists suggest that suicidal behaviour appears when a conflict seems to be escalating between the parents (Ferreira 1968; Minuchin 1974; O'Connor and Stachowiak 1971; Schuman 1970) and such behaviour attempts to reduce the conflict.

This pattern of reconciling conflict by problematical behaviour in a family member is reflected in family studies where children's problems are seen as attempts to unite parents and keep parents involved (Selvini-Palazzoli *et al.* 1973). Parental conflict is managed and kept in check by problematical behaviour on the part of the child. In this way, a pattern of conflict management can develop whereby any conflict that threatens to exceed a family threshold is reduced by symptomatic behaviour on the part of a family member to promote unity rather than divergence (see Figure 3:1).

Some theorists suggest that suicidal behaviour be regarded as 'benevolent', although misguided (de Shazer 1982; Waxler 1975). How such behaviour becomes manifested as suicidal behaviour is not clear but other authors suggest that there is often a direct contact with such behaviour in a family history (Brent *et al.* 1996; McCulloch and Philip 1972; Teicher and Jacobs 1966).

Rosenbaum and Richman (1970) propose a metaphorical communication about life and death. These authors go on to suggest that in family histories there are clues to how such behaviours develop. In self-poisoning families there is often a family culture of distress management by medication, by food

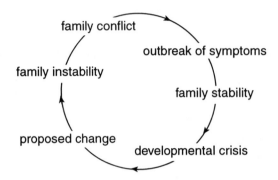

Figure 3.1 The circle of family conflict and developmental crisis

or by alcohol (Koopmans 1995; Martin *et al.* 1995). There is also a history of either suicide, attempted suicide or murder.

What we appear to be seeing in some families then are ways of managing distress that are passed on from generation to generation. Children with one or more family members who have committed suicide are at risk of attempting suicide than children who do not have such a family history (Gutierrez, King and Ghaziuddin 1996). We do not need to look for genetic markers, that would be biologically too specific and deterministic. However, from clinical accounts, we can say that certain behaviour runs in families. It is learned. Distress is managed as it is manifested. How distress can be expressed is also learned. Brent *et al.* (1996) couple the transmission of suicidal behaviour in families with aggression. As Shneidman (1993b) says, we can rely upon psychological descriptions of suffering to be adequate without having to have recourse to biological markers and chemical explanations. If the expression and management of distress is learned, it may well be that some suicidal behaviours within a culture of family distress management are indeed attempts to resolve distress.

Family suicide potential

From the previously mentioned research studies, it is possible to propose a number of factors that appear to be present in some families. We must be aware that these authors regard this behaviour in a family context and within a broader social matrix. In such a social matrix, suicidal behaviour may be considered as a strategy for controlling change and coping with stress within the family group to modify the environment (Lukianowicz 1972; Sale *et al.* 1975). The factors are:

1. A pattern of marked family hostility, with the prohibition that one member does not respond with hostility overtly. That member is not allowed to leave and there is a shifting coalition between that member and another family member against a third family member (Haley 1980; Richman and Rosenbaum 1970; Watzlawick and Weakland 1977).

2. A pattern of role disturbances and role failure in every area of personal functioning (Haley 1980; Murthy 1969; Schrut 1968), where failure by one member functions to stabilise conflict within the family. This is obtained at the price of estrangement and isolation from broader social contexts.

3. Suicidal behaviour occurs as a process of escalation when developmental crises have occurred in the management of family life-cycle transitions (Watzlawick and Beavin 1967) and these developmental crises have been managed by the presentation of pathological symptomatology to reduce conflict. In such families, individual developmental change is considered as disloyal, which places the suicidal member in a difficult position of maintaining a personal developmental coherence within his family milieu and a wider social milieu.

4. There is a symbiotic attachment between two partners that tolerates no strivings for autonomy on the part of either partner, both intimacy and separation are mishandled (Bowlby 1973; Byng-Hall 1980; Tabachnick 1961).

5. There is a high level of intolerance of crisis, where the developmental crises mentioned earlier are handled by hostility and conflict. This ties in with the epidemiological factors indicating that cumulative and rapid changes appear to precipitate suicidal behaviour, but particularly a row or argument with a significant other. The disruption itself is not the major factor but rather the way that a disruption is handled by the family or immediate social network.

6. The handling of crises is related to family conflict and organisation that is located within a family culture of crisis management, which itself has developed over a number of generations (Morrison and Collier 1969; Tuckman and Connor 1962; Tuckman and Youngman 1964). Such families appear to be socially insulated and protect the suicidal member from social change.

Above all, the occurrence of suicidal behaviour is seen as a pattern of communication. The suicidal member is not seen as initiating the process, nor is he a passive victim, but participates in the process together with the significant others who are involved in the suicidogenic situation. Somehow the suicidal act becomes necessary for the survival of the family system as a whole, whether this is to institute change or to prevent change is not stated clearly but points to the management and control of the rate of change.

The metaphorical nature of the communication expresses the nature of the family concern. It states the problem and is a solution. In this way, suicidal behaviour can be a statement of '*Treat this family as having a life or death problem*', '*This family has a problem with living*' or '*This family is dying as an entity*'. Self-mutilation may be a communication about '*See how cut-up we are*'.

The family researchers present a perspective that describes suicidal behaviour as a relational phenomena. Families organise themselves to manage developmental crises in varying ways. Some families accommodate change easily, and apparently naturally, without excess levels of distress. Some families develop, within their own cultural tradition, a means of accommodating change which involves hostility and conflict, leading to high levels of distress. The reduction of this familial distress and conflict is managed by one family member exhibiting symptoms (see Figure 3.1, p.???). When a pattern of distress management by the presentation of symptoms occurs, and developmental crises still occur, then distress escalates and symptoms worsen. This is the downward spiral that we read about at the end of Chapter Two. A characteristic of families with a suicidal member is that although coping mechanisms are exhausted, there is reluctance to involve external agents. In this familial perspective of suicidal behaviour it appears that families do not buffer the individual from stress but act as a social unity that manages change. What does appear to be critical for the resolution of problems is a family tradition of crisis management and the presence of intra-familial conflict.

CHAPTER FOUR

A Systemic Perspective

Stabilization of relationship has been called the 'rule of the relationship' and works in the interest of economy (it leaves many behaviours from the repertoire to be used no longer). (Jackson 1965a, pp.1–20).

Every individual exists in a continually changing world of experience of which he is the centre. The world of experience is for each individual, in a very significant sense, a private world. The organism reacts to the field as it is experienced and perceived. This 'perceptual' field is, for the individual, 'reality'. The world comes to be composed of a series of tested hypotheses which provide much security. Yet mingled with these are perceptions which remain completely unchecked. These untested perceptions are also a part of our personal reality, and may have as much authority as those which have been checked. (Rogers 1951)

My image is my aggregation and organisation of information about the perceived object, aggregated and integrated by me according to rules of which I am totally unconscious. I can know about these rules; but I cannot be conscious of the process of their working. (Bateson 1978, p.238)

So far we have the notorious plethora of views concerning suicidal behaviour and its multiplicity of perspectives. In this chapter I will attempt to present a theoretical perspective on suicidal behaviour that will begin to reconcile a number of those differing views and elaborate the interactional perspective raised in the last chapter. The focus that I will take is concerned with the process of escalating behaviour within a family context.

As families seek to maintain their viability they are presented with life-cycle changes that must be negotiated. The way these changes are negotiated is critical for the family as a system of individuals and as a systemic entity in a wider social ecology. Should these negotiations result in unacceptable levels of personal or familial distress, then attempted solutions resident within the culture will be tried. The difficulty of any such undertaking, as other theorists have pointed out (Atkinson 1978; Douglas 1967), is that of explaining situated concrete acts by abstract meanings. Individuals are material causes – without them there would be no attempted suicides – yet each individual can choose not to behave in a proposed way. It is society which can provide the necessary, if not sufficient, causes and restraints upon individual behaviour. At the same time, individuals are informing society in a self-referential way about the meaning of their behaviour and inventing new behaviours in different situations.

Which system?

A central feature of the descriptions in this chapter will be the understanding of persons in their particular social contexts. As Varela and Johnson (1976) propose, 'You can't study a rabbit without looking at his forest' (p.26). Systems are seen as organised like a collection of Chinese boxes, one within another; organs within a body, a person within a family, a family within a kin network and a kin network within a community. The key to understanding systems as wholes is that they are organised as a constellation, that is every part interacts with every other part giving a self-referential system. To try and make some understanding of such complexity it is necessary to understand that when these parts operate together, they have emergent properties as a whole (Bateson 1973). When split apart, and investigated as parts, the important emergent holistic properties vanish. It is this very point which will be amplified in later chapters concerned with family perspectives on suicide (Chapters Nine, Ten and Eleven). It might be possible to see two partners – father and adolescent, for example – but not the important emergent property – the pattern of the relationship between them. In this way then, individuals will be considered within a particular system of significant others. Although the separation out of such a family group perspective is an arbitrary choice, a choice of cleavage, it is one that makes sense from what we have read in the preceding chapters.

A general systems approach

In recent years social scientists and family theorists have taken a general systems approach to theory construction and the explanation of social behaviour. A system is defined as a set of objects together with relationships between the objects and between their attributes (Watzlawick, Beavin and Jackson 1967). Implied in such a definition is that a 'boundary' exists, which delineates the elements belonging to the system and those belonging to its environment. Such a boundary is selected which includes those units which appear to have a higher level of interaction among themselves than with units outside the system. However, in living systems such as the family, boundaries are more than arbitrarily chosen and passively observed lines of demarcation; boundaries are maintained and negotiated interactively. Who is in the family and who is not part of the family is a discussion many of us will have experienced at the time of wedding.

Circular causality

Systemic descriptions of the family are more than simply aggregating a number of individual descriptions. They are concerned with transactions between individuals. As we shall see in Chapter Six when a hospital ward situation is described, it is not a description of patient behaviour but a description of staff–patient interaction that is crucial for understanding suicidal behaviour.

Much of the previous research in the behavioural sciences, as we have seen in the previous chapters, has been devoted to finding causes for given observed effects. These causes are proposed as being linearly related to their effects – event B happens because event A has happened. Systemic descriptions take into account a phenomenon called feedback. This position proposes that information about event B impinges upon event A, which affects B and so on in a circular sequence of modifications. When a person threatens to leave a family, that threat influences the likely behaviour, which, in turn, influences the likelihood of leaving. In studying a related group of people who constantly influence each other, a circular causal model is more likely to reflect such notions as process and interaction than the linear model, which delineates event A from event B in a direct causal order (see Figures 3.1, p.48 and 4.1).

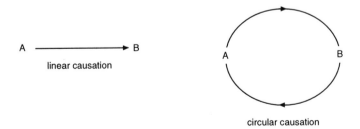

Figure 4.1 A comparison of linear and circular causality

Homeostasis: a steady state of change

A central feature of the previous explanations about how a person becomes suicidal has been the management of change. Homeostasis is a term borrowed from physiology and used by cyberneticians and systems theorists. It is a term used to describe how systems accommodate disruptive change in their parts by a capacity to absorb change to return to an equilibrial state (Ashby 1960; Buckley 1967; Jackson 1957). Family members change by growing up, yet somehow they stay together as a family and maintain a family identity.

Homeostasis is that constant systemic adaptation necessary to meet the demands of developmental change at the same and differing levels. An individual must develop himself but is also part of a family, and that must develop too. This adaptive, evolutionary view has been challenged by some authors who see homeostasis as the process by which systems return to a *status quo* that functions to prevent change (Dell 1980; Dell 1982; Speer 1970). Quite rightly, they argue that change cannot not occur and for one system to remain constant will mean that other systemic components will have to change to maintain coherence at a different systemic level.

Other theoreticians have pointed out that for a system to remain viable its stable point of equilibrium is not fixed and must remain on the move (Beer 1975; Maturana and Varela 1980). For the purposes of this chapter, this dynamic temporal view will be adopted. Systems maintain their viability in a steady state of change; homeostasis being the process of maintaining an equilibrial state. This stability is seen as a dynamic process of development and adaptation and is a gradual and subtle ecological balance of individual, social and cultural changes. If we were to follow the life cycle of a butterfly through its stages we might discover it had apparently different forms, but there would be a constant viable identity throughout its life. It all depends upon if we, as observers, have an epistemology that recognises life-cycle and metamorphosis. In addition, we know that the viability of the butterfly life-cycle is linked with that of the plants upon which it feeds. These, too, are bound to an ecology of the birds that feed upon the butterfly larva.

In a family we may observe two persons 'courting' each other, who eventually marry and have children. The children eventually leave the parental home and set up homes of their own and may themselves have children. Throughout this 'family life-cycle' there will be structural changes and individual developmental changes. The parents will be initially young adults. Eventually they will appear as old persons. The children will change from being dependent infants to becoming autonomous adults in their own right. Throughout this process the family members will change according to their own individual requirements and the demands of the culture in which they live. Similarly, these developments will be accommodated within family requirements which allow members to 'leave home' yet still maintain the identity of the family. Occasionally the adaptations to meet the requirements of the individual, the family and society do not 'fit' neatly together (Shibutani 1962). The debate about 'one-parent' families, for example, is indicative of how political considerations about the nuclear family ignore the fact that single parents also have larger family networks within which they are embedded. Indeed, some family workers (Hair 1996) suggest that the family structure of father, mother and children is rarely encountered and that other living configurations of linked systems are more commonly found in practice.

Like the butterfly, the family member will be part of a broader ecology of significant others, a cultural ecology and a social ecology. Leaving home and getting a job are important stages in individual development. But if you are in under-developed region, you may have to travel far away to find work, becoming dislocated from family and friends where accommodation and work are difficult to find. Indeed, Saunderson and Langford (Saunderson and Langford 1996) find that it is such a dislocation from social backgrounds when young people migrate to centres of urban poverty in big cities that we find concentrations of adolescent suicide and poor mental health.

The management of change and conflict in the family

The family studies theorists mentioned in the previous chapter have offered a number of descriptions of how such behaviour occurs in family and small group contexts. In such a social matrix suicidal behaviour is seen as a strategy for controlling change and coping with stress within the family group. Family or small groups, according to these studies, are stressed by developmental or life-cycle changes where symptoms of illness are used to reduce, manage or avoid conflict. Suicidal behaviour in such explanations is seen as a communicative process expressing a suicidogenic situation that reflects the survival of the family system as a whole. Whether this is a process to prevent change or institute change is not stated clearly, but there is an indication that suicidal behaviour is somehow involved with the management of the rate of change in a family.

Suicidal behaviour can be considered as a social phenomenon. Families organise themselves to manage developmental crises in varying ways. Some families accommodate change easily and naturally without excess levels of distress. Some families develop, within their own cultural tradition, a means of accommodating change that involves hostility and conflict leading to high levels of distress. How these differences evolve will be discussed later in this chapter. It is suggested that the reduction of this familial distress is managed by one family member exhibiting symptoms (see Figure 3.1, p.48) (Haley 1980; Madanes 1981). Effectively, one person acts as a material cause, representing distress at a different systemic level of interaction. The individual represents a pattern of social transactions.

Communication

Communication is a reciprocal process of inter-personal messages about relationship. Individuals engage in, or become part of, communication. In the presence of another person all behaviour is communicative. Activity or inactivity, words or silence all have message value: they influence others and these others cannot not respond. As we will see in Chapters Ten and Eleven, silence and withdrawal in the face of questions is a powerful response within a relationship.

Following on from this idea of communication as inter-personal relationship is the tenet that communication has two aspects to it: a report aspect and a command aspect. Communication not only conveys information but, at the same time, imposes behaviour. We will see in Chapter Six how the cutting of a woman's wrist is both a message about 'See how distressed I am' but also 'Do something about it'.

The report aspect of a message conveys information and is synonymous with the content of the message. The command aspect of a message is concerned with what sort of message it is to be taken as and is concerned with relationship. For those of us who remember our schooldays, we know that the report 'Thank you Sir' can be said in a number of ways, from the respectful to the insulting, according to the way in which it is said (and received). In later sections of this chapter I will refer to this report aspect in terms of constitutive rules and the command aspect in terms of regulative rules.

Communication in families

Since Stengel (1958) it has been generally agreed amongst clinicians that a suicidal behaviour represents a bid to communicate distress to key figures in an intimate social group. An implication of this view is that such acts may function as a language employed within such a group, where other groups would use less pathological forms of communication. This resembles Mechanic's (1974) 'vocabulary' of illness behaviour and places suicidal behaviour within the realm of social phenomena.

Kreitman, Smith and Eng-Seong (1969) point out that when persons in distress wish to convey that distress to others, they do not have to invent a communicational medium; such a medium exists within the subculture. All that the person has to do is to invoke it. What I am proposing is that there are shared personal meanings within families, as family meanings, and these meanings too are embedded in a larger cultural context of meanings.

Meanings in context

A difficulty of analysing communication both for participators and observers is that it is not always obvious what a person is doing when that person engages in communication. A given statement can mean different things in different contexts; it can be appropriate in one context but not in another. This has been the central problem facing the understanding of suicidal behaviour: 'What does the behaviour mean?' and, more appropriate, 'What does the behaviour mean in a particular context.'

A number of writers (Harré and Secord 1973; Mead 1925; Mead 1934; Powers 1973; Schachter and Singer 1962) have shown that the meaning of messages in communication resides in the interaction between sender and receiver, rather than in the stimulus, and that individuals differ in their interpretative processes. Yet individuals within a culture perceive most messages similarly enough to co-ordinate their activities to function as social entities. This commonality of meaning is ambiguous; individuals do differ and may differ in perception even when seemingly engaged in co-ordinated interaction. To understand each other they must continually negotiate that interaction. I am using the idea of negotiation deliberately here as the meaning of what we say and do in the context of a relationship cannot be taken for granted. We negotiate the validity of what we communicate and how we act. Kelly's approach, described earlier, reminded us that we must be validated in the world and this validation must be negotiated, it is not simply given.

Hierarchies of meanings

Immediately we begin to discuss individuals, individuals interacting and individuals interacting within a social context, we are faced with making an hierarchical understanding of meaning. These different hierarchical levels will be of a different order of abstraction and describe differing phenomena (Bateson 1973; Heyman and Shaw 1978; Korzybski 1958; Toulmin 1964). Meanings are made which contextualise and redefine meanings at other levels. At a simple level we can see this in the way that meaning has been assigned to acts of deliberate self-harm by authors taking differing theoretical perspectives. Although the same behaviour may be considered – the ingestion of a toxic substance – that same behaviour may be described as pseudocide, parasuicide, attempted suicide, self-poisoning or deliberate self-harm. This is the assignation of meaning by theorists. The assignation of meaning by the individuals involved, their families and friends may be quite different.

Even within professional groups with similar core trainings, differences of opinion will occur surrounding the same behaviour. Stotland (1997) describes a situation where an adolescent patient in a pediatric nephrology unit is described by the treating physician as being suicidal. However, when seen by an attending psychiatrist, who asks the patient why he is refusing to sign a consent form for treatment, the situation becomes not one of suicidal behaviour but reluctance to submit to a painful procedure. Once the patient's views are acknowledged, a satisfactory solution is found to what, at heart, is a relational problem between a sensitive patient and a heavy-handed clinician.

Punctuation

Social scientists have become concerned with the way in which we select 'meaningful' patterns from the ceaseless stream of events. This selective structuring of reality is given the name 'punctuation' (Bateson 1973). To an outside observer a series of communications can be viewed as an uninterrupted sequence of interchanges, but the participants may introduce definite episodes of interchange with, for them, clear beginnings and endings. Punctuation is seen as oganising behavioural events and is vital to interaction. Culturally, we share many conventions of punctuation which serve to organise common and important interactional sequences. We observe this when someone says 'He always starts an argument' or 'It first began when her husband died'. Such features of communication will be examined in Chapters Ten and Eleven where individuals and families describe their problems.

Disagreement about how to punctuate a sequence of events is suggested as a source of relationship struggles. In Chapter Eleven we will see how a wife tries to help, as she believes, her sick husband, who labels this 'help' as interference with his authority as the man of the house. In essence, their relationship is characterised by two understandings of a mutual interchange: 'I help because you are incompetent' and 'I'm incompetent because you insist on "helping"'. This concept of punctuation is particularly relevant to the descriptions of episodes of inter-personal behaviour that we will see in the later chapters.

Episodes

A regular feature of writing about deliberate self-harm has been descriptions of episodes of behaviour. Harré and Secord (1973) define an episode as 'any part of human life, involving one or more people, in which some internal structure can be determined' (p.153). Although imprecise, it does offer a valuable tool for considering behaviour in that behaviour is located inter-personally and structured (Pearce and Cronen 1980). Episodes can be described in ways which represent proposed 'levels' of construing. These levels are cultural, personal and familial:

1. Culturally: episodes are patterns of meanings and behaviours which are culturally sanctioned and which exist independently of any particular individual or dyadic meaning. This is represented by the 'cry for help' notion of distress. Such construings reflect the concept of significant 'symbols' described by Mead (1934) and Duncan (1968) which reflect publicly shared meanings. Such culturally significant episodes involving a public construing would be rituals such as marriages and funerals and ritualised ways of dealing with social events such as greetings, deference and leaving.

2. Personally: episodes can be seen as patterns of meanings and behaviour in the minds of individuals. This is a privatised meaning which represents an individual's understanding of the forms of social interaction in which he is participating or wishes to participate in. In a study by Parker (1981), episodes of deliberate self-harm are described by the girls performing the behaviour as similar to 'being alone and crying' and 'getting drunk'. This construing may be quite different to cultural construings of such behaviour which may see such an episode as 'manipulative' or 'punitive'. Or, as we saw in the earlier example in the nephrology unit, non-co-operation may be seen as suicidal behaviour. Difficulties occur when a personal construing of episodes is at odds with a cultural construing of episodes. What may be deemed valid individually may be invalidated culturally. We will see examples of this in Chapter Five where newspaper reports offer different descriptions of the same events of suicidal behaviour. In the nephrology unit, an individual refusal of treatment was at odds with the ward culture of automatic consent to a medical demand.

3. Familiarly: episodes are construed as common patterns of actions that assume a reciprocal perspective (Procter 1981). These familial construings have been developed throughout a number of

long-term interactions. In the way people live together, they co-ordinate an understanding of what the world means. A difficulty for co-ordinating meaning will occur when individuals construe their world quite idiosyncratically but engage in negotiating a common understanding with their significant others within a broader context of society. The Schachter and Singer (1962) experiments throw light on how, when individuals are not sure how to construe episodes in the world or themselves, the social context can 'offer' construings of those episodes (Tajfel 1969).

One way then to approach the stories people tell to make sense of their lives, is to begin to look at the episodes that lead up to suicidal behaviour or the episode itself. In the Chapters Five to Eleven I will be using such an approach where episodes are built into stories and interpreted by those involved. As we have just read, those episodes may be interpreted differently. A major task within the therapeutic endeavour is to seek out the sequence of episodes that have led the patient to the therapist – the punctuation – and what meanings those events hold for the patient – the construing.

Kelly's theory of constructive alternativism

Kelly (1955) proposed a way of describing how a person 'contemplates in his own personal way the stream of events upon which he finds himself so swiftly borne' (p.3). His theory proposes that each of us creates a pattern which we attempt to fit over the realities of which the world is composed. This is the way we make sense of the world, by making a 'fit' to our own understanding. These patterns, imposed upon the world to give it some regularity, he calls 'constructs'.

Early in his work Kelly gives an inter-personal example of construing which ties in with the notion of 'punctuation' earlier in this chapter:

> A man construes his neighbour's behaviour as hostile. By that he means what harm his neighbour will do him. He tries out his construction of his neighbour's attitude by throwing rocks at his neighbour's dog. His neighbour reacts with an angry rebuke. The man may the believe that he has validated his construction of his neighbour as a hostile person. (p.13)

These construings are not fixed, they are used and validated experientially and, if invalidated or of no convenience, they can be changed. In Chapters Nine, Ten and Eleven we will see how constructs are negotiated between persons in a close relationship. Constructs are approximations of the universe which can be tested for their predictive efficiency. Not only do they organise the world but they predict the world. The use of the term 'constructive alternativism' as used by Kelly emphasises the point that there are always alternative constructions available in describing the world. In this way, no one need be hemmed in by circumstance. This position lifts what may at first sight appear to be a determinist position of cognition to that of an existential position of creating knowledge. The theory implies that a person can enslave herself by her own ideas and then win her own freedom again by re-construing her life.

Kelly builds into his theory two corollaries of interaction: the commonality corollary, where if one person employs a construction of experience which is similar to that employed by another then his psychological processes are similar to those of another person, and the sociality corollary, where one person, in construing the construction processes of another, may play a role in a social process involving the other person.

We can speculate that as our intimate relationships develop we develop mutual construings of that relationship. The family systems theorists describe this mutual construing as if it were rules based and refer to it, as we have seen, as punctuation. This is not to say that we have rules in the head, rather 'as if' our social relationships accorded to some mutually agreed rules. In the understanding of mutual behaviour and the meanings that people develop together as families or small groups, we need some way of describing how they interact together. What I am trying to develop here is a way of seeing how differing meanings interlock with each other such that we can learn how distress is construed by individuals and their families and how we can begin to talk about such distress. Clearly, the communication of suicidal distress is not being made apparent to the statutory welfare and crisis agencies, as we have seen from the previous literature. In Chapters Ten and Eleven, where videotape data is analysed, we will see how family members construe the same events differently, although using similar sets of constructs. There are alternate opposing realities, although based upon the same shared premises. For example, becoming independent is a major issue in families with an adolescent. At the same time, remaining dependent is the opposite pole of that struggle for independence. An adolescent seeking to make a unilateral decision about staying out later at night may see this as a legitimate form of independent behaviour. His mother, however, may see this as an illegitimate bid for independence and his father may contend that as long as he is paying the bills, his son is dependent.

Construing in contexts and processes of negotiation

Individuals, with their own particular personal construings, belong to communities of intimates with whom they are inter-dependent and with whom they share construings. Shared construings are negotiated in social interaction. Rather than being located within individuals, these core constructs are located in the relationship. They are interactional rather than intrapsychic. It is these familial construings which define what a situation is and give meaning to the external and internal events faced by a family. It is important to understand that these construings are negotiated in interaction and are not necessarily fixed for all time. These construings will define what will count as a life event for a family and offer dimensions of seriousness, magnitude, legitimacy and content.

Furthermore, within families there will be negotiated understandings of how episodes are to be punctuated into events, beginnings and endings. The location of events, in terms of punctuation and magnitude, content and legitimacy, are contextualised further by considerations of accountability, duty and competence. In this way, as we will read later, constructs are combined into a rules-based understanding of interaction. The rules of ordering meaning (constitutive rules) and the rules ordering action (regulative rules) are negotiated, argued, stretched and ignored in the political interaction between intimate others.

In this way no normative inter-relational order is specified but must continually be constituted and regulated. This order does not reside in individuals but in the relationship between persons. Nor is this orderliness binding and indefinite but continually negotiated. What appears to be stable is a state of negotiated stability with a negotiated agreement about what would count as change and how that change is regulated to remain stable. However, this does not preclude individuals from having personal construings of reality which are negotiated within other social contexts, nor are these contexts separate. It is, perhaps, the negotiation of social construings in other social contexts, that is at work, at school, with friends, with lovers, which introduce change into the family context. In the context of the nephrology unit earlier it was the negotiation of the psychiatrist, first with the patient and then with the medical staff, that brought about mutual changes in understanding the behaviour.

In their description of shared and personal constructs in a commune Karst and Groutt (1977) taped their interviews with individual members of a commune and collated, grouped and hierarchically arranged the constructs they recorded. They reflected Kelly's position that subjective understanding based upon social interaction was the key to understanding the world of their subjects. In their paper they propose that what seems to be needed is a system to construe not just a single role relationship but a mutual role playing process – person A's role taking relative to person B and person B's role taking relative to person A – *at the same time*. Such reciprocal relationships are seen as a function of both commonality and sociality focusing on the processes between people: an inter-relationship.

Commonality and culture

Although Kelly's personal construct theory is concerned with the construe, the commonality corollary emphasises that a number of individuals can have the same constructions of experience. Living in a culture, we come to share certain constructs with others of the group. These shared construings are super-ordinate dimensions and are 'ideal' constructions by which the acts of individuals are construed. When individuals apparently deviate from such ideal constructions, categorising such behaviour is not sufficient. We need to know why it is being carried out in the first place. To do this we need to understand the construing of those intimately involved (as in Chapters Eight and Nine) and the implications for personal behaviour and the behaviour of others as a process.

Implication and process

By describing and observing process we can elicit the implications and links between construings that are resident within the process and which may not be available for description by the persons involved. It is only in considering process that inter-personal aspects become evident. Sometimes there are links between constructs that the subjects are unaware of. It may be that people are aware of these construings but they may only be invoked in the process of interaction. It must be remembered that constructs are essentially described as bi-polar. Not only do they group things together but contrast those things simultaneously. The process of simultaneously signifying same and different provides a differential network of implications for a family.

The stance that I am taking in this book is that personal meaning must not be sacrificed to scientific method. This does not mean that scientific rigour must be similarly sacrificed, rather that personal and relational understandings are the primary focus. The burden of discovery is placed upon the experimenter to discover what the subject means, rather than training the subject to respond in the experimenter's terms. The subject's frame of reference is given the paramount validity. A conception of meaning (Wright 1976) is central to this approach. Meaning is in the experience of persons and refers to a relationship. A thing, an event, has meaning when it is perceived within a wider field. It is the sum of these perceived relationships which confer meaning. When one person engages with others (and is engaged by others) and attempts to make sense of what they are doing, there are multiple frames of reference: self and other(s).

Apart from meaning being a negotiated field-dependent phenomenon, it is also a multi-level phenomenon. A characteristic of meaning is that immediate construings have implications not only for current behaviour but also for organising past explanations of behaviour and future action in terms of implication. If a life loses its meaning for the individual, it has occurred in a process of understanding carried out with others. Even if we turn to those that have become isolated from social contacts, the very process of becoming isolated is an element in the understanding that life has lost its meaning and purpose.

Relationships

Our construings as individuals are negotiated with those persons with whom we share our daily lives. As Bannister and Fransella (1971) remind us, personal construing is also influenced by those with whom we have shared our lives before. This is one way that the past contaminates the present. We bring our previously developed construings to current situations. Not only do we bring along our previous construings developed over the years in social interaction to new situations but also the previously negotiated rules for the understanding and regulating social interaction are brought to new situations. As we will see with Bobby Sands In Chapter Five, how he saw his behaviour was coloured by the group of people to whom he belonged and their understanding of a common history of Irish martyrdom.

New relationships may ask us to reconstrue our old relationships and challenge our former views. Some researchers (Byng-Hall 1980; Duck and Spencer 1972; Reiss 1981) propose that our relationships with friends and spouses are based initially on those construings negotiated within our primary reference groups. This means that we are often faced with seemingly conflicting evidence, spouses are not parents. In such a situation we can change our construing and accommodate change. We become changed or, alternatively, we try to demand that others accommodate within our con-struct system and change to confirm our construing. We become hostile. Such situations occur when young people are leaving home and negotiating new relationships. The young person leaving home is negotiating a change. The family being left behind is also being asked to construe its future organisation and to reconstrue the person who is leaving. Any new relationship will have ramifications for those persons immediately and intimately involved and their primary reference groups. It is this balance that is referred to as eco-systemic coherence. Realities are constantly being built, repaired and reconstructed in a number of contexts of meaning: individual, relational and cultural. These realities will, in turn, inform and contextualise each other. However, sometimes the same construct system is used repeatedly, even though it fails to be validated at one level of experience. This may be interpreted as single-mindedness or psychopathology, depending upon the context and the relative status of the participants.

Constructs and relationships

A number of authors have demonstrated the development of similarities in shared construing correlated with interpersonal relationships. Ryle and Breen (1972) related similarities of construing to marital adjustment. They discovered that patients, as opposed to controls, were more likely to see their relationships with their marital partners as resembling their relationship with their parents. When such a marital relationship was going badly they perceived their own role as more child-like, while that of their partner became more parent-like. My argument, then, is that although social order is continually open to negotiation, the range of constructs and available rules is subject to constraint. We have a repertoire of responses available to us. That repertoire is sometimes expressed as a tradition.

Similarly, Winter, Ferreira and Bowers (1973) discovered that spontaneous agreement about likes and dislikes increased with time in married couples. This appears to be a confirmation of the concept that who you live with influences how you think. Cognition, then, is placed within a relational and political frame.

Duck and Spencer (1972), in discussing friendship formation, hints at the way in which new relationships are developed. They suggest that people prefer others who have similar constructs. A new relationship provides the opportunity to validate those constructs. The depth of a relationship will depend upon different expectations being satisfied at different levels.

What I am proposing is that such an understanding is negotiated and rules based. Although initially having similar construings, those involved in the relationship may find that the implications of their construings are mutually incompatible. In this way, two persons may be attracted to their mutual capacities of adventurousness and attractiveness but find this incompatible with other construings of gender, religion or status.

The 'fit' of construing between marital partners has been investigated and described by several authors (Bergner 1978; Fry 1962; Holmes 1982). These researchers have looked at personal symptomatology within the context of marriage. The presence of a symptom such as anxiety, hysteria or phobia is seen as located within a marital and familial system. Although the symptoms are expressed by one partner, the non-symptomatic partner is also described as being potentially anxious, hysterical or phobic. The symptoms are seen as representative of the relationship and available to either partners. The presentation of such symptoms is seen as a means of managing change and in regulating inter-personal distance in the context of marital intimacy. Such management is dependent upon the rules and construings of what counts as change, how such change is to be managed, what counts as acceptable relational distance and how such distance is to be managed. Just as a hunger striker will represent his group and present a group grievance, the patient may be representing a family and presenting a family predicament.

Validation

Constructs are hypotheses tested out in experimentation. Experience validates construing. Kelly takes time to point out that persons are validated by significant others. The parent, for example, is the immediate validator of the child's testing of his construct system. The parent becomes a kind of solution for the young child's problem. The child sets a personal construct system to predict the parent. Parents will also offer constructs of a situation and direct the child away from alternative construings. As the child becomes older, the child becomes less dependent for validation. In so doing, the child becomes a validator of the parents' construct system. For example, he may say 'Like we are' or 'In our family we do it like this'. This reciprocal process of validation maintains a common negotiated order which structures both a personal and a collective reality. In this same way, significant others, bonded by mutual dependent interaction, reciprocally validate each other. In contrast, some adolescents will swing to the opposite pole and say 'I will never be like my mother' or 'That's how my father treated me and I won't impose that on my child'. Both poles involve the same common construing.

Suicide, hostility and conflict

The issue of validation of self and others is at the core of legitimising behaviour. Kelly (1961) views suicidal behaviour in a context of a decreasing ability to make sense of, interpret or react to one's personal world – most importantly, a personal world of people. Suicidal behaviour is considered a hostile act of demanding validation from others of a personal view.

Incidentally, Kelly also views such symptomatic behaviour as indicating the issues which are important for the person. Personal symptoms are a means of indicating what is important for the relational system. This would mean that individual suicidal behaviour raises questions about the life or death of a system. Such a perspective ties in with those family theorists who see suicidal behaviour as an act of communication about life and death issues. Those issues may be contextualised within a context of conflict – a metaphorical description of the political negotiation of relational power – or within a context of change – the negotiation of personal and familial boundaries.

Lester (1968; 1969) describes attempted suicide as a hostile act which seeks to extort validation and a confirmation of personal beliefs from significant others. Suicidal behaviour is seen as a reaction to information from the environment following social experimentation by the suicidal person. Not only are suicidal persons hostile but their immediate family or friends upon whom they are primarily dependent are also hostile. Both parties are engaged in cycles of mutual hostility demanding confirmation for personal beliefs. In effect, both parties are saying to each other: 'Stay the same, any move to change is a threat'. Yet, at the same time, all involved members are living in circumstances requiring change to meet either external or internal demands.

Conflict becomes the presence of mutually incompatible construing. This may not, of necessity, be negative. Conflict may promote a change whereby assumptions are changed or new commitments are made based upon a different super-ordinate construing. What appears to promote a difficult situation is when conflict escalates into a mutual avoidance of acceptance where all personal interactions by both parties are construed as hostile. Change has to be coherent such that levels of distress are not exceeded beyond their ability to recover. The ecological balance of all involved systems – personal, familial and communal – must be accommodated.

There is a concept, called desertification, whereby an ecology goes beyond the limits of its resources. We appear to see the same situation in suicidal behaviour where individuals, and their families, exhaust their resources, whether psychological, physical, emotional, filial, financial or social.

As a social group, the nuclear family is a special case of all possible groupings – the family has usually spent a long time together and have a common history. They have experienced a large number of events together to elaborate their mutual construing – sexual, marital, parental, filial and recreational. This is combined with an intensity of involvement in the simple day-to-day maintenance of survival needs. All these activities give opportunities for personal beliefs to be impinged upon, guided and formed. Within a familial context there are rules as to who may influence whom, who controls whom and who belongs to particular roles. The relationships of individuals within this context are, by and large, involuntary. Family members become dependent and only under certain conditions are they allowed to leave. This does not mean that persons cannot change within such a context, rather that change is negotiated within such a context and is constrained by the construings resident in such a context. Within this context there is a socialisation of understanding for all concerned, with consequences and implications for individual and collective construing. Love may become equated with violence, punishment with dependency and power with illness.

If personal constructs are cognitive determinants of how phenomena count as experience, then there are also familial and cultural constructs that determine the construing of phenomena in relational and social settings. In this way, the world is organised and stabilised for individuals and society. This construing is based upon a dynamic process of cognitive operations and can be represented by rules (Pleasants 1996). How these rules influence behaviour we shall see in the next chapter.

CHAPTER FIVE

A Model of Distress Management

A family rules hypothesis

From a family communication perspective, persons in a relationship continually offer each other definitions of that relationship. From a family systems theory approach, persons who interact together regularly relate in an organised repetitive manner (Reiss 1981). Taking these two ideas together, I propose a family rules hypothesis (Aldridge 1985). This hypothesis proposes that in any relationship, that relationship is stabilised into some form of regularity, an organised pattern. These relational regularities, or patterns, can be expressed as if they follow rules that prescribe and limit behaviour within a relational context. In this way, relationships are organised into a relatively steady state. Individual and family behaviour is regulated by such rules, but because individuals and families need to change, these rules are not fixed, they are open to negotiation. Indeed, when such rules are fixed, and become inflexible, then perhaps we have the ground for problem behaviour, and some problem behaviour is an attempt to change the rules. Deviant behaviour in this sense is an extreme form of negotiation and has to be understood in a relational context.

Relationship 'rules' explain the patterning of observed behaviour. These rules can be differentiated as two types: constitutive and regulative (Pearce 1976; Pearce and Cronen 1980; Pearce, Cronen and Conklin 1979). A constitutive rule says what an action is. An act of deliberate self-harm constitutes a 'cry for help' or it constitutes an act of manipulation. A regulative rule says what should be done. If this is a 'cry for help', then help. Both are forms of interpretation.

Constitutive rules

Constitutive rules (see Figure 5.1) function to say what a particular action counts as in the context in which it is being interpreted (the report aspect of conveying information). For example, a constitutive rule may say that if A performs a particular act, it counts as a manifestation of distress. This can be

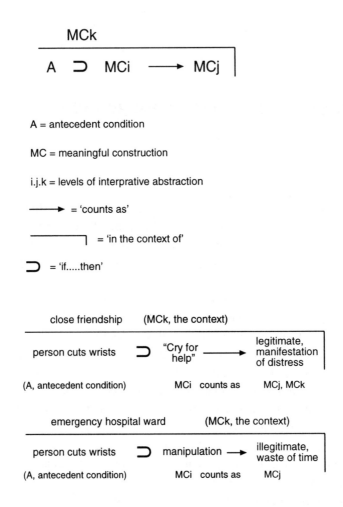

Figure 5.1 The construction of constitutive rules (after Pearce and Cronen 1980)

a personal construing of what A does or a familial construing or a cultural construing. In such a way, an act of wrist cutting may be seen as counting individually as a relief from tension, familially as a means of gaining attention and culturally as a means of an adolescent manipulating parents. We will see in Chapter Six how such self-mutilation is differently perceived by patients and caregivers. In Figure 5.1 we see how wrist cutting may be interpreted differently according to the context of close friendship or emergency treatment room.

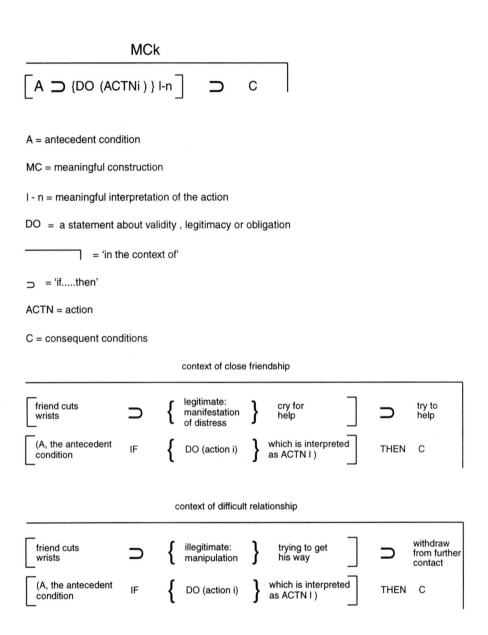

MCk

$$\left[A \supset \{DO\ (ACTNi\ )\ \}\ l\text{-}n \right] \quad \supset \quad C$$

A = antecedent condition

MC = meaningful construction

I - n = meaningful interpretation of the action

DO = a statement about validity , legitimacy or obligation

⌐ = 'in the context of'

⊃ = 'if.....then'

ACTN = action

C = consequent conditions

context of close friendship

| friend cuts wrists | ⊃ | { legitimate: manifestation of distress } | cry for help | ⊃ | try to help |
| (A, the antecedent condition | IF | { DO (action i) } | which is interpreted as ACTN I) | THEN | C |

context of difficult relationship

| friend cuts wrists | ⊃ | { illegitimate: manipulation } | trying to get his way | ⊃ | withdraw from further contact |
| (A, the antecedent condition | IF | { DO (action i) } | which is interpreted as ACTN I) | THEN | C |

Figure 5.2 The construction of regulative rules (after Pearce and Cronen 1980)

Regulative rules

Regulative rules (Figure 5.2) can be seen as representing what is appropriate to do next in an episode (the 'command' aspect of communication). Should a particular behaviour be construed as constituting a 'cry for help', the regulative rule may be to 'offer help'. If that same behaviour is perceived as manipulation, and another example of a partner trying to get his way illegitimately, then the consequences may be something entirely different. The other partner may withdraw (see Figure 5.2).

When persons communicate, should their constitutive rules be at odds or their regulative rules not be congruent, misunderstandings may occur (Cushman and Whiting 1972). As we saw in the nephrology unit example in the last chapter, a young man was considered to be a psychiatric emergency when he refused medical treatment (Stotland 1997). However, when he was questioned further, he revealed that his behaviour was not suicidogenic but reflected his anxiety towards the way the physician handled him during a painful treatment procedure in the context of a children's ward. Rules are essential for making sense of the world but need not necessarily be immediately conscious or explicit (Bateson 1978; Hoffman 1981). The task of the researcher is to find out what rules are being used to understand what particular behaviours mean in the contexts in which they are being applied. Understanding these rules of constitution leads to an understanding of what the consequences of such understandings are, as regulative rules.

We will see in Chapters Ten and Eleven how rules of constitution and regulation are woven together in cycles of family interaction. The elicitation of these rules is a formal way of presenting qualitative research data concerning personal and family narratives.

A hierarchical system

Rules governing the understanding of suicidal behaviour can be seen at a number of differing levels of abstraction and complexity. Varela and Johnson (1976) describe the process of choosing which systemic level to elicit as a choice of cleavage. At each of these levels there will exist constitutive rules of meaning and regulative rules of action governing the next act.

Such rules occurring in inter-personal relationships are subject to change and recreation. Understanding is negotiated and is a dynamic process. This is an important point. As Kelly (1955) argues, persons are prisoners of neither their history nor their heredity. There is then no deterministic psychology, in this sense, where behaviours must follow from understandings. There is almost always room for choice. Indeed, it is, perhaps, when in construing the world that there appears to be no room for choice that a person becomes suicidal. Hopelessness, then, would be the consequence of such a limited construing of the world where no choice appears to exist. And it is hopelessness that is linked by many authors to suicidal behaviour (Appleby 1992; Eggert *et al.* 1995; Glanz, Haas and Sweeney 1995). From a construct perspective, it is, perhaps, Shneidman's view (1993a; 1993b) that the person who becomes suicidal is constricted in his or her thinking that may be more relevant. Hopelessness is constriction in meaning, constitution and the regulation of choice.

Life events as promoters of change

If we consider episodes in the lives that people lead, those episodes will be composed of particular events. We have seen earlier that leaving home, leaving school, getting married and getting divorced are 'life events'. What counts as a life event will depend upon how the person considers his or her own role in the world.

A number of authors writing about self-poisoning or self-injury have considered how such behaviour is preceded by stressful life events (Horesh *et al.* 1996; O'Brien and Farmer 1980; Paykel 1978; Paykel, Prusoff and Myers 1975; Wetzler *et al.* 1996). Persons who have deliberately injured themselves are described as having experienced four times as many stressful life events compared with general population controls. Significantly, these life events usually involve a key person and are taken as indicative of difficulties in close personal relationships.

Mechanic (1974) points out the role that life events play in the occurrence of illness behaviour, but is careful to say that life changes, medical history, psychological distress and illness behaviour interact in complex ways. Life events appear to demand some adaptive change of individuals and their kin. In this book I am trying to understand how some families accommodate and adapt comfortably to change while some families adapt by developing various forms of symptomatology. Although life events research has been predominantly orientated towards individuals and pathology, it continually returns to understanding how life changes demand a complex response from the immediate social milieu of the individual (Davies, Rose and Cross 1983; Debats, Drost and Hansen 1995; Dohrenwend and Dohrenwend 1974).

Within the life events literature a general hypothesis is that life events play a role in the aetiology of somatic and psychiatric disorders and provide necessary, if not sufficient, conditions for such disorder (Dohrenwend and Dohrenwend 1974). There is a lack of consensus as to the nature of this role and to any specificity of life events correlating with particular illness or deviant behaviour. What is evident is the way in which major life events and life-cycle changes are handled, managed and adapted to is crucial. The question remains throughout: 'How do some families manage life-cycle changes and stressful events with the minimum of disturbance and some families adapt by one member harming themselves in some way?'.

A number of further questions are raised:

1. How do some individuals construe certain events in their lives as stressful (Folkins 1970; Hansen and Johnson 1979)?

2. How do some families construe certain life events as indicators of change or as stressful (Reiss 1967; Reiss 1971)?

3. How are some adaptations at the level of physiological or psychological functioning recognised as life events (Lazarus 1974; Lazarus and Averill 1972)?

4. What cultural construings are available to suggest which life events are stressful and how do these affect familial and individual perception (Mechanic 1966a; Mechanic 1966b; Mechanic 1974; Senay and Redlich 1968)?

It is Bateson (1973) who begins to offer a systemic understanding of events as 'news of difference'. Life events are not seen as causative but indicative. What is recognised as an event depends upon how individuals and social groups are informed by themselves and their culture as to what events make a difference, their's is a constitutive rule. There is a process of co-evolution where individuals and social groups inform their culture and culture informs individuals and their groups (Brown and Lenneberg 1965; Rippere 1981; Sapir 1949). Such an appreciation is noted by a number of researchers who describe the relationship between culture and symptoms and cultural components in response to pain (Schwab and Schwab 1978; Zborowski 1952; Zola 1966).

In Bateson's description of events as recognised changes, he points out that what happens to one member of a system may require changes elsewhere in his immediate social relationships – his family system – which, in turn, will absorb that change, that is the process of homeostasis.

Such changes, then, will impinge upon the whole of a family system and this, for life events research, is a major epistemological shift. Instead of looking at what happens to one person, it is necessary to look at what is happening at the systemic level of the immediate family. This has long been recognised in family practice by therapists from numerous fields. Hopkins (1959), a general practitioner, wrote of the way that families would present with a cluster of differing symptoms and that distress is not always solely located and presented by one family member. Family members would take turns in consulting their general practitioner over a period of time. There is a common ground of distress presented by various individuals from the same social milieu over time.

The 'breakthrough' metaphor and thresholds of distress

Beer (1975) writes that there are adapted neural pathways specific to the expression of pain. We rely upon our body organs to do their job and should they fail to do so, or if vital thresholds are threatened, this will be brought to our conscious attention. This is a precautionary measure and involves a threat to autonomy which the body politic cannot sustain. This special message will 'automatically' break through to whatever systems level is required to deal with it. If this signal is not acted upon, it will be expressed at the next level of systems organisation.

We can use this metaphor to consider deliberate self-harm, which may function as a special signal signalling distress in the family. When distress appears in a family, the thresholds of distress of a family member are being threatened. The expression of distress in a family follows learned and developed 'pathways' according to a family construing of distress. Should this manifestation of distress not be heeded, and is seen as a threat to the 'body politic' of the family, there are higher systemic levels of organisation at which the message can be expressed. In Western industrialised cultures this distress is often expressed as pain and a specific agent in the community is invoked to relieve that distress. A medical practitioner, as an agent of primary care delivery, is often chosen, although it could be a priest or a social worker depending upon how the distress itself is construed.

What we are seeing in the presentation of distress to medical practitioners and other helping agencies, in the case of suicidal behaviour, is that such distress is not being recognised within the immediate relational milieu of the patient or those charged with relieving distress within the community. For those 'sudden' suicides that appear to make no sense, the signs of distress are not being attended to and, in some contexts, are not being transmitted. Such a perspective directs us to understanding how the system of distress management is so constructed that distress can be expressed and attended to. Our attempts to individualise distress have effectively removed the communicative aspect of suicidal behaviour.

These thresholds of distress, then, can be considered as constructs; at the physiological level they will be set within physiological limits and exist as bipolarities. Blood pressure, for example, can represent thresholds that are 'too high' or 'too low'. From the work of the researchers in psychosomatics we also know that such physiological thresholds can be significantly altered by cognitive factors (Fishbain 1995; Greer 1979; Hill 1978; Latimer 1979; Lish *et al.* 1996). My point is that those thresholds, physiological and cognitive, are calibrated within the individual and within the context of the family. The thresholds of too much and too little, and all that is between, are set by rules of constitution. These thresholds can adapt. However, their adaptation is within the total ecology of the person.

In so far as a life event is recognised, and thresholds of distress are threatened, this may be expressed by the family or expressed by one member of that family. When this happens there will be a strategic move to reduce this distress if the stability of the family is threatened. This is the process of homeostasis and requires one member of the family to be temporarily 'sick' or 'deviant'. While this may be an acceptable strategy for managing distress, when the location of distress is not identified at its true source within the family, and located within the individual, the danger for that individual is that they may need to be the one who is 'sick' every time distress escalates. Should this occur, we have the phenomenon of the patient who makes repeat visits and who seems unwilling to respond to treatment. That person then gets labelled as being unresponsive or a difficult patient. It could just as well be that the problem lies with the practitioner who fails to realise the nature of the problem within the family milieu. If we take the analogy of a hi-fi system, it may not be the speaker that is faulty when the sound is poor but a problem with the amplifier, the compact disc player, the antenna for the tuner or a loose wire. Trying to repair the speaker will not bring any change if the problem lies elsewhere within the system. We will see an example of this in Chapter Seven where problems in a psychiatric hospital ward are expressed by the patients, yet the source of the problem lies within the broader system of the ward organisation.

Becoming ill

Illness behaviour, the sick role and deviancy

A common feature described by many authors of deliberate self-harm is the contact with medical services or 'helping' agencies in the community and the presence of physical illness. A feature of family research is that families organise themselves around, or consider themselves to be controlled by, a symptomatic member.

Butterworth and Skidmore (1981) propose that it is during childhood when we learn how to interpret and respond to sickness cues. This process is negotiated between the person who proposes sickness and those who are willing to validate that status of sickness. Not only do children propose symptoms to their parents for validation, as constitutive rules, but patients can scrutinise their children for signs of illness and prognose such a state. This personal and inter-personal behaviour is influenced by the cultural context in which the behaviour is embedded (Bursten 1965; Bursten and D'Escopo 1965). In such a way, the lay network can propose particular constitutive rules for determining what counts as illness and health. Furthermore, there will also be personal, familial and cultural expectations about how that illness should be treated. These are regulative rules. It may be personally validated to 'be off work with the 'flu'' but not familially validated if, after not being able to do the washing up on grounds of illness, you go out for a drink with your girlfriends.

Illness in context

Robinson (1971) points out that the empirical reality of illness, defined as the presence of clinically serious symptoms, is the statistical norm. The full understanding of symptoms requires a systematic consideration of the social and psychological context in which the episodes occur against the total background of daily life. It is necessary to discover the meaning of illness to those immediately involved and the available alternatives. Part of this understanding is to discern how people arrive in these situations and what decisions are taken. In an existing family culture of illness behaviour, particular persons are involved with validating illness behaviour. If you are feeling sick as a child, it is your mum who says you are able to go to school or not, even if you get a lot of sympathy from your grandmother. When you get older and go out to work, neither your mother nor your grandmother are likely to be of much help. This validation is based upon reference to past behaviours, family advice, lay literature and the example of others.

What is important is some kind of classification of episodes, evaluation of the nature and significance of common symptoms and predictions relating to the probable outcome of illness and their usual handling. It is with reference to this body of knowledge that the majority of illness decisions are made. Such a body of knowledge is an example of familial construing about the constitution and regulation of illness behaviour. In this way, individuals construing themselves as 'ill' negotiate that state within their family situation. It must be stated too that the personal construing of 'health and illness' is informed by, and informs, such familial construing. I know that I'm ill because I'm covered in spots and have a headache. My brother had spots last week and my mother said that he had chicken-pox. He stayed off school. So, its my turn to have spots this week and I ought to be able to stay off school. But, I have to show the spots and give a convincing act concerning having a headache before chicken-pox is validated.

The social construing of illness

Not only is illness negotiated in family contexts, the legitimation of illness behaviour and its management is negotiated in other social contexts.

Parsons (1951) points out that illness is used to give meaning to perceived deviance and that what is thought to be deviant does not arise through the deliberate, knowing choice of the actor and that it is essentially beyond his own control. In such a way, illness behaviour for those deemed to be sick is not seen as their fault. The Parsonian notion of the sick role is composed of four aspects:

1. The individual is not held responsible for his own sickness and some curative process is necessary for his recovery, not self-motivation.

2. The individual is exempt from normal social obligations.

3. Being ill is conditional on recognition that such a state is undesirable.

4. The sufferer is expected to seek competent help and to co-operate with attempts to get him well.

There appear to be certain societal expectations of occupying and entering the sick role. There is, generally, an absolution of blame, no matter what the rationale for it, and the sufferer is managed permissively and not punitively. This suggests a cultural construing of illness behaviour as to what legitimately counts as illness behaviour and how such behaviour may be regulated.

Freidson (1975) proposes that underlying and explaining the degree of exemption is an imputation of a degree of seriousness to illness behaviour. In such a way, different illness behaviours have different social expectations if they are to be legitimised. Further to this legitimisation, the sufferer is expected to co-operate with treatment. Freidson argues that the imputation of responsibility is a critical construct in the understanding of illness behaviour in social contexts. Deliberate self-harm violates the requirements for accommodation by the sick role because the individual is held responsible for his own behaviour and often does not co-operate with attempts to get him well. We will see how crucial this aspect of legitimacy and responsibility is in the following chapters.

Deviance

The axis of responsibility for behaviour is drawn as part of a social process of construing behaviour in context. In Western industrialised cultures the imputation of responsibility is made on the grounds of how the state of illness is achieved (see Figure 5.3). This can be seen in the way that some infections, as in venereal disease, are judged by the means of infection. In conditions such as obesity, due to overeating, or heart disease, due to careless exposure, illness behaviour is held in a different light to those same states ascribed to socially legitimated causes, for example hormonal imbalance or genetic defect. Significantly for these states, the co-operation with treatment and the motivation to recover is considered important. It can be seen from the label 'deliberate self-harm' that persons engaged in such behaviour are violating an important rule by being responsible for their own state. Similarly, the definitions of suicidal behaviour given in Chapter One have, at their core, the notion of personal intent. Studies by various authors (Glaser and Strauss 1965; Jeffrey 1979) have described how medical personnel place those people who attempt suicide into deviant stigmatised categories. They are referred to as 'rubbish, manipulators, malingerers'. Thus those who are discerned to responsible for their own behaviour, unco-operative in their recovery and illegitimate in their claims to be sick are in some way deviant. They are breaking 'the rules'.

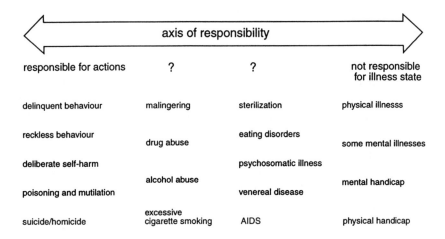

Figure 5.3 The axis of responsibility for particular illness behaviours

The politics of deviant behaviour

Becker (1963) volunteers, as do the family systems theorists, that all social groups make rules. Such rules define situations and prescribe appropriate behaviour. In this way, regularity and meaning is given to the world. A further function of rules is to maintain and draw boundaries around the person, around the relationship and around the 'particular system'. As we have seen earlier, rules are in constant use in defining behaviour both by saying what an episode constitutes and how it is to be regulated. For example, this boy has spots, keep him at home. However, individuals and groups differ in their rules and the application of rules. These rules themselves are negotiated. In judging what is deviant behaviour, Becker argues that behaviour is considered as to its characteristics and difference – very much as a process of construing is described by Kelly (1955).

This process of construing behaviour as deviant is a social and political process (Blumer 1972; Fagerhaugh and Strauss 1977; Laing and Esterson 1964; Lofland 1969) in that it is negotiated. Deviance is the failure to obey group rules, but it is an ambiguous state as a person may belong to different groups with different rules. The same behaviour may be construed differently in different cultures and at different times – one cultural rebel may be another culture's innovator. Indeed, we shall see in Chapter Six that one culture's martyr is another culture's terrorist. This relativistic view emphasises that the deviance is not the quality of the act, but a consequence of the act. Deviance becomes a political process involving the responses of other people to the behaviour. The meaning of behaviour as being suicidal, and therefore manipulative or communicative, is a political process of interpretation that must be negotiated after the act. This process is also at the core of all therapeutic encounters.

One of the dangers of classifying certain behaviours as deviant is that they may be considered as all of the same type. All overdoses may be seen as the same, whether an eighteen-year-old or an eighty-year-old. The same behavioural end can be reached by many differing processes. Further to this, the same behaviour may, in a sequence of events, operate as a cause and as an effect. This is a feature of the life-events research where the homeostatic adaptation to a life event becomes a life event in itself. This process is that of deviation-amplification and is a process of escalation. A small deviation feeds back into the family and becomes a biographical deviation by the way it is responded to and managed. How we categorise an act, as constitution, has ramifications for the way in which that act is regulated. Saying that suicidal behaviour is an attempt to maintain family coherence has different consequences as when it constituted as an example of pathological deviance.

Deviance as normality

Not all family theorists regard deviance negatively, as catastrophic or pathological (Coser 1962; Dentler and Erikson 1959; Erikson 1966; Penn 1982). They suggest that families require deviance to maintain that process of coherent homeostatic change mentioned earlier in this chapter. Deviance becomes the creative stuff of evolution in social systems and if deviance does not naturally arise, a family will induce a member to break its rules. Once deviance appears, a family will develop rules for sustaining it. Both constitutive and regulative rules can be used to describe the promotion, regulation and maintenance of behaviour.

The usefulness of deviance was noted by Durkheim (1958), who pointed out that upright citizens develop functional feelings of cohesiveness when a criminal offender is caught and punished. In this way, a common perspective and collective conscience is constituted. However, Erikson (1966) draws attention to the idea that once one type of deviance is controlled, another type of deviance is likely to take its place. This view is reflected by Markush (1974), who describes a number of mental epidemics throughout the centuries which last for a period, affecting many people, and then disappear, only to appear in another form at a later date.

These authors stress that deviance is required in social systems because it serves several important positive functions. Such behaviour is induced, if not arising spontaneously, sustained and regulated within a social context. Erikson's theory suggests that the occurrence of deviant behaviour in a family is a natural part of the role-differentiation process. Just as a family needs an emotional specialist or an organiser, so it requires a deviant. This suggests a construing of deviant-normal where family members can occupy such necessary poles for the purpose of family change.

The presence of deviant behaviour, and accompanying sanctions, serves an important purpose of defining normative boundaries. Deviant behaviour exemplifies the kinds of action which are not allowed (constitutive rules), and sanctions show what will happen if such acts occur (regulative rules). A rule maintaining a boundary works in the same way as the rule pi-squared is used as a rule to calculate the area of a circle. Deviant acts and their accompanying sanctions provide concrete models for family rules (Jackson 1965b). Only when a familial shared construing is present can interactions be smooth and predictable.

Families must negotiate their normative boundaries to promote predictable interaction. To do this, Erikson argues, families consistently apply sanctions to, not rejection of, a deviant member. Families seldom permanently stop deviant behaviour but maintain it at a level which promotes change. Once more, the rate of change appears to be a critical variable. It is this notion of applying sanction to, but NOT rejecting, the family member that is critical in considering suicidal behaviour. As we know, isolation is a significant factor in the process of becoming suicidal (Decatanzaro 1995; Draper 1996; Hawton, Fagg and Simkin 1996a; Hedge and Sherr 1995; Moscicki 1995) and rejection plays its part in such isolation.

Waxler (1975) begins to offer some explanation of how some deviant members become rejected. Deviation is accepted in a group:

1. When the deviation is limited in scope and when it does not pervade the whole person's being,

2. When the deviation is perceived as unstable and susceptible to change),

3. When the deviance occurs in areas that are not central to the groups values.

Suicidal behaviour transgresses these rules. It pervades the whole person's being and threatens central values of life and death and system viability. When group members begin to see the phenomenon not as deviant behaviour but as evidence of a deviant person amongst them, the deviant person is rejected. We will see later, in Chapter Ten, that it is when a family member is rejected, after all sanctions have failed to change his behaviour, that suicidal behaviour occurs.

Relative deviance

Erikson (1966) suggests that all social systems induce deviant behaviour and deviant possibilities are contained within its membership. The definition of deviance is relative to the social system in which it is found. Every family group will define what constitutes deviance in its own way, for example not working, drinking too much, being inappropriately sad, being noisy, not being dry at night, sleeping a lot, wearing strange clothes, talking nonsense, not concentrating, not listening, answering back or working too hard. This depends upon an actively maintained set of rules and is a familial construing which each member knows. In this way, individuals are informed by, and inform, such a construing; both personal and familial construings are interactive. The selection of deviant behaviour, it appears' can be selected almost accidentally. Any behaviour may serve as evidence of deviance to maintain family viability.

The presence of a deviant person satisfies a certain need for predictability. By occupying one pole of a construct 'deviant', the other family members are allowed to occupy the pole of normality by contrasting themselves with the 'other' person. However, difficulties may arise when the family member who has broken norms in the past may also come to be the expected deviant member in the present. Mishler and Waxler (1965) point out that the child who is 'always different' is likely to be selected as the 'family's schizophrenic'. In another study (Wiggins, Dill and Schwartz 1965), the family member who is construed as 'weak' and 'different' will take on the role of deviant. We will read later, in Chapter Eleven, that it is a history of one person taking on the sick role that is a contributory factor in identifying who is to become suicidal.

Once again, this points to a process of construing whereby a family construct exists as to which member will be chosen to be deviant. This may be present in some families as a construct about which age groups are allowed to deviate, since at certain ages deviations are believed to be normal. These too are contextualised by cultural construing about what transitional age groups are allowed to deviate legitimately, for example infancy, adolescence, senescence. Not only are these constructs about what age but also which gender is appropriate for deviant behaviour and the nature of that deviation. This throws a light upon the epidemiological studies which reflect the presence of particular deviant behaviours resident in particular age and gender groups, for example women aged 15 to 19 years for attempted suicide or women aged 25 to 34 years for depression.

Deviant behaviour, then, is a normal function in social systems which introduces necessary change to maintain stability (Sherif 1965). An accidental fluctuation can be amplified into a deviant behaviour, which can become an entirely new arrangement of the system. What is deviant is determined by constitutive rules based upon personal, familial and cultural construings. The maintenance of such behaviour depends upon regulative rules.

A model of systemic change

In the preceding sections a pattern has emerged which reflects a number of interactive variables: a recognition of a developmental crisis, a family tradition of managing crisis, the rate of experienced change and the presence of conflict within a context of rules which regulate and recognise such variables.

Suicidal behaviour is part of an interactional familial pattern of maintaining systemic viability. When we talk of change, we are inevitably considering change at different levels of organisation. Although we may take steps to resolve conflict or distress within our immediate significant relationships, that change of relationship will have ramifications for other relationships in which we are involved. This change in relationships at one level to resolve conflict may promote difficulties elsewhere which stimulate conflict or distress. Similarly, it may be that the presence of inter-personal conflict is maintaining a steady state for a wider eco-systemic context. In this way, we must endeavour to understand the politics of inter-personal conflict, hostility and personal distress in the management and negotiation of change – as we will see in Chapter Seven.

When the social environment changes (for reasons external or internal) but 'adequate rules' for managing or accommodating such change are not present, a crisis occurs. Any 'new' behaviour necessary to meet the demands of a developmental crisis will be labelled as deviant and the rules for the regulation of such deviance invoked. Should this regulation fail to maintain the homeostatic coherence of the eco-system individual/family/community, conflict occurs. The presence of deviant behaviour is a systemic move to promote the negotiation and development of new rules to regulate systemic development. When such 'new' rules are not negotiated coherently, 'old' rules are used and there is an escalation of that behaviour.

Within cultural contexts there are 'rules' for identifying what counts as a 'crisis' (crisis in Greek means 'judgement'). When there is this presence of distress within a familial context and no adequate rules for the regulation of that distress, it can be proposed that conflict is present.

Family processes are often represented by individual 'deviant' symptomatology. Previous research has indeed concentrated on managing suicidal behaviour by focusing on individuals rather than on understanding the systemic properties of such behaviour.

One of the difficulties of adapting to systemic change by the presentation of deviant symptomatology to reduce distress is that the symptoms become incorporated into the systemic tradition of managing change. In this way, Sluzki (1981) proposes that patterns are maintained within systems for accommodating change which may be detrimental to individual members. If an individualistic stance is taken that ignores the social context of the problem, that problem is not be resolved. We shall see in Chapter Eleven that the person who is always sick is regulating situations of escalating conflict and is the one likely to attempt suicide. There is a boundary of sickness behaviour beyond which some individuals are pushed that is to their extreme detriment.

A model of the systemic management of distress
Using the two previous models in this chapter, and the descriptions of regulating systemic change discussed earlier, I want to propose a general

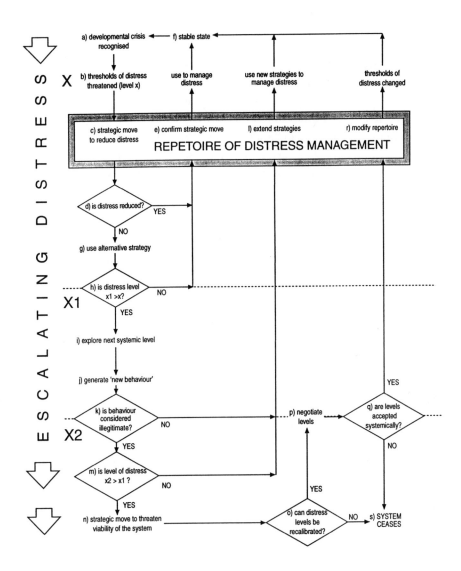

Figure 5.4 The systemic management of escalating distress

model of the systemic management of distress. This model understands the management of systemic distress at different levels of organisation: individual, familial or cultural (see Figure 5.4). Although conceived of as a circular process, it will be necessary for the purpose of description to interrupt this circularity and begin at one point – we have to start somewhere. The point chosen to start this cycle is that of a system facing a crisis. I am assuming here that any dynamic system is constantly scrutinising itself as to its current status. Homeostasis is constantly maintained.

In Figure 5.4 we see that a developmental crisis is recognised by a system (a), according to its own construings, that are, in turn, located within, and informed by, a cultural context. Something happens. A life event occurs. This event can be a change in blood pressure, the entrance of a virus to the system or an argument with a partner. Whatever, something happens that constitutes an 'event'. In Batesonian terms there is 'news of difference'. As a homeostatic adaptation to that event, thresholds of distress are threatened (b). There then follows a strategic move to reduce that distress (c) according to the systemic rules of regulation that have been developed as a repertoire of distress management. Blood pressure may be regulated by sitting down and relaxing, the immune system may react to the virus or an argument comes to some favourable resolution. What has happened is regulated successfully within the terms of the system itself. Distress is reduced (d), the repertoire is validated (e) and stability is maintained (f). This is a simple homeostatic loop (Beer 1975), as we see in Section X.

However, should distress not be reduced, an alternative strategy from the repertoire of distress management is used (g) and the system scrutinises itself for levels of distress. If distress is reduced, this alternative strategy is validated as a legitimate means of reducing distress (e). If distress continues to escalate (h), where levels of distress are higher than in Section X and systemic thresholds are threatened to excess to a point where the very viability of the system itself is threatened, distress management strategies are explored from a higher level of systemic organisation – stage (i) in section X1. A shift occurs from the organic to the personal, from personal to marital, marital to familial, familial to communal, communal to social or departmental to organisational (j).

This strategy will depend upon the systemic rules for distress management at this contextual level and will accord to the tradition of the system, that is the biography, memory and construing of the system (Maturana and Varela 1980). In this way, 'new' behaviour to the individual is generated. Patients suffering emotional distress in contact with the psychiatric service are introduced to new ways of expressing that distress. If this behaviour is considered legitimate then it effectively extends the repertoire of distress management (L) (Mechanic 1966b). Distress repertoires are extended by being informed within a cultural matrix – that is we learn about the most sympathetic general practitioner, alternative medical practices, other lay practices, differing psychotherapeutic techniques, the latest diets, exercises and alternative life styles to alleviate distress. It must be noted here that the current level of distress may be higher than at (b), although still within the thresholds of tolerable distress. In this way, some systems live with raised levels of distress by learning to live with pain, anxiety, depression and delinquency.

Current levels of distress may not fall to the initial levels (m). The system then calibrates itself to accommodate a higher level of distress. Distress at X2 is still greater than at X. When this occurs a family with a member who becomes symptomatic to maintain the family stability may become a family system with a necessarily symptomatic member, for example diabetic, asthmatic, problematic, anorectic, epileptic, tense, depressed or delinquent. Not only is the repertoire of distress management extended (l) but the initial thresholds of distress (b) are altered. The system returns itself to a stable state (f), but that state is altered.

If distress levels escalate, such that systemic viability is further threatened, then an overt strategic move is made to threaten the viability of the system (n). This move will be one which is culturally approved and based upon the systemic tradition of manifesting distress, for example blood sugar levels escalate into diabetes and then diabetic coma, essential hypertension becomes raised and develops into a stroke, delinquent behaviours escalate into deliberate self-harm or strategies of medication escalate into self-poisoning.

When a system becomes so threatened it will be necessary to implement measures to reduce distress and maintain systemic viability (o). This will be observed in those behavioural strategies used in a crisis. The vital question is: can thresholds of distress be recalibrated? For some physiological levels this may not be physically possible and the patient dies. For some psychological levels this calibration may mean a continuing psychotic episode. For some social situations there is withdrawal and temporary estrangement (p). Should these crisis strategies fail and the systemic thresholds are exceeded, the system will cease. Someone dies or leaves.

On the other hand, a crisis may successfully be negotiated and an attempt is made to recalibrate the systemic thresholds of distress and change systemic construing (q). Thresholds of distress are then changed within the repertoire of distress management (r). Should the negotiation of such systemic change not be successfully validated throughout the system to the satisfaction of all members, the system will cease (s). In this way, we see persons leave families by death, leave marriages by divorce, become expelled from school, sacked from an organisation and discharged from hostels.

In this model conflict can be seen as a means of promoting change and maintaining stability. Conflict may also promote further conflict and levels of distress are tolerated at a level higher than the initial level. Conflict may then itself become perceived as a life event.

Throughout the model, those strategic moves which attempt to reduce distress and recalibrate the system may act reflexively as 'life events' which, in their turn, are to be accommodated. This is the process of iatrogenesis. Treatment can also be a cause of further problems. Similarly, the act of diagnosis, or the results of a test, are events that have ramifications. How these events are handled depends upon the repertoires for how they are managed, and these are based upon rules of constitution and regulation.

CHAPTER SIX

Legitimating Suicide and the Politics of Dying

Not all things that look alike, are alike

We take it for granted for granted that suicides are the sorts of 'thing' that are sufficiently similar to group together, whereas, as we have already seen, there are often multiple patterns of meaning about suicidal behaviour present in the common culture (Atkinson 1978). Whenever suicidal behaviour is reported, cultural definitions of that behaviour are invoked that maintain the status quo and offer definitions to individuals by which they can understand suicidal behaviour. There are certain common motivational understandings about sudden death that define it as 'accidental', 'suicidal' or 'political' (Blumer 1972; Denzin 1970; Psathas 1968).

The categorisation of events is a means of perceiving regularities in behaviour and, although it means discarding some information, allows us to make predictions and expectations about the behaviour of others (Nisbett 1973; Pearce, Cronen and Conklin 1979). Without some idea of what events constitute, to organise the information our senses receive we would be subjected to a constant stream of unique events. The world becomes subjected to our construing of it into reliable expectancies, as rules, but we must bear in mind that there are a number of different available categorisations, a number of different windows on reality. In a cultural milieu we may have differing, even conflicting, constitutive rules based on differing logics of communication.

Newspaper reports of suicidal behaviour

Newspaper reports offer us particular construings of suicidal behaviour. In their reports they present gross cultural understandings of how to understand behaviour. In this direction 'to' particular understandings they also direct away from certain understandings.

News is constructed by those who write the news and is a gross representation of a constructed reality (Cohen and Young 1973). Even within 'The Press' there are differing orientations as to what is news. And even when there is a consensus about what is news, the significance and construction of that news differs. In a generalised way, these ideological differences, reflected in differing newspapers, are reconciled in the way they select and construct particular common items. Another feature to bear in mind is that news items which are concerned with suicidal behaviour lump such behaviour together and selectively represent particular examples from a wide variety of possible suicidal events. The items selected for national coverage are those suicides that contain elements of national concerns in the current climate of debate and which are open to construction, affirmation and validation. These items reflect the consensus not necessarily about suicidal behaviour (if there was a concern about suicidal behaviour it would be reported as an epidemic) but about those current concerns within the culture at that time, like unemployment and the rights of prisoners. It is items of local concern reflecting broader social and public concerns that are promoted to the status of national news.

This chapter will not attempt to compare the different reporting of the same events by different newspapers, rather it will address the concerns reflected in suicidal behaviour as reported by the newspapers. As is mentioned in earlier chapters, if suicidal behaviour is a communicative act, it is communicative act reflecting, by metaphor, a current concern within an interactive system – life and death issues, systemic change, conflict and escalating distress. Although different newspapers will inflect news stories differently, by picking up ideological themes, it is the generalised ideological theme which will be investigated in this chapter.

Although the direct effects of media content on opinion has yielded no significant results, what can be proposed is that people adapt the opinions promoted in news items according to their own prior dispositions. The presentation of news evidence will serve as validatory evidence for current opinions, which are reinforced by that reporting. The focus of news items not only validates what people think but also directs away from evidence of an alternative opinion. Newspaper constructions of reality offer some definitions for shaping people's common-sense knowledge of the world and ignores other definitions. Implicit in these definitions are cognitions of the 'way things are' (constitution) and 'what to do about it' (regulation). Newspaper reporting of suicidal behaviours implies what is right to believe and do. The contents of newspaper articles do not provide explicit models to imitate, nor do they say 'what to do', but offer representations that validate and reflect normative attitudes towards suicidal behaviour. These attitudes are embodied in rules of constitution and regulation.

It will be shown later in this chapter that particular issues of suicidal behaviour reflect both wider views of deviant behaviour and the political contextual understanding of such behaviour (Dentler and Erikson 1959; Erikson 1962). In the reporting of the death of Bobby Sands his hunger strike is represented as a political act but the same behaviour of self-starvation occurring in young women is seen as a 'disease' labelled 'anorexia nervosa'. No description, in the newspaper reports, is made that locates anorexia nervosa within the political context of the family as a means of gaining concessions and negotiating status.

The intention of this chapter is not to suggest that the only under-standings of suicidal behaviour we have are those offered by newspaper reports but that newspaper reports offer gross descriptions of suicidal behaviour available as constitutive rules resident in the culture. Another feature of such reporting is that it offers punctuations of behaviour that are not available for immediate first-hand experience or validation. Facts do not speak for themselves, they are given meaning in terms of the frame of reference provided (Bateson 1973; Cohen and Young 1973; Douglas 1967). The cultural construing of suicidal behaviour, as represented in newspaper articles, offers understandings that shape and control deviant behaviour. Behaviour is legitimated and controlled by such categorisations. Not only is behaviour controlled by constitutive rules – starvation as a political act, starvation as a disease process – but behaviour is also controlled by regulative rules – 'no backing down', 'treat with hospitalisation', 'put him in jail', 'put her in hospital'. The newspaper reporting offers both understandings of such categorisation but also presents commentaries as political statements in the form of editorials that offer pronouncements about the legitimacy of what is to be done about patients, poverty and the state of prisoners.

Equivocal situations

Sudden deaths are difficult circumstances to understand. The situations are often ambiguous and it is by referring to a Coroner's Court that a decision about the nature of sudden death is made. To make a decision about death, the circumstances are scrutinised for observed regularities. These regularities are observations structured by a cultural means of understanding. In this way, the presenting of observations and the reporting of observation act re-flexively. Artefacts of sudden death, like suicide notes, are also reflexive in that their presence is a means of construing that death. In the case of Roberto Calvi, a Vatican banker, his death was originally understood as a suicide following financial embarrassment and personal shame. A year later, following exhortations by his family, the attribution of death was seen as a homicide and the previous facts were reconstrued to fit that categorisation.

The dying of Bobby Sands

During the months of March, April and May 1981, Bobby Sands starved himself to death in the Maze Prison, Belfast. His claim was that the activity was a hunger strike and a political act. This was not an isolated incident and it is useful to investigate the political climate and attitude towards suicidal behaviour leading up to his death.

During 1980 there had been an increasing concern voiced in the Press that the number of cell deaths was rising. In the decade 1970 to 1980, 71 prisoners had died in custody – 59 of them by hanging. In July 1981 Ian Sherlock had been found hanged in his cell whilst on remand for murdering his mother-in-law. At Risley Remand Centre, Stephen Anderson had died and concern was being publicly voiced that prisoners were dying and obtaining the means with which to kill themselves. One of the other concerns raised was that a discrepancy had arisen over the judgement of such prisoners' 'mental states'. In the same period, Richard Campbell had refused food and been forcibly fed. When he died the verdict was 'death by self-neglect'.

Of those who killed themselves, the Press report that 30 of the men were jailed for crimes of violence. So, although concern is being raised about conditions of prisons, such that prisoners die and this reflects on the competence of the prison staff, there is the proposition that these men are violent and likely to perform such acts upon themselves. The same concerns of suicide and violence are still reflected today in both prisons (Bogue and Power 1995; Inch, Rowlands and Soliman 1995; Towl 1996) and psychiatry (Hughes 1996).

Over the period 1976 to 1993 the suicide rate in Scottish prisons showed an increase disproportionate to the rise in the overall prison population. Remand prisoners, prisoners serving sentences of over 18 months, particularly life sentences, and prisoners charged with, or convicted of, violent or sexual crimes were over represented. Hanging was the most common method of suicide. Most prisoners who completed suicide had harmed themselves previously. The majority of deaths occurred less than 3 months after admission, with a smaller number occurring less than 24 hours after reception into prison (Bogue and Power 1995).

By 20 October 1980, urgent demands were being made for prison reform. Brixton Prison had the worst record for prison deaths. The death rate for suicides in prison was estimated to be six times that of the general population (Topp 1979). The reasons were blamed upon poor conditions in prison. Recommendations put forward for prison reform revolved around releasing terminally ill prisoners as early as possible as a right and integrating the prison health service with the British National Health Service. Already it can be seen that a link is made between suicides and a condition that ameliorates suicide: the right to release when terminally ill. It is an interesting construing that terminal illness itself becomes a condition that reverses or terminates a custodial sentence.

There were moves, at this time, to select Coroners' juries on the same basis as other juries and make it binding to hold an inquest when a person died in custody. Merlyn Rees, the Home Secretary at the time, was also publicly concerned that during the year, 250 prison inmates were involved in 300 incidents of self-injury. The conditions in which prisoners were kept were blamed.

During 1980, then, there was a rising vocalised public concern over deaths in prison attributed to prison conditions. The release of terminally ill prisoners and improved prison hospital care were offered as conditions that would prevent suicide.

The first hunger strike

During October 1980, Brendan 'Darky' Hughes led seven men on a hunger strike which ended on 18 December 1980. One of the prisoners was close to death, which reinforced the position that being terminally ill gained positive benefits. The men had settled for a package of prison reforms that broadly met their demands. The principal demand that had been proposed, and not met, was the recognition of political status to those convicted of terrorist crimes in Northern Ireland and the corresponding accession of visiting rights and day-to-day treatment.

By January 1981 their new leader, Bobby Sands, described as a 'hard-liner', confronted the prison governor, Stanley Hildith, over the implementation of the reforms. It was here, the Press note, that the seeds of the hunger strike were sown. Within days of Sands starting his fast, the other prisoners ended their 'dirty' protest and ceased smearing their cells with excrement. They accepted bedding and beds for their cells and allowed their cells to be cleaned. The 'dirty protest' itself had revolved around the issue of the treatment of prisoners and the recognition of political status. While such 'dirty' protests were not uncommon then, this trend has decreased and has been replaced by self-mutilation (Hall 1997). Both activities are related to a strong sense of injustice when they occur in prisons.

It was stated quite clearly in the Press that the motivation for the hunger strike was to gain political status and was recognised as a political act.

Who killed Bobby Sands?

Bobby Sands eventually died on 6 May 1981. The leader article of *The Times* pointed out the political motivation for the death and saw it as no justification for granting privileges to a large number of criminals convicted of very serious crimes merely because they professed political motivation. It was also stated that it was unfair to ordinary criminals who were subject to normal prison discipline.

The death of Sands, and his treatment, were clearly and concisely represented in the British National Press. The British Government was vindicated of blame for his death and was congratulated for not bending to meet his demands. His death was seen as being self-inflicted and that he knew full well what he was doing. Sands had also, it is reported, rejected all initiatives designed to save his life. Here then was a personal act within a political context. However, at the end of the leader article it is hinted that Sands was following the orders of his masters. However, a later report in 1981 (*The Times*, 13 September 1981) suggests that Sands was not following orders during this period. He was seen by the Press as the leader of the men in prison (a misconception) and his act was said to be one of personal leadership and example. The Provisional I.R.A. leadership outside the prison at that time, it was reported, had spent a year trying to talk the prisoners out of launching the campaign of hunger strikes.

An historical tradition

On the same day that the leader article appeared in *The Times*, an historical explanation of the behaviour also appeared. The use of hunger striking as a political weapon was placed within the context of Irish history and protest against the British. Bobby Sands had been the thirteenth Irishman to die whilst on hunger strike during this Century.

The act of starvation fitted into an Irish political tradition of attempting to gain concessions. At no stage was Sands' mental health questioned. The act was clearly seen as a political move. In a political context of conflict and bargaining, no precipitating circumstances for his behaviour were proposed. It can be shown, however, that this behaviour occurred in a tradition of political expression and amongst a climate of concern over cell deaths. Terminal illness, it must be remembered, was a condition in English prisons of granting concessions. Although Sands died in May 1981, the strikes continued throughout the year. However, the reporting lessened and a number of consequent deaths failed to secure concessions and reinforced the hard line of the British Government. Here we see the 'hunger strike', with its overt personal intent to die, not being described as suicide and also not being accepted as a political act. It is the ultimate exercise of power that any legitimation of an act is denied and, in this case, ignored. Death ceases to have any impact.

We have a similar sense of such denial today where, although suicide rates are seen as a problem in the young and the old (Diekstra 1996), there is little reported in the popular press and little being done in terms of allocating budget resources for prevention.

Two martyrs

On 28 August 1981 the national press in Great Britain gave prominence to the coroner's statement about the deaths by suicide of Graeme Rathbone, aged 18, and his friend Sean Grant, aged 19. The Coroner reported that:

> These two boys had the courage to take their own lives. It is not an easy thing to do. But they felt that the world didn't hold a future for them.

> This is a clear result of the economic situation in this country. It looks to me as if there are going to be more cases like this where youngsters who have not got jobs feel the only way out is to take their own lives. (*Daily Telegraph*, 28 August 1981)

The comment was placed within an article that gave prominence to youth unemployment and mentioned that the deaths occurred in an unemployment black spot. The boys had left a note that was destroyed by the family but reconstructed for the coroner (we saw in Chapter Three how suicide was seen to be a family communication of distress). The reconstruction was quoted as follows:

> What have we left to live for now there is no work for anyone? All teenagers have to do is hang around street corners getting moved on by police who think you are up to something. The way this country is going no-one will be able to get jobs. That's why the young are turning to crime and violence – what else is left?

> We've not got much time to live now. But whatever happens to us doesn't matter. It's the rest of you we feel sorry for.

Not only is suicide seen as promoted by unemployment, but the societal view that unemployment is responsible for crime and violence is proposed.

Mrs Rathbone, the mother of one of the boys, said that she often found her son crying and that he was depressed. Mr. Grant said that his son was depressed too. At the foot of the article the Coroner mentioned that Grant had been due to appear in court but he did not believe this had led him to take his life.

No martyrs

On the following day, 29 August 1981, *The Daily Telegraph* ran a front page story that featured two photographs; one of the coroner and one of the former school headmaster of Rathbone and Grant. The headmaster attacked the coroner's view of the case saying that he had made the two young men into 'martyrs' because they were unemployed. He claimed that the tragedy was a prank that had gone wrong and that the boys had been worried by impending court appearances. The coroner said that he regretted using the word 'courage' to take their own lives but he did reiterate that committing suicide was not an easy thing to do. The families supported the coroner's view and accused the headmaster of 'stupidity'. The girlfriend of one of the young men said that he had talked for weeks before of committing suicide and that on the day the men died she had tried to talk him out of it.

However, the headmaster is reported as pressing on with the opinion that although they were 'likeable lads', they had been troublemakers and Rathbone had done a term inside prison. He saw the act as a tragedy, not as one of courage, and that other people without jobs may see suicide as a way out.

Two understandings emerged of this suicidal behaviour. The view of the coroner represented the boys as victims of unemployment without a future, who had become depressed and legitimately took their own lives. The headmaster saw them as unfortunately unemployed, likeable but troublemakers, who killed themselves accidentally not courageously. The first view seemed to be a warning to heed the concern over youth employment. The second view seemed to propose that only the deviant would behave in such a way and death would only ensue as a consequence of incompetence.

'Why the dole can lead to suicide'

The Sunday Times (30 August 1981) presented a prominent and lengthy article entitled 'Why the dole can lead to suicide' as a commentary on the case.

Jobless teenagers were described as becoming increasingly vulnerable to severe depression and suicide unless they were found proper counselling. This view was presented as that of a psychiatrist, Dr Leonard Fagin, who also predicted an epidemic of such behaviour (Fagin 1978). Fagin had produced a document for the Department of Health and Social Security documenting unemployment and health in families. Unemployment was seen as triggering psychological changes in the breadwinners, resulting in clinical depression, hopelessness, self-blame, lethargy and insomnia, withdrawal, loss or gain of weight, suicidal thoughts, violent behaviour and a greater dependence on alcohol or tobacco.

Other reports were considered and the general tone of the article was that unemployment is bad for you, but how it is causally related to suicide is not known.

A disgraceful comment

In the same Sunday newspaper, the editorial drew attention to the coroner's words – which were described as 'frighteningly irresponsible'. The editorial comment was:

> In a single sentence, he (the coroner) thus inverted the whole Western tradition that suicide is, with rare exception, the opposite of courage and flinching from challenge. Second, he made the quite unsubstantiated statement that the suicide was a clear result of the economic situation in this country and opined that 'it looks to me as though there are going to be more cases like this where youngsters who have not got jobs feel the only way out is to take their own lives...'

> The coroner's words fit well with the fashion that justifies almost any action by the underlying circumstances. The first contrary instinct when violence or vandalism is committed is not to condemn but to seek the 'grievance' which can be said to have predetermined it – as though there were no choice. Mr. Hibbert has extended this kind of fatalism to unemployment and suicide without the least justification. He has also risked assisting the birth of a cult of imitation. (*The Sunday Times*, 30 August 1981)

This editorial comment raises an important point about the categorisation of suicide. The Parsonian notion (Parsons 1951) of the 'sick role' emphasises that occupation of the status 'sick' prevents group formation. We can see that individualistic depressive descriptions of suicide confirm this, but the description of suicide as a courageous response to unemployment leads to a notion of group identity and legitimate grievance. The threat of suicide can then become an important political tool for demanding concessions and for organising groups of unemployed. If crime, deviancy and violence are laid at the door of social problems rather than examples of personal inadequacy, a necessary political change in the *status quo* is proposed in terms of describing behaviour and attributing motives. We have seen earlier that the death of Bobby Sands was actively misconstrued by the British Government as not being a political act but one of personal deviance.

Newspaper reports in 1982

During 1982, 31 cases (22 males, 9 females) of suicidal behaviour were reported in *The Times* newspaper (The Times Index 1982). These reports were brief and usually occurred on page 3, the page for home news. These reports were placed among reports of domestic crises, murders, court appearances, personal misadventures and political scandals. Apart from their being laced in a general context of general folly, they were described and reported in recognisably stereotypical ways. The ramification of such construing based on limited facts is that in new situations, stereotypical solutions may be found and facts ignored that offer an alternative construing of behaviour.

The reporting of suicides not only presents information but resurrects and confirms the cultural construing of social reality. The way facts are collected and organised are important processes that affect our understanding of behaviour. There appear to be rules which say: 'in understanding behaviour, these facts are the ones to consider and put them together in this particular way.' This circular process may well blind us to other understandings of behaviour. It is these gross cultural understandings that will be considered here, particularly the way in which facts are reported and put together.

Depression

For sudden deaths which have clear causal attributes, newspaper reports are straightforward. When males die their deaths are understood within a particular causal framework. An incident occurs of social loss that either causes subsequent depression or depression is already present. This depression is usually reported by a close member of the family or a friend. Such a causal understanding is reported, along with the means of completing suicide. The coroner takes into account the method of death and the presence of depression as evidence of suicide.

For the man in Table 6.1(a), his death was described straightforwardly. The man's name was given, he was described as a former detective superintendent and had stabbed himself through the heart. He was both anxious and depressed. During the weeks before his death he had attempted suicide and his wife said that something was causing him great distress and continuous worry (*The Times*, 21 January 1982).

Depression reflects the psychiatric perspective on suicide (Morgan 1979) and is mentioned in ten of the reported deaths (see Table 6.1).

Table 6.1 Reported suicide and the occurrence of depression

Case	Gender	Age	Context	Precipitating factor	Marital status	Method
a	male	58	anxious and depressed	something causing distress and worry	married	stabbed himself
b	male	34	depressed about broken leg	demoted in football league	married	stabbed himself and drank weedkiller
c	male	37	severe depression	death of mother	separated	overdose
d	male	70	depressed, concerned about medication	wife died four years previously	widowed	overdose
e	male	31	manic-depressive	father dies	not known	gunshot
f	male	20	regarded self as failure	read of the death of former girlfriend	single	drugs and alcohol
g	male	36	depressed over financial, social, emotional and marital problems	deserted his ship	married	hanged himself

Criminality

If we turn to Table 6.2, we can see that the precipitating factor is that of facing, or having faced, a criminal charge. This precipitating factor is much closer in time to the event of suicide. The contextual descriptions are varied and not nearly as clear as in the attribution of depression. Again, the method of death is sufficient to presume suicide. This was to be disproved eventually in the case of 6.2(c). Signor Roberto Calvi had become involved in a political scandal and was due to appear in Italy for currency offences. The day before his body was found, his secretary had killed herself in Milan. Although the coroner passed a verdict of suicide, his family challenged this view and after a year, and the presentation of new evidence, the verdict of suicide was rejected in favour of homicide.

Two of those who died after being faced with criminal charges died whilst in custody. The youth, 6.2(d), who hanged himself in custody was awaiting a sentence for throwing petrol bombs into a police station. He had been remanded for psychiatric reports on a charge of arson. The judge said that the evidence disposed of the case. This appears to further perpetuate the notion of a disturbed balance of mind and that there must have been some psychiatric problem. The method of death, then, was used to organise previous events into a coherent understanding. What was previously ambiguous or speculative, his state of mind, was made clear retrospectively to the judge by the act of suicide.

The idea of the balance of mind being disturbed was given as the causal context for the man who jumped in front of a lorry – 6.2(e). He was described as the co-director of a firm and was alleged to have killed his wife. After receiving an insurance payout of £63,000, the police had investigated the circumstances surrounding his wife's death. The woman he lived with said that he had been totally destroyed by his wife's death and the police questioning. The man's diary was produced that had an entry to his dead wife saying: 'I cannot live without you'. The verdict of suicide 'while the balance of the mind was disturbed' was given.

A striking point of these descriptions of suicide after an alleged crime is the direct or indirect imputation of guilt to the deceased. The overall assumption appears to be that if an act is committed following criminal charges then the charges are true and the act of suicide is sufficient grounds for believing such an assumption. As the Judge said of an elderly man, 6.2(d): 'The evidence disposed of the case'. If the man killed himself, he must have been psychiatrically disturbed and, therefore, guilty of the offence.

Table 6.2 Reported suicides facing criminal charges

Case	Gender	Age	Context	Precipitating factor	Marital status	Method
a	male	37	not known	detective facing rape charge	married	gas
b	male	56	in a bout of severe depression	demanding money with menaces	not known	exhaust fumes
c	male	62	due to appear in court	political scandal	married	hanged
d	male	youth	remanded for psychiatric report	throwing petrol into a police station	single	hanged in custody
e	male	35	balance of mind disturbed	alleged to have killed his wife	widowed	jumped in front of a lorry
f	male	18	clever boy hoping to go to university	killed two boys with a shotgun	single	shotgun
g	female	31	believed to have murdered children and then herself	divorced six years ago	divorced	overdose
h	male	34	tried to break drug addiction	previous prison conviction	single	hanged in custody

The only female representative, 6.2(g), was discovered unconscious in the presence of her three dead children, aged ten years, seven years and sixteen months. The children were believed to have been murdered by her. It was also reported that she had been divorced six years before.

Fifteen of the reported cases are represented by concise descriptions of method, precipitating factor and context. Such episodes consist of patterns of behaviour and meanings that are culturally sanctioned. These reports are the public symbols, albeit gross, by which meaning is shared. In this way, they are ritualised forms of describing episodes; they are cultural construings of events.

In describing such episodes, the reporter organises explanations by presenting certain facts to invoke those patterns of meaning resident within the culture of both reporter and reader. In the reports of depression (6.1(c), 6.1(d)), causal information from four years and more prior to the event is presented. Although the victim is seen as having become depressed about something, the descriptions are predominantly concerned with an intrapsychic connotation. The same intrapsychic interpretation holds true for the description of criminal causality, although the causal factors are much more immediate.

Do not ask why?

The same may be said for the man, 6.2(h), who hanged himself in police custody. He had been found collapsed on a grass verge and taken to a police station (*The Times*, 10 November 1982). In the police station he was examined by the police doctor, who said that he would recover from his drug overdose in about six hours. The man made a statement and was charged. Although the police thought he looked unwell and called in another police doctor, he was passed fit to stay in custody. He was visited in his cell by a police officer and he asked for a cigarette. Twenty-five minutes later the man was found hanged in his cell. He had been in prison before and convicted 30 times for drug offences. After his last conviction he had decided to try a drug rehabilitation unit as he hated prison so much.

The Coroner at Hammersmith Court instructed the jury that they must not ask 'Why?', they needed only to consider when, where and how the death had occurred. This seems to be the principal reason for a rather longer newspaper article where the reporter questions the description of what happened in police custody and the direction by the coroner that motivational questions were not admissible (it must be remembered that there had been a vociferous concern over deaths in custody and allegations made against the police in the previous and current years). 'Why?' is the valid question to be asking, yet the coroner is deliberately directing the jury not to ask such a question.

During the same month, in the same newspaper, two suicides were reported (6.1(e), 6.3(a)) where clear reasons were given for suicide. These episodes were reported in the home news section and were as follows:

> Father's death led to suicide. The Company Secretary of Debrett's, aged 31, shot himself after becoming a manic depressive following his father's death. The coroner said that he had killed himself while the balance of his mind was disturbed. (*The Times*, 12 November 1982)

> A Royal Artillery Officer, aged 54, was found dead with shotgun wounds. After having an affair with a woman his wife had started divorce proceedings when she had discovered the relationship. The officer had made several threats to take his own life. (*The Times*, 13 November 1982)

What distinguishes these reports is that they fit into stereotypical episodic descriptions of suicidal behaviour with recognisable causal trains and precipitatory events. For the man who was a drug addict, his death occurred in circumstances where his death may have been averted, where there was already public concern over cell deaths in police custody and the suicide verdict was debatable. Again, not asking 'why' means that the public are directed to accept the *status quo*, not to question it.

Table 6.3 Reported suicides and marital problems

Case	Gender	Age	Context	Precipitating factor	Marital status	Method
a	male	54	having an affair with a woman	wife started divorce proceedings	married	shotgun
b	female	61	depression following a breakdown	marriage broke up	widowed	overdose

Table 6.4 Reported suicides with financial and employment problems

Case	Gender	Age	Context	Precipitating factor	Marital status	Method
a	male	not known	financial difficulties	actor living on social security	not known	overdose
b	female	26	unemployed	unemployed	single	self-immolation

Financial difficulties

Only two cases are suggested as being direct results of financial difficulties (6.4(a), 6.4(b)). One is an actor who overdosed with sleeping pills. He was said to be living on social security and had been faced with financial difficulties. The other case is a woman, aged 26, who was unemployed and set fire to herself after pouring paraffin oil over her body. The brief article is headlined as 'Fire Death', (*The Times*, 23 August 1982).

In May of that same year a report was made expressing concern over suicidal feelings in the unemployed and that many unemployed had experienced feelings of depression after being out of work for more than six months (*The Times*, 3 May 1982). The unemployed were seen as needing counselling and the resources of the Health Service to deal with depression and suicidal thoughts. Although depression and concomitant suicidal thoughts are seen as results of unemployment, particularly in the young, the solution to this problem is seen not as a political or economical solution but as a 'mental health' solution. Such deviant behaviour is channelled into an individual perspective as reflecting personal health rather than a legitimate expression of social distress. The recognition of the social causation of problems but individual resolution of such problems is a common theme of suicide prevention and rests on the assumption of some personal weakness in those who engage in suicidal behaviour. In this way, the descriptions of suicidal behaviour invoke descriptions within the *status quo* and reinforce those same descriptions (Ovenstone and Kreitman 1974). The idea of legitimate grievance would place suicidal behaviour within the realms of legitimate distress, as we saw in the previous chapter, and focus on the social causation of such acts and episodes.

Table 6.5 Reported suicides with miscellaneous causal descriptions

Case	Gender	Age	Context	Precipitating factor	Marital status	Method
a	male	22	obsessed with violent death	wanted to be a psychiatrist	single	overdose and alcohol
b	female	29	public relations consultant		single	overdose
c	female	21	hidden torment	raped two years previously	single	jumped from high building
d	female	28	depressed	vicar's wife	married	not known
e*	female female	not known		'cries for help'		overdose of paracetemol
f	male	52	a policeman			fell to death
g	male	†	Mahler predicted that music would lead to suicide	finished his article		

* two women who died together
† unreported

Miscellaneous descriptions of suicide

In Table 6.5 we see a number of cases where idiosyncratic descriptions are presented of episodes of suicidal behaviour.

In 6.5(a), a music student, aged 22, locked himself in a room at Claridge's hotel and killed himself with drugs and alcohol. His mother is reported as saying that he had tried to take his own life when he was 17 years old. He had wanted to be a psychiatrist and had been obsessed with violent death from an early age (*The Times*, 17 June 1982). This description invokes the description of the personal psychological disturbance of a young man. To justify this, his mother presents a biography of his personal obsession.

Both Atkinson (1978) and Lofland (1969) bring our attention to the way deviant acts are described by a retrospective reference to a deviant biography. Of all the previous biographical incidents, particular incidents are selected to fit the social description of the suicidal act. What may have been defined as 'previous interests' become retrospectively defined as 'obsessions'. The negative reframing and selection of incidents is a means of making biographical events consistent with a classification of suicide. The effort to make known facts consistent with categorisation is an act of social construing and it is this construing which is invoked and perpetuated by newspaper reports. The commission of a deviant act appears to necessitate an understanding which seeks prior evidence of deviancy. The formerly neutral becomes reframed negatively.

For some descriptions of suicide a complete account is not available. In 6.5(d), a woman, aged 28, was found dead in a field. She was said to have been suffering from depression and was a vicar's wife. This was not a report following an inquest but a description of a news event. However, it does highlight the attitude towards suicide in women, that depression is a sufficient explanation and that somehow by being a vicar's wife some profile of her previous life can be reconstructed from our cultural assumptions of how vicars' wives live their lives.

'Death Risk of Popular Pain Killer'

During December 1982 two young women died as a result of paracetemol poisoning (6.5(c), *The Times*, 4 December 1982). The London Coroner recorded verdicts of accidental death on these two women. He is reported as saying that '...a lot of people do not know how dangerous they (the drugs) are and take them like sweets'. He also added that the deaths were accidental rather than serious suicide attempts and young women who died in this way were making 'cries for help'. This is the dismissal of serious intent in young women and a presumption of their ineptitude.

There was, at this time, and there still is now, a growing concern during 1982 about the availability of paracetemol as a medicine (Hawton and Goldacre 1982). On 22 July 1982 newspapers and television were urged by the Pharmaceutical Society of Great Britain not to print details and quantities of medications taken when reporting suicides as reports could prompt imitative suicides. The concern was raised that 200,000 persons had attempted suicide, and a further 4,000 persons succeeded, in England and

Wales during the previous year. This had meant an incident of suicidal behaviour every two and a half minutes. The Pharmaceutical Society wanted the press to be free to report the circumstances and details but not the name of the drug and the quantity used.

This case does appear to highlight the general opinion that whereas men complete suicide, women only attempt suicide. These attempts are perceived as cries for help when made by women and, if completed, are examples of accidentally achieving death. For men, however, death before dishonour appears to be an acceptable description for suicide with no overtones of accident. In 6.5(f), we see that the policeman who fell from the bridge was categorised by *The Times Index* as a suicide, although few details were supplied. Nobody suggested that it was a gesture and that he accidentally fell through his own incompetence.

In 6.5(g), we see an example of an explanation being tailored to fit the death of the records editor of *Hi-Fi News* (*The Times*, 25 August 1982). After writing the final paragraph of an article on Mahler's *'Das Lied von der Erde'*, the man took his own life. In *The Times* article, the story is reported of how Gustav Mahler had been reluctant to have *'Das Lied'* performed. He feared that the stark imagery of the music might induce those who heard it to commit suicide. This is juxtaposed with the report of the man's death. No attempt was made to place the death of the man in any other context either social, financial or relational. This view reflects the romantic notion of rational suicide in men by suggesting how a sensitive man, moved by music, takes his life. Contrasted with descriptions of suicide in women, it appears that few examples of completed suicide are legitimate for women, whereas suicide in men is a legitimate activity. This may account for the greater rate of suicide in men in that suicide is seen as a legitimate solution to insurmountable distress. Just as violence is legitimated in male behaviour and not in female behaviour, so violent acts of suicide may not be culturally available in repertoires of legitimate female behaviour, although that may now be changing. With a change in gender role expectations, we may see a change in completed suicide rates and the methods that are used to achieve death, with a move towards more violent methods in women.

Attempted suicide

The reports of attempted suicide (Table 6.6) are sketchy as there is no coroner's report. The reports appear to be considered for their novelty value. The report of Lady Lucan's overdose is typical in that it is an incident considering an individual on the periphery of public life. Lord Lucan had been the subject of newspaper reports during the previous year following his disappearance.

Table 6.6 Reported attempted suicide

Case	Gender	Age	Description of events	Method
a	female	43	Lady Lucan overdosed and taken to psychiatric hospital	overdose
b	male	50	found trying to hang himself from Law Court's balcony	hanging
c	male	28	deceived authorities and gained free hospital accommodation	overdose
d	male	31	the woman he wanted to see arrived in the car park	leaping

The cases 6.6(c) and 6.6(d) represent the negative construing of attempted suicide. They present the element of manipulation associated with suicidal behaviour. The 28-year-old man (6.6(c)) was accused of taking overdoses to gain free hospital accommodation and of further threatening suicidal behaviour to secure such accommodation. The tone of the article is that the man was deviant and manipulated the authorities. A similar description of illegitimate behaviour is presented for the 31-year-old man (6.6(d)). Once the woman he wanted to see appeared in the car park, his suicidal behaviour ceased.

Social knowledge; a political act

In describing episodes of death deemed to be suicidal, there appear to be three principal considerations: the presence of violence or the nature of the act itself, the presence of a particular event associated with criminality and a contextual element usually associated with depression or some psychiatric disturbance (see Table 6.1, p.99). To validate the description of suicide, a causal train is invoked from a past biography where ambiguous incidents are reframed as evidence of prior deviance. Where there is the presence of violence and criminality, less evidence is needed to pass a verdict of suicide. The context becomes inferred from the immediate events and a circular process of description occurs where events themselves become contexts.

newspaper reporting

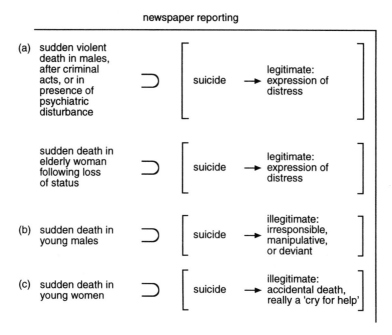

Figure 6.1 Constitutive rules for the legitimation of suicidal behaviour in newspaper reporting

A critical factor involved in describing suicidal behaviour is the legitimation of such an act. There appear to be a number of categories where suicidal behaviour is seen as legitimate for certain males: political protesters, police officers, criminals, those who are violent, depressed or psychiatrically disturbed, those who have lost a significant other and for men over 40. Such legitimate status is denied to women, males under 40, those who are not depressed or disturbed, the unemployed or those whose primary significant relationship remains intact (see Figure 6.1).

We will see in the next chapter that the assessment of legitimacy is critical in the management of distress when it occurs in the psychiatric hospital. The validation of legitimate status has important political and social consequences for the person being judged, as we saw earlier with Bobby Sands. In Figure 6.2 we see that there are more pathways to becoming labelled

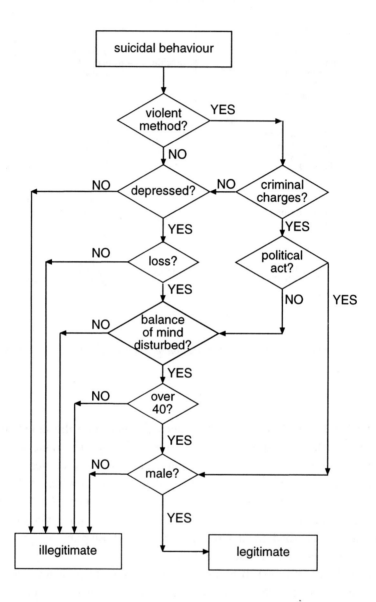

Figure 6.2 Paths to the legitimacy of suicidal behaviour

illegitimate than legitimate for those who are distressed and deemed to be
suicidal.

Constitutive rules for assessing legitimacy

The cultural constructs associated with the description of suicidal behaviour
recognised in this chapter appear to be: legitimate/illegitimate, de-
pressed/not depressed, disturbed/stable, male/female, violent/non-violent,
criminal/non-criminal, employed/unemployed, relationship disrupted /re-
lationship intact.

The validation of behaviour, and the person, as legitimate appears to be
an important factor in the process of becoming suicidal and in describing
such behaviour in the newspapers. I am speculating in this chapter that
ascribing the crucial label of 'legitimate' to behaviour depends upon how
both the individual construes his own behaviour and how that behaviour is
construed by his significant others (Garfinkel 1956; Heider 1946). In times
of ambiguity, there are understandings present in the social stock of knowledge. Should the suicidal behaviour be labelled as a political act by the
individual and those others in his social milieu, as part of a tradition of
martyrdom, the behaviour becomes an acceptable means of negotiating
concessions. If this tradition is not accepted by one party in such a
negotiation, as in the case of the British Government and Bobby Sands, and
the behaviour is not therefore overtly labelled as a political act, suicidal
behaviour is taken as an illegitimate attempt to manipulate others, avoid
responsibility and gain control.

This issue of legitimacy will be investigated in the following chapter in
its implications for how suicidal behaviour is construed inter-personally and
the ramifications this has for women in distress. What is of concern is that
media publicity about suicide can offer a 'mode' for suicide (Martin 1996)
and violent activity (Cantor and Sheehan 1996). Stories about celebrity
suicides appear to trigger further imitative suicides. Several authors, writing
after the death of the pop star Kurt Cobain, suggest that these suicides may
be averted by responsible handling by the media and the establishment of a
provision for handling crisis calls (Jobes *et al.* 1996). In England, although
Simkin *et al.* (1995) found no significant changes in overdosing episodes
following a television drama depicting a teenage girl's overdose of
paracetemol, they too suggest that the presence of guidelines for the sensitive
presentation of such material are essential.

CHAPTER SEVEN

The Politics of Self-Mutilation

Patients and staff members wheedle, argue, persuade, bargain, negotiate, holler at, shriek at command, manipulate relevant contingencies, and attempt to deceive. (Fagerhaugh and Strauss 1977, p.8)

This chapter is concerned with describing suicidal behaviour in the context of a psychiatric hospital ward. The basic premise presented here is that self-mutilating behaviour is part of an interactional pattern between persons. An attempt is made to see how such behaviour is maintained in the interactive context of a hospital ward. The emphasis on the maintenance of current behaviour is a deliberate choice. Rather than focus on the reconstruction of the cause or origin of the behaviour, I hope that a contextual description in a particular setting will offer a metaphor for describing the behaviour in other interactive settings, such as the family home. Although the psychiatric ward may appear to be a special and extreme case, we will see in the stories of the women who come to be in such a hospital that the dramas of their lives are played out in other locations too.

The political context of the ward

The events described here occur in the setting of an acute admissions ward in a psychiatric hospital. At the time there were a number of women on the ward who were engaged in self-harming behaviours involving cutting their wrists, burning their bodies with cigarettes, breaking windows and overdosing with medication. In addition, some of these women were mutilating themselves with razor blades, cutting their arms and thighs. This latter activity is not considered to be suicidal behaviour by some authors and is regarded as a means of tension relief (Callahan 1996).

In any arena where groups of individuals co-ordinate their collective behaviour there will be differing philosophies about consensus. There will also be cultural differences between patients and staff, between patient and patient and between staff member and staff member about illness, health, the expression of distress and how people are expected to behave in hospital. The same arguments apply to the psychiatric hospital, where the expression of distress and the management of distress are part of a politicised arena. Collective behaviour is a coping dialogue where all parties are actively striving to meet their various responsibilities, to control their environment and to make everyday circumstances more tolerable and certain.

The presence of conflict

A number of authors (Bursten and D'Escopo 1965; Caudill *et al.* 1952; Fagerhaugh and Strauss 1977) describe how outbreaks of problematic behaviour occur on hospital wards when there is a discrepancy between two warring staff authorities who define their overall position as benevolent and attempt to conceal their differences. Hawton (1978) reports that ward staff frequently indicate a conflict between the desire to withhold attention, to manage the physical consequences and to try and understand the act through discussion when dealing with suicidal behaviour.

Haley (1980) hypothesises that symptoms such as self-mutilation reflect an organisation with a confused hierarchy where no clear lines of authority are present. When the hierarchy of an organisation becomes confused, symptomatic behaviour becomes adaptive and stabilises such confusion. Bursten and d'Escopo (1965) reiterate this position. They suggest that it is tempting to see patients who 'refuse' to get well as being in conflict with society or their family. This 'refusal' may be seen as resistance to social norms, defiance or seeking an aggressive control of others in the same situation. However, what appears as deviant or defiant behaviour may really be compliant. By such behaviour the organisational hierarchy is clarified and symptomatic behaviour becomes appropriate.

It is this perspective of patterns of behaviour constituting conflict that Sluzki (1981) pursues. He suggests that the presence of a 'conflict' or a 'crisis' does not mean there is a 'pathology' preceding or underlying the conflict, rather that the current management and systemic organisation of behaviour is the conflict. In this same way, Ross and McKay (1979) describe how young women were successfully encouraged to stop mutilating themselves by changing the organisational pattern of managing self-mutilatory behaviour. Instead of trying to stop, prevent, control or punish the behaviour, Ross and McKay adopted a different, but coherent, policy of approaching self-muti-latory behaviour which reorganised the pattern of management of that behaviour. Instead of treating behaviour they studied it, instead of punishing the behaviour they asked that it might continue in order to understand it better.

Such political collective behaviour occurs when people have common shared understanding and expectations about behaviour. If self-mutilation is indeed a communicative act, communicating rage, rejection or abandonment, then this communication is within a relationship (Callahan 1996). Behaviour is co-ordinated by expectations about relationships. These expectations are governed by rules and constructs designating what a behaviour counts as and how it is to be handled. The construing of self-mutilation is critical to its management.

How behaviour is construed

In a paper about deviant patients in casualty departments, Jeffrey (1979) suggests that the moral evaluation of patients is an important feature of their treatment. Two principal categories are used for describing patients in hospital casualty departments: the good, interesting patient who is legitimately ill, who will give the staff a chance to practice their skills and will test their competence and maturity and the bad, rubbish who present trivial, irrational, insoluble problems, who are illegitimately seeking the status of sick, who offer little chance of therapeutic success and who are emotionally blackmailing their significant others.

As we have seen earlier in Chapters Four and Five, suicidal behaviour is negatively construed and evaluated. Negative construing is a handicap to the successful management of such behaviour and the negative connotation of behaviour is part of a degradation ceremony (Garfinkel 1956). Degradation ceremonies are communicative acts where the public identity of a person is transformed into something seen as lower in the scheme of social types. Deviant women that do not conform are degraded into mental cases. Such a process depends upon the social rules about suicidal behaviour and how the person is seen in the context of his primary reference group. In the process of degradation a person becomes construed as an 'out-of-the-ordinary' deviant. Added to this, further negative labels are ascribed: 'abnormal', 'illegitimate' and 'unco-operative', for example. Garfinkel emphasises that when a negative construing of behaviour occurs, it is supposed that the person is choosing such an illegitimate behaviour in contrast to the positive poles that exist of being co-operative and normal and, thereby, legitimate.

In the preceding chapter a number of core constructs were elicited which were repeatedly used to describe suicidal behaviour by the news media. These descriptions centred around the descriptions of criminality or depression and the conferring of personal legitimacy. From the authors describing suicidal behaviour, it is clear that the self-mutilating behaviour of women is not considered to be legitimate by health care workers and transgresses the demands that patients are responsible for conforming with treatment and do not form a group.

Four women

Women were harming themselves repeatedly on the ward of a psychiatric hospital and they were willing to talk to me as a researcher interested in suicidal behaviour. It is important to emphasise here that I was in the position of a researcher, not a therapist. The reasons for this will be clearer later in the chapter but the primary reasons were that I did not want to establish any immediate expectation of help and that I needed the co-operation of the women themselves, which was in itself a turnaround from most of their daily contacts. I was primarily interested in the way in which women talked about their problems and what they believed would help them. When we talk about our lives we use stories to make sense of what has happened to us and, in some way, to legitimate what we have done. While the nursing and medical staff refused to confer legitimacy upon these women, I wondered how they, the women, saw their own lives. This approach has recently been labelled as the use of illness narratives in research (Hydén 1996).

All of the four women overdosed with medication and mutilated themselves. Self-mutilation is, in itself, not necessarily considered to be suicidal behaviour in the psychiatric literature and is one possible indicator of a borderline personality disorder (Favazza and Rosenthal 1993). However, both the staff involved on the ward and the patients themselves regarded the behaviour as suicidal. And, as Callahan (1996) writes: 'Two of the central issues in working with borderline clients are their self-destructive and "manipulative" suicide attempts. However, borderline clients also *complete* suicide' (p. 444, original author's italics).

However, if we consider that women who make suicide attempts are more often lacking in social support and have been previously admitted into hospital and these factors are aggregated with unemployment, the presence of a mental disorder and the use of anxiolytic medication, then these women were indeed at risk (Runeson, Eklund and Wasserman 1996).

Sally (aged 24)

Sally was admitted to a psychiatric hospital after an overdose of medication. Her parents were unwilling to have her at home as they said that they could not cope with her continual abuse of medication. Although the admission was to have been a short stay, the stay lengthened and Sally's behaviour became more and more damaging to herself. Sally's parents were unwilling to have Sally home. Her daughter (aged 5) was living with Sally's parents and Sally returned home at weekends. During her visits home she mutilated herself, or overdosed, and was promptly returned to the hospital by her father.

Sally described an adolescence characterised by a narrative of sexual adventures and disasters. At fourteen she was engaged to a soldier who drank and beat her up. She broke off this engagement at the age of seventeen. Following this she was involved in a liaison which produced her daughter, Jane. Eighteen months later she was pregnant again by another man and this pregnancy was terminated surgically. Sally was nineteen. During her pregnancy in 1975/76, Sally was described as a difficult and defensive patient. Her gynaecologist describes her as resentful and unhelpful. Following an interlude abroad, and return home, she sought medical help for abdominal pains, diarrhoea, loss of weight, eventually leading to a diagnosis of Crohn's disease. She was prescribed steroids and a high-protein diet. By March she had put on weight and by August was described as in static remission. It was suggested that all medication be left off completely. However, by February 1980 there was a relapse of the Crohn's disease, followed by remission, followed by relapse in the following August.

The following period was characterised by increasing tension and irritability, difficulties with her parents and her friends. She was abusing codeine phosphate and using alcohol to relieve tension. She had asked her general practitioner for sleeping tablets and further psychotropic drugs, which were prescribed, but the medical notes also acknowledge that she inevitably abused those very drugs. Her general practitioner wrote that it was difficult to establish a working relationship with her. Numerous attempts were made, after a referral to a consultant psychiatrist, to engage Sally in therapy but all proved to be fruitless.

She was admitted to the general hospital after an incident of self-poisoning using paracetemol and codeine phosphate and discharged home after three days. Three weeks later she had poisoned herself again and this was the episode which precipitated her admission to the psychiatric hospital.

Sally was seen as a difficult, unco-operative patient who had attempted to solve her physical health problems by a number of previous solutions. These solutions had failed. Finally, her physical symptoms were questioned and she was seen as illegitimate in her claims to the status 'sick'. As we have seen in Chapter 4, one of the criteria for occupying the status 'sick' is to co-operate with treatment and not to be responsible for the state of disease. In Sally's case she was seen by her general practitioner as contributing to her own demise and that her symptoms were functional in basis. We see the progression, previously schematised in Figure 5.4 (p.85), of continuing cycles of escalating distress and failed solutions that are integrated into a repertoire of distress management.

Kelly (aged 21)

Kelly had been a regular in-patient at the psychiatric hospital for two and a half years when she was first interviewed. She had repeatedly mutilated herself. She was first admitted, aged 17, to the adolescent unit in the psychiatric hospital in 1979 after an overdose. There was a question raised at the time that she may have been three months pregnant. There was concern too about her mental state.

Throughout her case conference in the September of that same year, Kelly cried continuously. Even then the idea was being raised by Kelly that her mother wanted her transferred to the psychiatric hospital proper. Kelly had been staying with an aunt but this relationship deteriorated as the aunt blamed Kelly for a poor relationship with her daughter. Her mother had shown no interest in Kelly since she arrived at the hospital and there were continued outbursts of aggression and self-mutilation. During that time she was placed legally confined to the hospital.

This young woman was considered to be aggressive, maladjusted and deviant. Her physical symptoms, like Sally, were seen as illegitimate and 'hysterical' in origin. Although described as having personal problems, much of her difficulties were blamed on her familial antecedents.

Her mother was also reported to be aggressive and her father was a criminal. Kelly had undergone numerous attempted solutions to physical problems, which had failed. The inference was made that the symptoms were illegitimate attempts to enter the status 'sick' and that when faced with life's difficulties, she would escape her responsibilities by overdosing or mutilating herself. She described herself as 'Queen of the Slashers', referring to her ability to mutilate herself in a variety of ways.

Kath (aged 28)

This woman voluntarily sought admission to the psychiatric hospital as she feared for her own safety. She had been discharged recently from the general hospital after an overdose of vodka, lager and aspirin.

Leaving home at the age of 17 to live with her husband-to-be, she discovered that she was already pregnant. Her mother and step-father were moving and she did not want to move with them. The parting was difficult and she had no further contact with her parents until her daughter was born.

Following the birth of her daughter her pelvis became infected and a hysterectomy was performed. She was 18 years old. Her parents rallied round to help her and throughout her marriage she would turn to her parents in times of stress. The marriage had many areas of conflict. Her husband was unemployed but played in a rock band. She worked full-time and in the evenings. There were recurrent depressive interludes and a twelve-week stay in a psychiatric hospital. She says that she stayed in the marriage for security and to be with her daughter. During these depressive interludes she would return to her mother.

However, her husband eventually petitioned for divorce and she became involved with a young man of 18. Her former husband was awarded custody of the child, which she did not contest as her new boyfriend said that he would not live with her and her daughter.

There had been a previous episode in the spring when she had lacerated her wrists and been admitted for a day at the psychiatric hospital. Her boyfriend had heard about this and subsequently 'rescued her' (her terminology). He had moved to be with her so that they could make a new start but had since returned to his old job in another part of the country.

This woman voluntarily sought admission to the hospital and initially received sympathetic treatment by the staff, who saw her as being emotionally disturbed by a disruption in a key relationship. This sympathetic understanding was dispelled by her subsequent actions when she repeatedly mutilated herself by locking herself in the lavatory, beating on the door, plunging her hand and arm through the window until her wrists were lacerated and then screaming loudly. The accompanying attempts to break down the door and the rush to stay her bleeding all added to an increased tension and heightened drama. Increasingly, she was seen as illegitimate and unco-operative, aggressive and uncontrollable. It is, perhaps, ironic that she was admitted to a psychiatric hospital at her own request because she felt suicidal, yet during her stay she engaged in behaviours of self-harm that caused increasingly greater physical injuries to herself.

In a family interview her father told me that she had never had been any good and that if she were a dog he would have had her put down. It was to this family background that she had turned when distraught and to which she returned from hospital.

June (aged 51)

June was the eldest of the four women described here and had four children. She was admitted to hospital after an overdose of alcohol and medication.

She had been involved in an argument with her husband before her admission to hospital.

There was a history of psychiatric admissions. She had been diagnosed as manic-depressive. This psychosis, she said, had been precipitated twenty years previously by an incident abroad whilst she was in the women's navy service. In the past five years she had repeatedly been admitted for episodes of mania and episodes of overdosing. During the previous years she had complained of gynaecological problems until eventually she was sterilised, an ovary removed and a hysterectomy performed.

June was seen by the ward staff as a chronic patient who was 'crazy' but 'likeable and harmless'. When she first engaged in self-mutilatory behaviour she was not regarded as manipulative or hostile, as were the other women. However, as her stay lengthened and the number of episodes increased, becoming part of a number of collective incidents of suicidal behaviour, she was seen as 'difficult'. Sometimes on the ward she would be seen laughing with the other patients and she was construed as making no effort to leave. If pressed to make a decision about leaving, or challenged in a meeting, an episode of manic behaviour would follow. This led the staff to conclude that she was manipulating the staff and making no effort to get better.

The staff perspective on the women

The staff of the hospital ward, both medical and nursing, saw these women as difficult patients who presented a management problem. They were unresponsive to treatment, hostile, manipulative, aggressive, illegitimate in their claims, difficult, unco-operative and seeking control. They were not accorded a legitimate place in the order of being mentally ill but as deviants, even within the context of mental illness. In fact, they were not seen as 'mentally ill' but 'disorderly'. Their behaviour was not regarded as legitimate once treatment strategies had been implemented to manage such behaviour. The patients had not responded as the staff expected. This perspective is not unique. Lawless, Kippax and Crawford (1996) describe how women that are stigmatised as deviant, impure, undeserving and guilty have difficulties in obtaining appropriate treatment and support from health care workers.

A profile of these women was constructed by the staff which saw them as illegitimate in their claims to illness, although they had gained admission to a hospital on the grounds of a fear for their own safety. Despite this admission for asylum, they had repeatedly harmed themselves. When the staff had introduced strategies to help these women, they had not co-oper-ated and were, therefore, illegitimate in the eyes of the staff. Not only were they seen as illegitimate but also as responsible for their own condition when they continually harmed themselves. Mutilation was a direct result of their own action. These actions came, in turn, to be seen as hostile acts against the staff. These women were no longer considered to be sad or mad. They were, in the eyes of the staff, bad.

The construing of suicidal behaviour

The staff, as a collective body, began to consider these women in the context of the psychiatric patients on the ward using six core constructs:

- Individual patient – collective patients: These women were considered by their actions as women with emotional problems precipitated by personal crises. Yet despite this understanding, they were considered as a cohort of 'slashers' who set out to disrupt the smooth working of the ward, who failed to be reasonable in their demands and who provoked each other to upset the staff. The word 'slashers' was used both by patients and staff in a common language referring to self-mutilation.

- Legitimate – illegitimate: Their behaviour on the ward was seen as illegitimate in that specific treatment strategies had been formulated to combat their self-mutilation. Although initially seen as legitimate by some of the staff (because the women were either suicidally distressed through emotional loss or just plain 'crazy'), the women came to be seen as illegitimate. Once seen as illegitimate, all suicidal behaviour came to be seen as manipulative too. Furthermore, other behaviours by the same women – the questioning of medication, answering back, getting up late, demanding psychotherapy – also came to be seen as illegitimate and manipulative.

- Responsible – not responsible: With the ascription of legitimacy there was a concomitant ascription of responsibility. For suicidal behaviour to be legitimate, the person has to be considered not responsible for their continuing plight. These women were seen as contributing to their demise by active participation in defiant behaviour, making choices that deliberately exposed them to further pain and rejection and for deliberately harming themselves.

- Co-operative – non-co-operative: Any event which indicated a deterioration in the patient's mental health status became seen as evidence of the patient's lack of co-operation with the treatment strategy. The staff spent time working out what to do with the women, what medication to give them and what ward programme they should pursue after hours of talking, reassurance and nursing concern. When an incident of self-mutilation occurred, it was seen as non-co-operation with these efforts and taken by some staff as a rejection of their personal help and nursing skill.

- Personal – social: The understanding of the causes for suicidal behaviour varied around the two poles personal–social. When the women were engaged in mutilating themselves on the ward for no apparent reason, or following a ward meeting or were seen to be tearful and depressed, personal causative factors were proposed. These centred around having a personality disorder, a depressive illness, pre-menstrual tension, tiredness, a disturbed adolescence or being downright awkward. However, when incidents of self-mutilation occurred during home visits, after telephone calls or visits from significant others, the causative factors were seen as social in origin. These centred around marital conflict, familial conflict, loss or rejection by an important other.

- Punitive – permissive: With the oscillation between construct poles of legitimacy, responsibility and co-operation, the staff were caught in a bind about treatment. Some staff considered that a punitive line should be taken where non-co-operation by patients would result in a lack of privileges. However, some other staff thought that this treatment of patients as a collective was unjust and that punitive measures should only be taken against certain mutilating women and not against other patients. Some staff believed that although the behaviour was illegitimate, it was necessary in the context of a mental hospital, where, perhaps, people were expected to act 'crazy' to follow a permissive regime.

Of all these considerations, the discussions returned eventually to how the behaviour could be controlled and how this control by staff over patients could be implemented. This control, however, had to fit in with the beliefs of members of staff about what degree of control one human being could have over another. Eventually both sets of behaviour, the strategies of the staff and the acts of mutilation by the patients, were seen as mutual steps in the dance of maintaining control over ward life. This symmetrical escalation of mutual control seeking, with more and more extreme attempts to exhibit power tactics, meant that all members of the ward experienced continuing distress.

As we can see in Figure 5.4 (p.85), distress escalates when attempted solutions fail. It was at this point that I was contacted by the staff to suggest a strategy to reduce the escalating conflict and distress. It should be noted that the staff requested this meeting. This raises a consideration for any therapeutic intervention by a researcher. Any strategic intervention is a political act if involved in controlling the social and personal behaviour of others. A means of accommodating this will be suggested later in the chapter.

The organisation of the staff hierarchy

Haley (1980) suggests that disturbed behaviour occurs when there is a covert hierarchical conflict. This was evident in the behaviour of the staff, or rather in the way that the staff were organised. The staff were divided into two hierarchical structures. There was a nursing hierarchy which was organised into three working shifts. The nursing staff were involved in the day-to-day routines of handling patients, handing out pills, supervising meals, changing beds and some psychotherapy. The practice of psychotherapy is an important part of mental health nursing and an activity which nurses pursue and enjoy.

The other hierarchical structure was that of the medical staff, who were responsible for diagnosing the patient's illness and formulating treatment strategies. The medical staff, apart from the consultant psychiatrist, were not trained in psychiatry and were only resident on the ward for six months. The six months residency was part of a training in the general practice of family medicine. As the practitioners themselves said, they had no previous experience of psychiatry and were initially unused to the terms and the strategies of treatment used. What was significant was the emphasis by these medical practitioners on an epistemology that saw events in linear terms of cause and effect and that illness could be cured by finding the appropriate strategy. The bio-medical model pervaded the strategies for controlling patient behaviour. Failure to respond to a treatment strategy, or a repeated strategy, meant that the patient's responsibility was questioned. As patients were seen to deliberately harm themselves, they violated the primary maxims of the bio-medical status of sickness: to co-operate with treatment and not be responsible for their own demise.

Both sets of staff changed at regular intervals. The nursing staff were rotated on a shift system within the ward. Any formulations of strategies had to be made when all staff were present. However, some nursing staff had differing perspectives on how patients were to be treated, particularly those patients who mutilated themselves. The discussions between all staff centred around a permissive approach or a punitive approach based on a restriction of privileges. The medical staff favoured a perspective that formulated

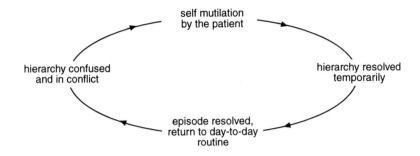

Figure 7.1 Self-mutilation in patients and the resolution of hierarchical conflict in a psychiatric hospital ward

strategies for dealing with individual patients. The nursing staff believed a policy towards the patients as a collective should be pursued.

The episodes of self-mutilation effectively thwarted any co-ordinated, planned attempt to implement either of the two policies. Once a patient mutilated herself, a recognised course of action began that resolved the crisis temporarily by staff physically treating the patient. There was no need for a negotiation of crisis procedure, the staff occupied their learned and traditional roles of 'nurse' and 'doctor'.

The circularity was a regularly repeated pattern of confusion and lengthy debate over policy, followed by attempted strategies, followed by episodes of self mutilation (see Figure 7.1).

The ward situation

The ward situation was exacerbated by its reputation as a difficult place to work on. Not only were the patients 'difficult' but a charge nurse on the same ward had himself recently taken an overdose. The staff morale was low and the nursing staff confessed anxiety about their own futures by working on such a ward. The general impression was that there were not enough nurses to actively nurse the patients and that nursing attention had to be given 'on demand'. The nursing staff saw this as a reason for their colleague overdosing coupled with an unsympathetic nursing hierarchy unwilling to listen to their claims. As one nurse said of the patients: 'The squeaky wheels get oiled first'.

Both nursing staff and patients complained of a lack of continuity of medical and nursing staff to maintain some therapeutic stability. As Haley (1976) suggests, when persons from two differing hierarchical levels conspire against a third, in this case nurses and patients against the doctors or doctors and patients against nurses, distress is likely to occur. In this way, when conflict gets out of hand, symptoms take over; when symptoms become out of hand, conflict takes over. The cycle of interaction began to escalate and it was at this point that I was asked by the staff to become involved in formulating alternative strategies to resolve their collective distress.

It is interesting to note here that an 'overdose' was an attempted solution shared by both staff and patients and is a vital factor in considering a shared construing of their commonality of experience. However, the charge nurse was expelled from the 'staff' group. Similarly, the concept of 'slashers' was a meaning shared by patients and staff.

When violent suicidal behaviour was used, a search for long-term causal explanations was abandoned by the staff. These women, when behaving in a violent manner, breaking windows or engaged in self-mutilation, were deemed to be illegitimate in their demands by the ward staff. Any former legitimating factors associated with loss, depression, age or gender were rejected in favour of immediate contextual demands. There was a circularity built into this process. Once a former set of legitimating grounds were abandoned for an immediate causal explanation, those former events became reframed negatively and previous episodes of violence 'discovered' in the patient's biography. This ties in with the similar pre-emptive construing of suicide presented in the newspaper accounts in the previous chapter. Constructing a retrospective 'bad' biography stigmatises the patient and absolves the therapeutic staff of responsibility.

Finally, some patients were also distressed by the continuing acts of self-mutilation and the events surrounding that mutilation. Some had indeed sought peace and quiet in what they thought to be the safe harbour of a psychiatric hospital. Others were sensitive to the emotional tone of the process of escalating distress and this disturbed them, particularly when their own therapy was targeted at bringing some emotional stability and calm to their lives.

Meaning in context

There was a situation of considerable distress and, as can be imagined, much chagrin on behalf of the senior staff who wanted to make some meaning out of what was going on. Although the suicide literature suggests the meaning of such behaviour, what was apparent was that meaning is not an abstract cognitive reasoning that can be sought in books.

Meaning is performed in action (Kirmayer 1993). These women were articulate in their distress as it was embodied and performed, not as it was expected to be related in the format of therapeutic interviews. Life has not the consistency we are trained to expect. Suicidal behaviour, then, is an activity, something that is done, it is not only an idea. Even though it may be dismissed as a gesture, the gesture has occurred, it has been performed and, therefore, done by one person who intends to influence another.

Baerveldt and Voestermans (1996) refer to the body as a 'selfing device' – a means of self presentation of expressing emotions and feelings. Wrist cutting may not be a communication about, or a protest against, a social order, it may be symptomatic of that social order. With non-verbal or non-discursive expression it is not easy to spilt that expression into meaning units. The meaning derives from the simultaneous conditions of the whole and the whole is comprised of the others involved in the action. While self-mutilation, by its reflexive use of the term 'self', refers to the individual, the use of mutilation in a psychiatric ward is the embodiment of a disrupted social order. Such ritualised expressive forms are common to psychiatric institutions and prisons and are part of a repertoire of expressive acts. While it may be counter-intuitive to talk about ward mutilation behaviour, the use of self-mutilation directs our understandings to an individualised and linear causality and away from the communicative performed meaning in terms of its relationship. To use a previous metaphor, we are still looking at the speakers to discover the disturbance in a sound system rather than the source of the noise in the system as a whole.

The management of suicidal behaviour on a hospital ward

I was repeatedly asked by the staff for my opinions about what was happening systemically and how the patients' behaviour could be handled. 'That's what experts are here for', I was told. In this context, as researcher, I was expected to be an expert, although I did try and explain that a researcher is there because he doesn't know. As I was attending meetings, talking to staff and patients and known to be interested in the systemic description of suicidal behaviour, this was maybe a reasonable request. However, it did mean that one faction was attempting to co-ally the help of a member of the larger system – staff/patients/researcher – to manage the behaviour of a cohort of seemingly misbehaving deviant patients. Although I was involved by being an observer, I could not help but influence matters by the questions I asked. I was, therefore, part of the political system of the ward. What I had to do was to find a strategy to circumvent any potential alliance between myself and the staff and provide a model for continuing procedures.

What I did was to tell the staff that I could comment once I had found out how the patients saw the situation, that is what their views were and what they wished. One of my primary considerations was to make an understanding of the possible function of the deviance and not to ignore the further possibility that the behaviour was a powerful message about the ward system itself. By delaying a reply, and canvassing opinions, I was able to imply that a total systemic strategy must be formulated acceptable to all members of the system – patients and staff. The delicate part of this explanation was to talk about both staff and patients without switching the blame from manipulative patients to incompetent staff. This mutual blaming was itself contributing to the difficulty.

Furthermore, delaying a reply was a message that a policy must be proposed that would not be reactive to immediate events. One of the difficulties present was that crises appeared to determine behaviour and disrupted other policies. These policies were never worked out systemically but by various *ad hoc* staff groups or by individual patients and therapists. Also, delaying, consulting, legitimating all present and negotiating resolutions were a modelling of a process that was necessary.

Co-operation

Ross and McKay (1979) took great pains in their work to co-opt the assistance of patients. By involving patients they made a change from previous strategies of treating patients. By taking a research stance they became interested in what the patients were doing in terms of mutilating themselves and this was a powerful positive connotation of the behaviour of the self-mutilating patients. I took such a position in interviewing the patients. Instead of offering psychotherapy and attempting to change the women, I made it clear that they were skilled and expert in what they were doing and could help in my research about self-mutilation and overdoses. I also asked them about what would help should they wish to be helped, at what times they felt suicidal, what they believed promoted this behaviour, how should they be treated and when would they do it again? This mirrored the approach made by Ross and McKay. Where Ross and McKay went wrong, as they say themselves, is that they forgot to co-opt the staff. Without the staff co-operation, their strategies 'failed'. In this study the same questions were asked of the staff that were asked of the women and so further emphasised the need for co-operation. This was a strategy for bringing about systemic closure, that is getting all 'parts' involved in working together (Beer 1975; Scheff 1968).

The first step in understanding the ward behaviours was to see how the ward system was organised such that it did not disintegrate totally. This appeared to be a process whereby policy disagreements between the staff were associated with rising distress throughout the patient body. Once certain threshold levels of distress were reached, an episode of self-mutilation occurred that precipitated concerted action, relieved collective tensions and temporarily co-ordinated action. What became apparent was that both patients and staff had begun to place an increasing number of negative connotations on each other's behaviour. No matter how ambiguous behaviours were, each faction saw such behaviours as being against them, as examples of non-co-operation and as further evidence of illegitimacy.

A policy for action

After talking to both ward staff and patients, it appeared that both groups wished that the episodes of self-mutilation would end and that some of the patients would be allowed home. It was agreed by all concerned that if the staff implemented a policy towards the patients, they should carry it through consistently. The patients and staff agreed on this before they knew what the policy was to be (this is a strategy known as the 'Devil's Pact' (Watzlawick, Weakland and Fisch 1974). What is important is that there is a general atmosphere of trust and agreement. Co-operation is established.

At a meeting of the staff it was proposed that they formulate a policy together based on what concrete steps of action would be taken in particular situations. Instead of a debate at an abstract level of future policy open to differing interpretations, the staff were encouraged to develop particular concrete solutions. These solutions were also expected to be different to those previously suggested that had failed. These previous solutions were discussed and the staff admitted that they had not worked. The important emphasis was made that the staff had made legitimate attempts to solve the problem despite the failure of those attempts.

The staff also proposed that I be put in charge of organising further strategies, which I resisted. Such an attempt to put me in charge appeared to put me in a separate place, where any failure could be laid at my interventions not on the behaviour of the staff. Furthermore, it was a neat way of setting me up directly against the medical and nursing hierarchies. The staff were encouraged to nominate amongst themselves who was to be in charge of particular strategies. This meant that the staff negotiated away their conflict publicly by reaching a consensus choice of leader amongst themselves. If I had accepted the role of organiser, the hierarchical difficulties between the groups would not have been resolved.

New frames for old

McPhail (1972) proposes that to generate new behaviour there is no need necessarily to generate 'novel' behaviours, but that different sequencing of old elements of behaviour can be used. Combined with this, he suggests that new relationships between the participating units facilitate new behaviour. Acting on this principle of establishing a new order, it was arranged that staff co-operated collectively and negotiated their relationships afresh. Staff carried on in their former roles but these were arranged in different sequences. For example, a principal therapist was named for each patient who would co-ordinate the therapeutic strategy for that patient and to whom all others would refer. This was to establish therapeutic consistency and was a change from the previous conditions where therapeutic strategies changed according to shifts and who was available.

Specific strategies were worked out for treating certain aspects of behaviour. If an act of mutilation occurred, the patient was to be stitched and cleaned up but receive no psychotherapy or prolonged comforting until the next therapeutic session. This session was mutually arranged between therapist and patient. If an act of mutilation occurred or a window was broken, no members of staff were to rush to the scene but to ask the nurse-in-charge what to do. This reduced the drama of the occasion and meant that the immediacy of reacting was replaced by a policy of deliberation. The staff believed that the patients could manipulate them and these strategies put control back into the hands of the staff. So far, no mention had been made of stopping the behaviour. Not to try to 'stop' the behaviour, as had been happening, was emphasised as a first step coupled with how the staff may organise themselves if the behaviour occurred. An additional factor was that the so-called 'nurse-in-charge' became the nurse in charge, not the incident of self-mutilation.

To achieve a commitment to these strategies and to encourage the staff to carry them out once they had left the meeting, the suggestions of Pelz (1965) were used. Pelz found out that when decisions were made in a group which expressed a common purpose, publicly indicated commitment and also specified concrete actions, the decisions were likely to be implemented. As Pelz suggests, the process of making decisions and the degree of consensus obtained and perceived are important variables. To this end I acted as a secretary who wrote down what happened at these meetings (for the ward notes), duplicated the strategies to be shown to absent staff and also asked staff members if they agreed to the strategies by a show of hands. The constant emphasis was that concrete specific actions should be formulated and an agreed consensus be made.

The second stage was to agree specific treatment strategies between therapists and patients.

A positive reframing of suicidal behaviour

As part of my systemic description of suicidal behaviour, differing constructions of the suicidal behaviour were offered. First, the staff were told that it was an opportunity for them to try out their skills in managing behaviour which was notoriously difficult to handle. This helped to separate the staff group from the patients and place a boundary around the staff group, uniting them in concerted action, rather than joining some staff and patients against other staff or a group of patients.

Second, I suggested that maybe we should accept that one of the self-mutilating women would indeed one day be successful in killing herself. The staff did not have a right to take away the existential choice between life and death, although they must abide by the legal requirements under the Mental Health Act. The same approach was made to the patients. Death, or life, was her choice and it was irresponsible for anyone to take that choice away, even though they were patients in a psychiatric hospital. From what we know about suicidal behaviour there is always the likelihood that someone would one day succeed. This effectively reduced the attempts to immediately stop the behaviour and some of the anxiety surrounding the possibility of death. It must be remembered that previous attempts to prevent suicide had resulted in behaviours whereby suicide might have occurred. This tack was just the opposite. One of the reasons for this may have been that everyone felt responsible for what was happening, rather than accepting the delegated responsibility within the ward. By not accepting the ward hierarchy, everyone behaved as if they were in charge and ultimately responsible. Such therapeutic omnipotence is counter-productive and, in the face of suicidal behaviour, misplaced.

The issue of successful suicide and the death of a patient is a troublesome prospect in psychiatry. There are legal ramifications for the psychiatrist in charge of the hospital ward (Cheung 1992). In addition, the question is raised about whether we are offering treatment for a sick patient or are we responsible for preventing the death of a sick patient (Gralnick 1993). These women were initially admitted for treatment but the circumstances were changed such that they were either admitted or detained for their own safety.

Third, the patients were asked who their next of kin were, what sort of funeral they wished, how many stitches they had had, if their anxieties had been relieved by mutilating and what would happen to their families should they die. The intent was to contaminate the 'when I'm dead and gone' fantasy (Whitaker 1973). Instead of avoiding the issue of death, patients were actively encouraged to talk about their own deaths and the consequences. This elicited how these women viewed the future, what they would want to happen to their estates, what the ward staff would tell the patient's next of kin and what to tell the coroner if a death occurred. All the women involved said that they did not wish to die and that anyone, namely me, who believed that they did wish to die 'had got it wrong'. What they did want to do was to live differently and for specific things to happen.

Once it was established that these women wanted to live differently and that they had specific goals for that life, commitments to a future action and to alternative behaviour could be made. The specific goals for each woman was written down in her notes. As we will see in the next chapter, these wishes may appear to be mundane but they fit the context of the woman's own life and are her solution to her problem.

At this time I was also able to watch videotapes of interviews between therapists in training, including junior doctors as part of their psychiatry rotation, and patients. What appeared over and over again was that at the mention of suicide, or suicidal behaviour, the clinician would immediately change her sitting position, move forward onto the edge of her seat and become noticeably more interested. Not only that, the emotional tone of the interview would change and the practitioner would later admit to being more anxious, believing that they had to do something. This is indeed precisely the trap of such behaviour and why, perhaps, clinicians regard the behaviour as manipulative. Their expectations expect that she should do something immediately, yet it is the patient that is described as being manipulative. Indeed, the legal requirements are that clinicians respond to the threat of suicidal behaviour. How that behaviour is assessed and responded to is another matter. But the situation changes from that of listening to a difficult and distressing story, a patient's sad tale, to one of an expected therapeutic intervention. A chance occurs for the novice clinician to do something in the field of psychiatry. Yet, working with such patients, we know that a threat exists to the novice clinicians competence and projected efficacy. How strange that, under a challenge to that professional efficacy, it is concluded that the patient is being manipulative and not that the expectations of the practitioner are misplaced.

The encouragement of legitimation

The patients were asked about their past lives and how they described particular events that had happened to them which were seen as traumatic or influential in some way. These women had developed a biography which they had re-iterated at their frequent previous consultations with medical personnel. They had had a succession of therapists and numerous hospital contacts in which their biographies, or 'sad tales' (Goffman 1959), were well practised. These biographies were reframed positively as a series of events that could precipitate feeling suicidal (as indeed the life events literature suggests). This biography was then written down and a copy given first to the patient and then to the staff. The biography was discussed for discrepancies and for alteration, if necessary, with the patient and the staff.

Instead of being seen as deviant and manipulative, the patients were reframed as having been faced with a number of tragic life events and legitimate as persons (McFarlane *et al.* 1983). The act of suicidal behaviour was described as yet another sacrificial attempt which women make to get everything right and that some women do give up their lives, their health, their future and their sanity for the sake of their loved ones (Chesler 1971; Chesler 1972). The significant losses in their lives were listed: loss of health, loss of a future, loss of a child, loss of a loved one, loss of a long-term relationship, loss of adult status, loss of freedom, loss of a home, loss of friendship and a loss of sanity.

The staff, too, saw these losses as legitimate causal grounds for distress and, while not legitimating the behaviour of the patients, the patients as persons were legitimated. This was a turn around from the total negative construing of illegitimacy to a partial positive construing of a woman legitimate in her own right, although questions about the legitimacy of the behaviour remained. The act is challenged, not the integrity of the person.

Before the research intervention

At first, there appeared to be mutual interlocking roles for describing self-mutilatory behaviour. The core construing of legitimation was validated by the ward staff (see Figure 7.2). Although the women believed themselves to be legitimate, the ward staff would only validate suicidal behaviour if certain factors were present. Eventually this process of withdrawing validation escalated until any act by the women became construed as deviant, illegitimate and unco-operative. In the same way, the women became hostile towards the staff, who were seen as unsympathetic, uncaring and unable to help, which negated their professional skills. In Kellyian terms (Bannister

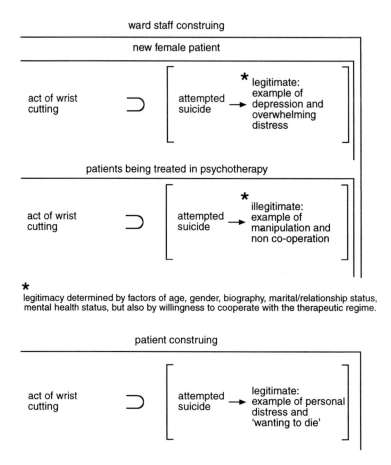

ward staff construing

new female patient

act of wrist cutting ⊃ [attempted suicide → * legitimate: example of depression and overwhelming distress]

patients being treated in psychotherapy

act of wrist cutting ⊃ [attempted suicide → * illegitimate: example of manipulation and non co-operation]

*
legitimacy determined by factors of age, gender, biography, marital/relationship status, mental health status, but also by willingness to cooperate with the therapeutic regime.

patient construing

act of wrist cutting ⊃ [attempted suicide → legitimate: example of personal distress and 'wanting to die']

Figure 7.2 Constitutive rules related to the legitimation of wrist-cutting

and Fransella 1971), hostility is the continued effort to extort validational evidence from others to support our expectations. Both the women and the staff had expectations of each other that were not met. Both groups interacted in a cycle of mutual negation (see Figure 7.3).

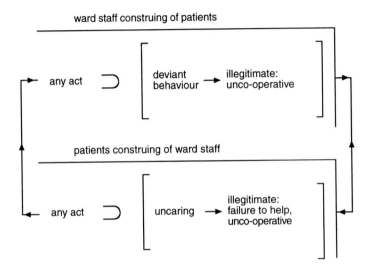

Figure 7.3 The mutual negative construing of ward staff and patients

In terms of regulative rules, acts which constituted treatment, that is acts by patients on a hospital ward which did not respond to professional treatment strategies, were seen as further acts of deviancy. The staff would alter their perception of the patient rather than alter their treatment strategies. Bannister and Fransella (1971) point out that a difficulty with the stuttering child is that an elaborated network of constructs develops concerned with speech and disfluencies. The 'thing that keeps a child stuttering is its inability to construe its fluencies and so it never comes to construe itself as a normal speaker' (p.89, 2nd edition). Patients, in this sense, were always perceived as illegitimate in their demands and themselves unable to construe their own legitimacy.

It might well be said that the ward staff construed the patients in a continuing way, which elaborated the construing of deviancy. There became more ways of construing the patients as deviant than normal. Likewise, in a

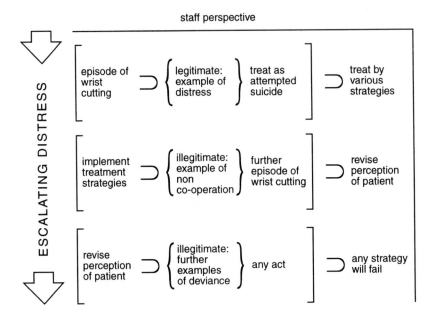

Figure 7.4 Self-mutilation, regulative rules and the escalation of distress from a staff perspective on a psychiatric ward

circular process of mutual escalation, there became more ways for the patients to construe the staff as failing and fewer ways to construe the staff as successful (see Figure 7.4). This same cycle of mutual negation will be reflected in later chapters.

After the research intervention

The research intervention sought information that was already in the competencies of staff and patients alike. By setting mutual concrete goals, construings of success rather than failure were offered. Rather than confront either group that they were wrong, each group was encouraged to see each other as legitimate in their own way and as trying to get things right. Once the elements of control were satisfied and co-operative endeavour established, the levels of ward distress fell. Furthermore, the conflict in the staff hierarchy was temporarily resolved. Suicidal behaviour was no longer needed to clarify the organisation of the ward and symptomatic behaviour was no longer appropriate. The patients, perhaps the most socially sensitive in this context but least articulate, were no longer required to express the difficulties of the psychiatric personnel. Indeed, if suicidal behaviour is a communication, the articulacy of mutilation was redundant given that the distress was located and resolved through negotiated treatment strategies and common therapeutic goals.

In the other social and familial contexts of these women, where a similar process of negative connotation had occurred, the reframing of their behaviour as positive rather than negative brought about a change in the relationship and a consequent lowering of levels of distress and hostility. Staff talked to family members not about how difficult the patients were on the ward but about what difficulties the patients must have had in their lives and how the carers must have suffered too.

The previous literature about suicidal behaviour stresses that such behaviour is not homogenous. There are many varied paths to suicidal behaviour, as we have seen in Chapters One, Two and Three. Previous researchers have concentrated on considering past experiences and identifying particular individual characteristics. However, if current interactive behaviour is considered as maintaining systemic organisation, a different picture emerges. Suicidal behaviour becomes yet another strategy for maintaining systemic coherence, reducing conflict and clarifying the systemic hierarchy, albeit temporarily. The conflict is seen as residing in the way the system is organised rather than located in any one individual. Once the system labels one of its members as illegitimate and deviant as a person, rather than a person exhibiting deviant behaviour, systemic distress will escalate. This escalation of distress threatens the future viability of such a system. It is this escalation which will be investigated in Chapters Nine, Ten and Eleven.

Coda

The suicidal behaviour reduced within a week of this new approach being made. Within a month, three of the women were discharged from the hospital. A month later, June was discharged home to her husband. For Sally, the same principles of intervention were used with her and her family as were used on the ward. She was returned home within a week. Death was discussed with her and her family, as were the arrangements to be made should she die. She was construed as legitimately ill by her parents and allowed to return home. As other authors have found (Aldridge and Dallos 1986; Aldridge and Rossiter 1983; Aldridge and Rossiter 1984; Payne and

Range 1996), and as we will see later in Chapter Nine, a family perspective on alternative coping behaviour and problem resolution offers an alternative to prolonged hospitalisation if the family support services exist in the community. Simply expecting a family to cope alone is to return to the *status quo*. Indeed, repeated attempts (King *et al.* 1995) and poor problem solving capabilities (Sadowski and Kelley 1993) appear to be features of adolescent suicidal behaviour and, if family dysfunction is implicated, families need support not condemnation.

One year later, Kath was re-hospitalised for a night and then discharged herself. The last I heard of her she was engaged to be married, again.

All the women had an episode of deliberate self-harm within a month of being discharged but were not admitted to psychiatric hospital. This initial period after discharge from the hospital is a time of particular vulnerability for further suicidal behaviour, including fatal suicide, even when clinical improvements have taken place (McGovern 1996). As previous hospitalisation for suicidal behaviour and a history of non-fatal suicide, particularly multiple attempts (Rudd, Joiner and Hasan Rajab 1996), are risk factors for completed suicide, the challenges to these women were significant. What is perhaps important to mention here is that clinical changes must be located within the social milieu.

One of the reasons for there being no further admissions to the psychiatric hospital was because a psychiatrist colleague and myself had implemented a catchment provision for attempted suicides (see Chapter Nine). Former patients and their families were interviewed together in a problem-solving approach that included the immediate family (Aldridge and Rossiter 1983; Aldridge and Rossiter 1984). After eighteen months, none of the women was actively harming themselves and all were getting on with their lives in the community. Perhaps more importantly, no further immediate outbreaks of such behaviour occurred on the hospital ward. The staff believed themselves to be coping and that their morale had improved.

Within the year there were outbreaks of suicidal behaviour on the ward and these involved patients new to the ward. Changes occurred in senior ward personnel and the rotation of junior medical colleagues continued. What is negotiated in one staff context, then, is not necessarily carried over to another context, further emphasising that social meanings are continually being maintained and negotiated. A therapeutic culture must not only be established but has to be maintained with some consistency.

CHAPTER EIGHT

Everyday Descriptions of Suicidal Behaviour

Personal stories are not merely a way of telling someone (or oneself) about one's life; they are the means by which identities may be fashioned. (Rosenwald and Ochberg 1992, p.1)

The advantage of studying illness narratives is that they make it possible to study the experience of illness form as number of vantage points: as social and cultural construct, as a transformation and expression of bodily suffering, and most of all as the suffering person's attempt to construct his or her own life-work and life context. (Hydén 1996, p.65)

Narratives of distress

A number of studies have presented the reasons people give for taking overdoses (Bancroft *et al.* 1979; Bancroft *et al.* 1977a; Bancroft, Skrimshire and Simkin 1976) but few have concentrated on finding out what descriptions suicide attempters make of their own behaviour (Heather 1979; Hjelmeland 1995; Michel, Valach and Waeber 1994; Parker 1981). Few studies have tried to describe what suicide attempters themselves say what they have found helpful or how they see themselves after the event. As one purpose of this book is to formulate strategies for therapeutic intervention, it seems sensible to ask those previously engaged in such behaviour what has helped them.

While listening to patients is accepted within psychiatry, the question remains as to what language is to be used in such conversations and how such language is structured (Brown *et al.* 1996). We read in the previous chapter that mutilatory behaviour is expressive and a performed meaning. Meaning, however, is gained by considering the context of its occurrence and the relationships involved. In the following accounts by women that are suicidal, we will see how varying selves are presented. What is important to remember here is that the self varies and it varies in interaction with others (Sands 1996). Like the apparently deviant women in the previous chapter, who were competent informers for my research, we will see a similar process repeated in this chapter, where women who have been non-fatally suicidal are expert and informed participants. It is important, then, to consider in our health care initiatives that it may be we, the health care providers, that are damaging to some women by restricting the selves that they can present to us in a therapeutic relationship. Stories are told to us in interviews. The purpose of that interview will structure the narrative for both narrator and listener. For the narrator, their identity is provisional and may contain elements of the dominant discourse of psychiatry, if told to a psychiatrist, as well as a submerged voice, if told to a friend or confidant. An institution may foster asylum for the disturbed, and facilitate knowledge through therapy, but the individual still remains vulnerable to a dominant ideology (Wilbraham 1996).

Typologies of attempted suicide

Within this study so far, some attempted suicides have been considered as expressing inter-personal conflict and escalating distress. In the literature, conflicts involving key relationships are correlated with episodes of suicidal behaviour and are seen as being prompted by a quarrel in such a relationship, particularly in female attempters (Bancroft *et al.* 1977a; Birtchnell 1973). Although many suicide attempters contact a helping agency during the week prior to the attempt, those attempters state that they need someone to talk to. In the Bancroft study, 69 per cent of the group studied actively sought help prior to the event. It may well be that a possible source of difficulty for the treatment of suicidal behaviour is recognising that requests for help are not being met by practitioners. This would seem to indicate that practitioners are not able to recognise distress as it is presented, not making an interactive, relational understanding of distress and not having sufficient strategies for dealing with such behaviour. To do so reflects the proposition that general practitioners are open to bias in that they stereotypically perceive what counts as healthy and miss distress when it is presented outside of that stereotype (Marks, Goldberg and Hillier 1979). In Norway, for example, seven out of ten female and male patients who exhibit suicidal behaviour have been in contact with a health or social services agency within the previous month (Hjelmand and Bjerke 1995).

We know from the recent studies of attempted suicide that certain characteristics are significant – that is age, gender, living alone or socially isolated, divorced or separated, a matrix of social problems, precipitating life events and chronic persistent problems (Farmer and Hirsch 1980; Hawton and Fagg 1992; Hjelmand and Bjerke 1995). Surely it is within the understanding of health care professionals to recognise these factors, yet the same factors are also present in a variety of other disorders. What is of most clinical significance is that the medical practitioner cannot do anything directly about poor housing, isolation or marital strife. Nor will any amount of pharmacological preparation bring about a change in such conditions. The question that we must ask ourselves, then, is how we as a community restrict the source of resolving distress to one particular channel. Distress has become medicalised. Subsequently, the expressions of distress are increasingly somatised and appear as symptoms. We come then full circle to the argument about the expressive body as performed, that the presentation of distress is an activity. The language of symptoms has an articulacy and a logic, the logic of which is not readily accessible to being broken up into meaning units and is not structured in the dominant verbal language of health care professionals.

Symptomatic behaviour (Tschudi 1977) is the behaviour that obliquely gets at the issues that are important for the person. Kelly (1955) proposes that ill health forces people to return to childlike dependency patterns where validation is only offered when the person is ill and dependent. He suggests that both the child's and parents' perception of ill health are considered for an interpretation of their mutual lives together. This position is also reflected by Haley (1961), who emphasises that the crucial aspect of a symptom is the part it plays in a relationship with another person.

Levine and Reicher (1996) also ask how people make sense of their symptoms. Symptoms are related to how people see themselves, that is symptoms are related to identities. These identities are personal and social but not necessarily medically dominated. Indeed, lay beliefs about the causes of mental disorder are predominantly psychosocial explanations related to unemployment, isolation, stress in the family and occupational stress (Matschinger and Angermeyer 1996). Unfortunately, we are so dominated in our health care delivery by medical and psychiatric descriptions that we see illness and health as opposing poles of a spectrum. What is more important is that common sense understandings about health and illness are many-sided and not dependent upon one particular logic. Indeed, once a person becomes isolated and identifies her problems as being located solely in herself, she loses the benefit of an alternative identity and, more importantly, the possibilities for alternative action. If in the presentation of symptoms, the activity of expressing distress, she comes up against a psychiatric epistemology that locates those problems within her too, she is further isolated and becomes a deviant person. While the patient and the therapist may be talking the same language, it is essentially a monologue. Once her self-identity is stigmatised, and she believes it, we have the grounds for hopelessness. The danger of isolation and hopelessness is that a damaged identity cannot be repaired alone.

What helps

I wrote to the health care editor of Cosmopolitan Magazine asking her to insert a small paragraph asking for information by letter (see below) about what had helped after an episode of attempted suicide:

> STAVING OFF SUICIDE
>
> A research psychologist is studying how best to help people who make suicide attempts. Often, he has found, the attempts arise from stressful circumstances, such as unemployment in the family, rather than through problems specific to the person making the suicide attempt.
>
> He would be grateful if women who have tried to commit suicide in the past would write and tell him what helped them most, after the event, and how they have changed as a result. He hopes to use the information, which will be treated in confidence, as a guide to devising practical help before a suicide bid is made.

These letters were collected and their contents analysed according to the types of information present. A standardised set of data was generated from the letters themselves about what women themselves found important to include (see Figure 8.1). If any of the categories were missing from the letters, I wrote to each respondent asking for that missing information. The criteria used were those presented in the letters as important to the respondents. What I wanted to know was how do people talk about what they have done, the reasons they give for doing those things and what they did afterwards. Of primary interest, as in the previous chapter, was what would help people when they regarded themselves as being suicidal. This is another example of treating the persons who are engaged in the behaviour as being experts on what they are doing and as valuable resources as to what might help them.

One of the difficulties about clinical research has been the opinion that everyday descriptions are clouded by considerations of social desirability and so are biased in their reporting. This part of the book removes some of that bias by not being a clinical study. None of the respondents were dependent upon me for any therapeutic activity. To do this the contact with respondents

Age now:	Occupation:			Code:
Present marital status:		Children:		
Reasons for attempt:	Relationship at attempt:	Method used:	Age at attempt:	Medication used:
....	....	....	....	....
....	....	....	....	....
....	....	....	....	....
....	....	....	....	....
....	....	....	....	....
....	....	....	....	....
Number of attempts:		Regret surviving, current suicidal ideation:		
Support offered:				
What helped:				
Attitude of professional contact:				
Attitude of significant others:				
Life cycle stage(s) at attempt(s):				

Figure 8.1 The form for the collection of standardised data from the letters

was conducted at a distance and as research after the event, not as a gateway to treatment. Each correspondent was treated as knowledgeable, socially aware and an expert informant. This, in itself, is a positive connotation of the person. Consequently, some of the respondents reported that the process of describing was itself therapeutic. Again, this raises the question for me about the way that we structure our modern communities. It is comforting and helpful to write to a stranger because we have removed those contacts within the communities themselves or channelled distress such that we must become stigmatised as sick, weak or foolish before we can ask for help.

All the respondents were women. The sample itself is hopelessly biased and skewed from a statistical approach or even as a sample of people who have attempted suicide. The intention was to gather in a number of reports and examine them for their content. Although the analysis has no statistical validity, it has a demonstrable validity of presenting everyday descriptions by people of their behaviour. All this chapter aims to do is to propose that people, when describing their situation, make causal attributions to which we must give credence. Such informant credibility is a central plank of the following chapters where families are interviewed. Because people are distressed, it does not mean that they are illogical. And because their logics do not conform to my logic does not mean that they are wrong, nor is it evidence of illness.

People interpret and re-interpret themselves and their situation

The use of biographical material is, for Kelly (1955), an important tool in reconstructing an explanation of an individual's view within a social context and explains those pivotal points about which a person's thinking revolves.

Implicit in the notion of ourselves as individuals is that we exist in relation to others. Kelly himself argues that our construing of ourselves is developed as a bipolar construct of 'self versus others' and that this whole construct elaborates the system whereby we construe the world at large. This self construing is firmly located within a social matrix and develops from within a social context:

> Perhaps it would be better to say that his behaviour in comparison with other people is particularly affected. It is, of course, the comparison he sees or construes which affects his behaviour. This much of his social life is controlled by the comparisons he has come to see between himself and others. (Kelly 1955, p.131)

In his guide to understanding biographical material, Kelly says that:

> First of all, it may be seen as factual material out of which a person has had to make some kind of sense at some time in his life. Second, it reveals something of what the person's system must have in order to account for his behaving in certain ways in the past; hence it suggests the kind of thinking and behaviour to which he may have recourse if his present way of life suddenly becomes invalid or unpredictive. In the third place, it indicates the kinds of social expectancies with which the person has been surrounded and hence the kinds of validators with which he has had to check his construct system. (Kelly 1955, p.752)

What the women said in their letters

Categories of age and transition

The majority of the respondents were under 30 years old at their attempt, which reflects the general population figures (See Table 8.1).

Table 8.1 Distribution by age at attempt

Age	%	n
14 years +	6	(3)
16 years +	22	(10)
20 years +	32	(15)
10 years +	19	(9)
50 years +	4	(2)
Not known	17	(8)
Total	100	(47)

Age alone is rather a static variable, it does not really tell us anything about a person. However, we can hypothesise from the age of a person in a looser sense by considering the possible developmental stage of that person and what transitions are occurring in their lives. On scrutinising the data it is possible to see groupings of the women that are reflected in their age but contextualised by their relationship status at the time.

Some writers have become concerned with describing transition and stress in social groups. Other researchers interested in adolescent suicide attempts (Aldridge 1992; Barter 1968; Hawton and Fagg 1992; Hawton *et al*. 1982b; Hawton *et al*. 1982c; Schrut 1968) have commented upon the way that such behaviour fits into a pattern of disrupted family life. The life event researchers have also commented on transitions as life events which promote episodes of suicidal behaviour (Andrews 1981; Brown, Harris and Peto 1973; Eggert, Thompson and Herting 1994; Finlay-Jones and Brown 1981; Isometsa *et al.* 1995a; Myers, Jacobs and Pepper 1972; O'Brien and Farmer 1980; Paykel, Prusoff and Myers 1975; Wetzler *et al.* 1996).

In the letters from the women, using the broad categories of age, seven transitional changes can be discerned:

1. Adolescent; at home (sometimes with an absent parent).

2. Adolescent; leaving home (for training or further education).

3. Early Adult; leaving home (becoming independent).

4. Early marriage; marital adjustment.

5. Relationship/Marriage; breaking up.

6. Marital Adjustment/Failure; children leaving home.

7. Late Marriage; marital difficulty.

It is important to note that these categories are not discrete, they blend into one another. What is important is that rather than see age alone as a variable, we begin to consider what may be going on in a person's life at a particular age. As our children grow up and leave home, we change as parents and individuals. Examples of transitional categories are presented below that represent both family problems as presented in the correspondence and attempted strategies of change to allay those problems.

Adolescent: at home

This first letter describes how attempted suicide was used on a number of occasions and became part of a collective interactional sequence of managing distress and promoting change.

> Letter 7
>
> I have attempted suicide on three occasions. Once at the age of 14, once at 17 and once at 20.
>
> The first time I had been referred to a psychiatrist after a severe nervous breakdown...I was not able to communicate to the staff the extent to which I was suffering at home.
>
> The second time I was under such stress from home, college and a relationship with an extremely unstable person that suddenly

something snapped and swallowed a bottle of tranquillisers on the way home from college.

The third time I was a day-patient at a neurosis clinic severely depressed and spending the day crying uncontrollably... I was still in the bad relationships, home dire, so this last time was an expression of anger and desperation...

The majority of clinical interventions used in common practice would have focused on this girl's apparent personal distress and pathology. However, she locates her difficulties within a family context and a relationship context.

Adolescent: leaving home

This young woman was aged 19 years at the time of her episode of deliberate self-harm and was training to be a nurse, away from home.

Letter 12

I had been depressed for about six months... I failed my exams, had money problems and a lot of other problems and the most worrying fact was that my mum (who was always very cheerful and strong) got very depressed. No-one seems to have the time to listen or give any practical help... I took an overdose and slashed both wrists. I really meant to end it all.

She then moved home to live with her parents and improved enough to leave home again. Within a few months in a flat, she was arrested for being in possession of controlled drugs. She then moved back home to live with her parents. This appears to be a classic example, the process of which Haley describes, where a person attempts to leave home and fails, returning home once more to maintain the family stability (see Chapter Three).

Early adult: leaving home

The next letter describes a young woman who took two overdoses when aged 20 years and 21 years. She had been seeking help for two years for a suspected problem with her fallopian tubes. She was living at home but had then moved in with a boyfriend. After her overdose she moved back home for her family to take care of her. She says of her family:

Letter 17

...just after I came out of hospital... I was bursting to tell someone so I told my brother. But only after he told me that he had got so desperate and lonely one night he rang the Samaritans. My mother has feelings for another man which she has kept hidden for years or so… I think my father may sense this and feels that perhaps she is rejecting him for someone else. When they fight he attacks her character pulling her down badly, and then she comes to me feeling guilty and worthless, useless…she says if he thinks so little of her and if she can't arouse the right loving feeling towards him that they, to coin a phrase, should 'knock it on the head'…I do try to talk to dad; my father finds personal communication very very difficult.

Once we see suicidal behaviour located in a social nexus, we see how difficult it is for this woman to leave home. On the one hand she serves a function in the family of a communication bridge between her parents and as a means of resolving marital conflict. Yet, on the other hand, she must satisfy both her own needs and desires as an individual and broader social normative expectations that she will leave home and become independent.

Early marriage: marital adjustment

Letter 53

…I tried to commit suicide when my first child who was spina bifida died. My husband told me to shut up, stop crying and get back to work. He had been dead a week. The funeral was over and my mother left on the train. I was alone with 150 pills the doctor had prescribed. There was no purpose in living. I opened the bottle… I phoned the Samaritans. They kept ringing me back and offered to come, but I was afraid of my husband, a violent man – I begged them not to phone after 5.00 pm when he got home from work.

This woman goes on to say that she had no support after the death of her child. Her doctor advised her to 'go home and try for another one'. Sound advice, perhaps, yet in total ignorance of the marital context of conflict. This lack of understanding of context reflects the paucity of training which general practitioners have (Marks, Goldberg and Hillier 1979) in understanding individuals in families. 'Good advice', when presented as a prescription in the face of such overwhelming distress, is no longer good, nor is it advice. Perhaps such formulaic responses are the result of general practitioners not being able to cope with their own distress when child deaths occur.

Relationship or marriage breaking up

This letter describes how the episode of suicide facilitated the ending of a difficult relationship. Within this family there had been a history of com-

pleted suicide and attempted suicide. This woman, aged 29 at the time, had
been previously engaged to be married.

Letter 22

My mum put on a very brave face but I learned later that she was
extremely disturbed by the incident. She herself had been an
extremely anxious, phobic personality. My fiancee was
dumbfounded and agreed readily to breaking off our relationship
right away. I was relieved as we had not made the right decision in
being engaged. She says of her parents and her relationship with
them...he and my mother had a stormy marriage. My relationship
with my mother has been full of tenseness and strain but we continue
to make efforts... When my father was killed at work the storm of
guilt, relief and anger was never quite resolved within our family.

This illustrates the contextual elements of relationships within relationships
and how common-sense descriptions incorporate such contextual elements
(Garfinkel 1972; Rippere 1981): a suicide attempt brought about a positive
resolution in her relationship with her boyfriend. While the literature
suggests that suicide attempts are related to relationship problems, it may be
that the attempts are not intended to manipulate the other person, rather to
resolve the problem.

In this family death and its consequences was never properly resolved
and death and dying appear as recurring issues. In this way, the past
contaminates the present and, as we saw in the last chapter, it is important
to talk about death openly. Indeed, talking about death and suicide does not
promote suicide but allows an openness to talk about distress.

Marital adjustment or marital breakdown

In this next letter the respondent describes her stressful circumstances
following her marital separation when she was 38 years old. She goes on to
say that these difficulties are not located solely within herself.

Letter 20

...stressful circumstance was – in my case – one of the main factors,
i.e. redundant from work, single parent with no maintenance from
ex-husband...no help from D.H.S.S. ... However, in my case there
are also specific problems which added to the attempt. For example,
my age, my overweight and out of condition body, migraines, skin
allergies, no sex and no hope for the future – when my youngest son

leaves home for the Army (in September) and the cat and dog (who are 14 and 12 respectively) finally go to the Kingdom in the sky.

My husband left me…in the hope that his lady friend would move in with him. He's very unhappy and drinks too much. I also drink too much.

She then goes on to explain that she intends to take her own life eventually and that this hopelessness is reflected in her children.

Nobody knew about my suicide attempt except my youngest daughter and she was very upset and asked me not to try again but as her life is now a mess too she understands how I felt and often says she feels like trying to kill herself too.

I will tell you this much – if I haven't got a job to occupy me and provide some money to live on by the time my son has been in the Junior Leaders for a few weeks and I an still depressed and lonely, I shall feel very tempted to try and kill myself again.

Not only is attempted suicide a strategic device for managing distress, it is also seen as a real alternative if events cause further distress or the quality of life does not improve. This woman recognised, too, that the leaving home of her remaining child will be a difficult stage of transition. Contemplating suicide is a means of accommodating such transition. This strategy is also passed on to other members of the family. What we may have to acknowledge is that there is such a thing as a family culture of distress management and within this culture there exists a repertoire of behaviours to manage distress. One of these is suicidal behaviour. The danger is that it may lead to completed suicide. I am not arguing here for a genetic base for suicide but that it does indeed run in families.

Late marriage/marital difficulty

For the woman who wrote this letter, a suicide attempt occurred after being, as she says, 'deeply disturbed' at the way she saw patients being treated in hospital. She had been disastrously married when she was 21 years old and had borne a son but that marriage had ended. She married again.

Letter 11

Until the second world war I was happy… The War changed a lot in our lives, my husband returned from service overseas a different man I did not realise how traumatic service life had been for him; and so we just stayed together.

I had taking Nembutal for about a year. I had never a good sleeper and my husband was having broken sleep patterns because of my restlessness – I moved into a separate bedroom with his agreement so that he was able to sleep peacefully again.

Although we can only speculate that the sleeplessness was symptomatic of the relationship, we can see how a change in that relationship, and an attempted resolution, that is the moving into a separate bedroom, itself promotes further distress.

The presentation of symptoms and problems

Most of the respondents offered detailed descriptions of their problems. As the respondents had time to write and no treatment was being offered, they had the opportunity to describe their problems as individuals and the context in which these problems were experienced (see Table 8.2 and 8.3).

Although these women presented individual problems, they located these problems within a problematical context. It would seem sensible that any therapeutic interventions be aimed at the problematical context as much as the presented symptoms, as we saw in the last chapter. In their descriptions, 81% of the women said that their problems involved a significant other. In addition, they describe a process of escalation in conflict and the consequent presentation of symptoms. This point will be seen again in the following chapters. To illustrate this contextual argument I will present a number of case examples that represent the cells in Table 8.4, that is individual symptoms in an individual context, individual symptoms in an interactive context, interactive problems in an individual context and interactive problem in an interactive context.

When we categorise behaviour in terms of why we suppose it occurs, we offer interpretations and explanations of behaviour that render such behaviour predictable and intelligible. Heider (1946) proposes that the means by which we predict social events is by looking for necessary and sufficient conditions for events to occur. A central endeavour is the distinction between personal and impersonal causes and internal and external attributions. These women appeared to locate their difficulties as legitimate means of avoiding confrontation with a key other. It is interesting to speculate upon what history of confrontation avoidance is evident in such relationships and this speculation is investigated in Chapters Nine and Ten.

Table 8.2 The coding of individual problems

Psychological problems	f	Isolation	f
depression	16	alone	8
nervous breakdown	4	single parent	2
schizophrenia	2	no-one to talk to	1
unable to cope	2	alone with baby	1
psychosomatic illness	1	no sex	1
anxiety	1		
phobia	1	**Personal stress**	
panic attacks	1	broke and money worries	6
unhappy	1	no job	3
deeply disturbed	1	build-up of personal problems	2
angry	1	lots of responsibilities	1
		leaving hospital prematurely	1
		stressful circumstances	1
Personal motivation		homeless	1
cry for help	3		
escape misery	2	**Death**	
no hope	2	of a lover	1
wanted out of life	2	in a family	1
desperate	2	of a child	1
NOT cry for help	1	abortion	1
be out of way	1		
want to die	1	**Somatic problems**	
didn't want to exist	1	sleep disorder	7
life not worth living	1	persistent pain	3
didn't want to be around anymore	1	anorexia nervosa	3
everyone better off without her	1	migraine	2
self-dislike	1	pre-menstrual tension	2
lack of self confidence	1	persistent illness	1
blow to self image	1	allergies	1
no longer belonged anywhere	1	arthritis	1
avoid stigma of being ill	1	constant vomiting	1
mother depressed	1	overweight	1
		constant lethargy	1

Table 8.3 The presentation of symptoms and interactive problems

Individual presentation of symptoms	Psychological	%	n
	personal motivation	40	19
	somatic	30	16
	isolation	24	13
	personal stress	22	12
	death	7	14
Interactive problems	with key other	43	23
	in family	22	12
	school	11	6
	work	9	5
		N=53	

Table 8.4 The presentation of symptoms and problems in individual or interactive contexts

	Individual symptoms	Interactive problems	Total
Individual context	15%	4%	19%
Interactive context	64%	17%	81%

Individual symptoms/individual context (15%)

Both of the cases here are concerned with 'depression'. Although interactive contextual elements can be read into these descriptions, the women themselves did not propose them as being important.

> Letter 34
>
> Before, I had tried to hide how bad I was feeling, ashamed to talk about my depression, and afraid of boring or worrying everyone or seemingly self-centred. Yet at the same time I had been resenting everybody for not realising what a crisis I was going through.
>
> I explained the reason for my depression – that my husband and I had just been told we would never have children.

Although this woman locates her problem of depression within the context of childlessness, we may well speculate that 'childlessness' is not necessarily an individual status and had major implications for her marriage. However, the problem of her depression was worsening. Interestingly enough, although she was feeling ashamed about how she felt, she was also hostile towards her family and friends for not allowing her to express herself. Sands (1996) writes that women's depression is a response to relationships in which they are silenced, where they silence themselves out of fear that if they act on the basis of their own needs they will lose a significant relationship.

Letter 35

The trigger points for such depression (which suddenly enveloped me in a compulsive desire to take as many tablets as I could, and a wish to die…) seem to have been pain and incapacity from three road traffic accidents, the change of life style, inability to follow leisure pursuits, the permanent ending of permanent employment, a significant lack of cash and death in the family.

This woman made two suicide attempts. In the face of overwhelming problems, which forced a change in life style, she decided to overdose with tablets. It is striking that 'depression' is seen as causal for the suicide attempts, rather than the personal circumstances which contextualise the depression. For both women, an escalating process is described where difficult, unacceptable personal circumstances are followed by depression that worsens and leads to a suicide attempt. Both of these women reported that the support of friends following the episode of attempted suicide was significant in their recovery.

Individual symptoms/interactive context (64%)
This was by far the largest group of explanations presented by the women.

Letter 4

I am now 51 and happily divorced, and therein lies the key to my present tranquillity…I was absolutely desperate. This was not caused by family conditions but by lack of sleep. I had two young daughters and a husband who went out with women night after night. He would come in about 2 a.m. and berate me calling me a slut and saying the house was in a mess.

I finally formed an attachment with a married vet who wanted to go away with me but I could not leave my daughters. I then became very ill and had constant vomiting if I attempted to eat.

I never quite got fit. Gradually…a lethargy or 'numbness' crept over me and all I wanted was peace, and restful nights… I took about two-thirds of a jar of barbiturates and went to bed.

During the years this woman was married she was treated for a physical problem and sleeplessness with medication. At no time does it appear that any attempt was made to resolve these problems in the context of the marital conflict. She locates the source of her distress within a context of marital conflict, however she still places the causal genesis as being an individual problem.

However, towards the end of her letter she does say that 'I have always avoided confrontation'. It could very well be that attempted suicide is not necessarily a 'cry for help' but a communication of a different sort, as we saw earlier in the letter when a suicide attempt helped her to separate from her boyfriend.

The meaning of this communication is dependent upon the interactive context and, in this woman's case, is a form of confrontation. A circular process appears to occur whereby physical symptoms and psychological symptoms are used to manage conflict within a systemic context (see Figure 8.2).

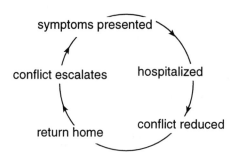

Figure 8.2 The cycle of conflict reduction and escalation

Interactive problems / individual context (4%)

> Letter 40
>
> I have been treated for manic depression for seven years. 2 years ago I took an insulin overdose whilst in an anxiety state due to an unsatisfactory relationship with my live-in lover and the strain of working in an intensive care unit.

The immediate problems in this group are seen as relational but placed within a causal train of individual pathology.

> Letter 41
>
> I became more and more isolated, hoping and trusting that if he saw I was willing not to push him he might back to me...all the time I was getting dispirited. I saw him going into the theatre with the girl, just ahead of me and I snapped. I just went mad, destroyed some valuable sound equipment and no-one could calm me. The hysterics stopped, to be replaced by a deadly stillness. He didn't say a word to me, until I asked him, 'Why'.
>
> He replied, 'But you knew', which I had not because suppositions and half-thoughts are not certainties. So while he watched I searched for and found a razor blade used for splicing tapes together and slashed my wrist.

This woman had gradually become isolated from her family by distance, her friends by volition and from her lover by estrangement. On seeing him with another girl, believing that he was 'sorting himself out' she realised that she had been wrong about him. As Kelly (1955) points out, in the face of a massive invalidation of such core construings hostile acts are an attempt to affirm that previous validation. For both these women, the immediate causal problem is seen as a relational conflict.

Interactive problems / interactive context (17%)

The letters describing interactive problems present a situation where a relationship has failed and a new key relationship is proving difficult.

> Letter 24
>
> The circumstance where that I had been living alone since my divorce in 1976. I came across this man, got involved, then he told me he was married and with children (how could I have been so naive). He was going to live with me – he wasn't going to move in etc. etc. I was 10 feet or 6 inches tall alternately. I wanted to be

pregnant (glad I wasn't that silly!). I suppose I just found it too much like hard work to go through life alone. When I took my tablets he had left me but my overdose was not to 'show him', nor a cry for help, I just didn't want to be here.

Letter 29

My last O.D. was when my youngest daughter was two. Previous to this I had tried to act in a mature way and sought the help of a marriage guidance counsellor... With my first two O.D.'s I said I was having difficulties with my eldest daughter. Before my last O.D. I again asked for help with my eldest daughter...

In desperation I range the N.S.P.C.C. for guidance. They advised a child-guidance visit and I felt relieved to think there was someone to listen and offer support... I hadn't taken an O.D. for three years, but here was this going into my past and saying my daughter needed to go into care... Over the next two days I panicked as arrangements were made for her to go into care. I took an O.D. and the following day she went into care.

This woman says in her letter that she was desperately unhappy and seeking attention. Unfortunately, the agencies to which she presented her desperation for attention implemented a train of procedures which heightened that desperation. One of the difficulties present for this woman was that taking an overdose became a strategy which she repeated at times of distress and was part of her repertoire of distress management.

For both these women, their key relationships were difficult.

A worsening situation

The majority of the letters present a worsening situation within a relational context which itself is construed as difficult. The worsening situation is temporarily resolved by new alternative strategies of resolution but as these strategies are rarely aimed at a systemic resolution, the situation escalates. As we know from studies of the ecology, partial solutions that deny the ecology only exacerbate the problem in the long term. This worsening situation also intrudes upon other spheres of activity causing further problems and a gradual estrangement and isolation. Many of the letters present individual symptoms which affect the varying social situations the person is experiencing. Finally, when the person perceives no viable alternative strategy, when distress levels have escalated, an overdose takes place (see Figure 5.4, p.85).

For some of these women, it appears that their depression, insomnia or distress could not be escalated any further.

Such a worsening situation will be seen in the next chapter when families are interviewed after an episode of deliberate self-harm.

Current suicidal ideation

On examining the letters, 32% (15) of the respondents were found to be currently suicidal or contemplating suicide. Paykel *et al.* (1974) investigated the presence of suicidal feelings in the general population and found 13.3% had suicidal feelings. The figure found in these letters was greater than those studies. It would appear that having once engaged in suicidal behaviour, such a behaviour is actively considered as part of a behavioural repertoire. For young women, repeated suicide attempts are a risk factor for fatal suicide (Rudd, Joiner and Hasan Rajab 1996). Suicidal feelings are correlated with depression, psychiatric disorder and somatic illness. These problems are prevalent in the letters from these women.

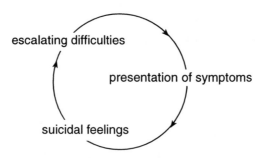

Figure 8.3 The cycle of escalating difficulties and suicidal feelings

We see, then, a cycle where escalating difficulties are followed by somatic or psychological symptoms that are, in turn, followed by suicidal feelings, followed by escalating difficulties (see Figure 8.3), as we saw in Figure 5.4 (p.??) and in the previous chapter. Once a person is labelled as illegitimate and deviant, distress escalates. It must also be emphasised that this negative connotation is a mutual description of interactive behaviour. The person is labelled as deviant, the welfare system is labelled as being uncaring.

What helps

The majority of the letter writers regard their distress as being 'personal' but caused within a context of relational difficulty. These women attribute their actions to situational requirements, whereas observers of attempted suicide usually attribute the same actions to personal dispositions. Similarly, these women invoke a processual account of escalating difficulty within a fraught relationship. The suicide attempt is construed as a legitimate means of avoiding conflict within that relationship. This ties in with the accounts of the ward process in the last chapter and will be seen reflected in accounts in the following chapters.

The women said that they were best helped by someone objective to talk to, some concrete activity to engage themselves in and practical financial and social support.

Professional caregivers, psychiatrists, therapists and psychologists fared rather poorly in their estimation. What women need, they write, is a person whom they believe understands them best, listens to them and recognises their view of the problem. Unfortunately, as professionals we fail to meet these needs. What we cannot do so easily is to telephone spontaneously and invite a patient out to eat or to come round for a chat. And this is what some women said helped. Such spontaneous friendship falls outside the capabilities of a professional therapists role, not to say his or her diary. Strikingly, friendship was seen as being more objective than therapy. Perhaps it is the acceptance that lies at the heart of friendship, that forms the basis for this objectivity. As Wilbraham (1996) says, '…the difficulty of confession and advocated, professionally facilitated, psychic work elevates those practices above the realm of ordinary activity and experience and, indeed, denies effectiveness of coping strategies and resistances available to women' (p.165).

Friends can tell us that we are making a fool of ourselves because the relationship has already been established. Friends are also not asked to 'treat' us. Whereas the Samaritans place great store on objective listening, which they do admirably, they are also restricted in what they can do actively. Friendship demands that we do something. It demands an active role, even if it is that we cannot do very much.

What we can take on board is the practical steps to recovery that these women recognised. Concrete activities like buying new curtains, getting a cat or planting new bulbs all helped. In these practical activities is the smallest seed of hope for the future. None of them are based upon clever psychological interventions, nor do they depend upon any dynamic insights about personal growth or resolutions of past trauma. However, the decision to plant a garden in October as preparation for the coming Spring is indicative of a decision to live for the coming year. Similarly, being given a kitten by a friend changes the focus from being solely upon the self and shifts to that of caring for a dependent creature. One woman decided to buy new curtains and asked a friend to accompany her when she bought them. This decision and the accompanying act of friendship, she decided, was the activity that helped her.

Such small concrete steps are, perhaps, the keel around which we can build the ship of therapeutic endeavours. We have, however, to beware of making checklists of such activities and volunteering one from each list to a person that is suicidal and then suggesting they find a friend with a cat to invite them out, perhaps stopping off at the curtain shop on the way home.

These initiatives remind us that the dominant discourses of medicine and psychiatry stigmatise patients. Friendship allows for an emergent self that, despite vulnerability, is essentially competent, whole and valued positively.

What therapists, counsellors and social workers can do is to help organise social support in terms of welfare when material needs are the identified problem. However, some of the demands for income and housing support can only be achieved by political change. Individual therapy cannot bring about structural changes in the nature of poverty and unemployment.

The women who had repeated a suicide attempt were also the women who saw the problem as being solely individual within the context of themselves. It was these women who were still feeling suicidal. If the medical and psychiatric contact emphasises such an individualistic perspective and that is the only contact for the resolution of distress, the treatment itself becomes part of the problem – that is, iatrogenic.

Meaning is dependent upon relationship. To discover what another person means, we must begin to understand how those meanings are constituted and how those meanings are used in practice. As Kirmayer (1993) writes, 'Meaning, on this view, is equivalent to use – whether that use involves an overt action or an inferred cognitive transformation – and use is irreducibly triadic: the use of something by someone for some end' (p.162).

In the next chapter we will see how meanings about behaviour are negotiated in family contexts after an episode of suicidal behaviour.

CHAPTER NINE

The Strategic Assessment
of Deliberate Self-harm

Throughout the previous chapters a perspective has developed which proposes that an understanding of familial and individual distress is the key to
the successful management of that distress. In the last chapter a number of
suggestions were made for the therapeutic management of patients that came
from the personal experiences of women who had suffered. On the basis of
these suggestions and a systemic understanding of suicidal behaviour, I
structured an assessment schedule suitable for working with patients after
admission to hospital following an episode of suicidal behaviour (see Figure
9.1). An aim of this book is to formulate, and propose, therapeutic strategies.
This schedule is a step towards that end. In this Chapter I will present a
practice-based means of assessing suicidal behaviour in families.

Chapter Seven describes a strategy for preventing an escalation of distress
and for reducing attempted suicide in the psychiatric hospital. The strategy
is to assess neutrally the current situation, positively connote all behaviour,
seek to resolve conflict by a public commitment to a common goal and not
to precipitately engage in attempts to 'change'.

In Chapter Eight we see that individuals present problems that are located
within interactive contexts and the escalation of unresolved distress is
correlated with the repetition of attempted suicide. As a major consideration
of any treatment agency is reducing the repetition of suicidal behaviour, any
practical steps in this direction will be welcome. My argument is twofold.
First, if we understand suicidal behaviour as it occurs interactively, and target
our treatment strategies to such a systemic understanding, then we can reduce
recidivism. Second, if we take those engaging in suicidal behaviour seriously,
and that such persons are not deviant but attempting to actively solve a
problem, then we listen to their suggestions and incorporate them in our
therapeutic endeavours. The aim, then, is to establish a therapeutic dialogue.
Third, people are able to suggest ways to help themselves that are perfectly

Name	General practitioner:	Age:	Sex:

Address:	Other agency involved:	Current relationship:

Means of referral:

Life events:	Family map:

Details of the episode:

The problem(s) as presented:

Previously attempted solutions to the problem(s):

Expected changes:	Observations:

Hypotheses:	Response of significant others:

FUTURE ACTION:

Figure 9.1 An assessment schedule for the systemic understanding of suicidal behaviour

valid given the necessary support that understands the behaviour in an ecological context.

The strategic assessment of deliberate self-harm

The assessment design presented here takes a perspective that a systemic understanding must be made that includes all the significant others involved with the patient, the assessment of the problem understands both the process of genesis of the behaviour, and the way that the behaviour is currently maintained, the process of assessment is a therapeutic strategy that informs the system by the very nature of the questions that are asked and invokes answers about relationships and the resolution of problems can be generated from within the ecosystem – individual – family – treatment agency.

The researcher as therapist

In Chapter Six a neutral research approach was successful in the systemic management of distress on the ward of a psychiatric hospital. The same approach is proposed here. By neutrally researching rather than being overtly therapeutic, a de-escalation of symptomatology and reduction of distress can occur. Basically, the principle is that before doing anything therapeutically, observe what is happening and what has happened before.

Decisions must be made, and sometimes urgently, but these decisions have their own consequences. By the time an episode of suicidal behaviour has occurred, there is a window in time through which we can take a steady look at what is going on. Therapy appears to be about change but, as we shall see, sometimes people are dealing with too much change in their lives. Thus therapy can be also about stability and 'not changing'.

This schedule was developed together with a colleague who is a psychiatrist. We asked questions from the schedule as a means of gathering information in terms of assessment, not as therapy. The individual and the family were told this at the time. By working together, both researcher and clinician can ask questions that are pertinent and the family is not subjected to another lengthy, possibly harrowing, interview. The psychiatrist is also responsible for the consequent management of the patient and takes the necessary responsibility in terms of further referral and any possible medico-legal requirements and patients are informed of this. When I use the terms 'we', or 'us', in this chapter, I am referring to my psychiatrist colleague and me. Although the assessment was for the purposes of research, it was also used later as a foundation for therapy.

Reasons for the schedule

Prior to the current research, patients seen in a general hospital had been referred on to other professional agencies or returned to the community at large. The clinical use of the strategy presented here allows a unification of clinical information suitable for immediate use but also bearing further referral in mind. I was also concerned to see how a systemic understanding of deliberate self-harm fed back into the practice of the psychiatric day hospital and the practice of referring general medical practitioners. We knew that it was necessary to make links with the broader community practice agencies involved in managing suicidal behaviour. It is important that this is done in a way which is acceptable to those agencies, as consultation, rather than confronting them with a 'holier-than-thou' systems perspective as expert advisers.

Inevitably, the management of suicidal behaviour must be seen as an eco-systemic strategy and to alienate other involved agencies is a mistake (Auerswald 1968; Keeney and Sprenkle 1982). To accomplish this we built into the procedure a practice of informing all involved practitioners of the understandings which were made after assessment. Practitioners were also informed of what could be offered in terms of therapeutic management and their active co-operation was sought. While this places the expertise in the hands of those who have to make the immediate decisions, it also lets the general practitioner and social worker, for example, know what is going on and what has been decided. They can then react to such initiatives. An important part of this procedure was to ensure that any subsequent suicide attempts were then seen by us in the general hospital. This resulted in a continuity of management and the idea that all the practitioners were working in co-operation rather than one working against the other. For the unfortunate patients and their families, there was no escape from us.

Which system

At the general hospital we were presented with a person who had attempted suicide. This person was generally seen alone for a first assessment interview. If a member of the family or significant other was present, a joint interview would be made. Such an approach emphasises that even the presentation of the symptom by a particular member presents important information about the system as a whole. It is important to accept this perspective of individual presentation as it positively connotes the family as attempting to solve a problem. However, whilst accepting the initial presentation by the family, this does not mean that the researcher has to continue with an individualistic perspective. It is possible, by careful questioning, to discover and arrange data concerning the patient and his or her community of intimates. In our questions we were trying to discover how the behaviour of the individual was maintained and stimulated and promoted other behaviours within a familial context (Selvini-Palazzoli 1983; Selvini-Palazzoli *et al.* 1973; Selvini-Palazzoli *et al.* 1980).

Once a systemic understanding was made of who was involved in the interaction, it was possible to arrange another information gathering session that involved those significant others. When a family is seen together, quite different properties emerge from those initially presented by an individual, or the same properties may emerge but are located in a different individual. For example, in one family where a woman of forty years had taken an overdose of medication it was her elderly mother who presented the familial distress when all were seen together. No amount of treatment for the daughter alone would have resolved the distress of the mother or, more significantly, the family as a whole. The daughter was the spokesperson for the family distress but the source of that distress lay elsewhere.

Although the term 'family' will be used throughout this chapter, it is important to say that it is not always 'family' configurations that are seen together, nor are other systemic configurations ignored. Madanes (1981) uses the term 'community of intimates' and this is, perhaps, a closer description of the configuration of relationships seen in this chapter. As Hair (1996) writes, 'For many family therapists, the word "family" no longer accurately describes the great diversity of relational systems within which they work' (p.295). Following on from the premise of starting with what the system presented, the second assessment interview invited and incorporated those individuals presented as significant by the identified patient. By doing so, we avoided reifying the 'family' and moved towards a flexible systemic orientation. Who is involved in the management of distress is, perhaps, more important than trying to think strictly in terms of 'family'. However, as Bourdieu (1996) says, while the family may indeed be a fiction reproduced by the state, 'it receives from the state at every moment the means to exist and persist' (p.25).

Preliminary hypothesis

Before the patient was seen in hospital, the hospital notes were carefully read so that a preliminary hypothesis could be made using the patient's age, current status and previous medical history. This gave a broader focus other than on the episode itself and gave some idea of what questions to ask, although it is important to bear in mind that case histories are not neutral

(Schwarz 1996). As we saw in the Chapter Seven, histories are constructed according to the context in which they are related.

Gathering the data

The epistemological basis for gathering data was that described by Weakland *et al.* (1974) for focusing on current problems. This approach concentrates upon:

- predominantly current problems and how they are maintained by behavioural interaction
- the concrete manifestation of 'what is wrong'
- the situational and interactional nature of the problems
- what life changes have been made or are imminent
- what solutions had been developed and used to solve the problem before.

The principles for interviewing the subjects are based upon those recommended by Selvini-Palazzoli *et al.* (1980). These are:

- hypothesising – where an unproved supposition is made about the interactive systemic nature of the behaviour
- circularity – where specific interactive behaviour is discovered to gain a full systemic understanding of the behaviour
- neutrality – where the interviewer(s) take a position of assessment, taking, metaphorically, 'one-step back' from the involvement with the subjects.

Basic demographic data was collected, such as name, address, age, gender and marital status. This gave basic data to compare results with other research and from which initial hypotheses are made. As in the last chapter, if we take a developmental perspective on suicidal behaviour (Graber and Brooksgunn 1995; van Geert 1996; Yang and Clum 1996), age, gender and marital status may point to important life-cycle transitions that would be expected to take place.

Means of referral

This category is concerned with how the patient arrived in the current situation. It gives clues to what significant others are instrumentally involved with the patient and also that there may be a complainant other than the patient. It may well be that those patients who are feeling suicidal have been coerced into attending a hospital for help. By asking how the patient came to hospital and how such a process was generated and who was involved, it is possible to gain a systemic description of the referral process. If some significant other was involved, it was necessary to include that 'involved' person in any assessment procedure.

For example, if a husband had continually urged a wife to attend for treatment, or brought his wife into hospital after an overdose rather than call for an ambulance, it would be necessary to see the husband and wife together. In a similar way, if a general practitioner urges treatment by the psychiatrist and a crisis consultation, it is necessary to include the general practitioner in the systemic understanding of the crisis. That practitioner has had a previous contact with the patient that is significant and he or she has attempted to relieve the patient's continuing distress.

Family map

This section deals with who is significantly involved and lives under the same roof as the patient. It is a practical means of discovering who is immediately involved in the patient's living situation. By asking who lives under the same roof as the patient, further questions can be asked about the location of other significant members such as a spouse, partner, parents or children. These questions then promote secondary relational information. For example, if asked about the location of a spouse, the answer might be: 'My partner was living with me but left after a row last night.' Or, if asked about the location of a parent, the patient may say: 'My father moved in next door with his girlfriend when my mother died last year'. This will raise further questions about the daughter's grief for the death of her mother, her relationship with her father, as a neighbour and the presence of a 'girlfriend' following a bereavement. If suicidal behaviour is a communication about life and death issues, it may be the management of the mothers' death and the grieving process of the daughter, or father, that become the focus for the presented problem. The young woman presents the distress, the problem may be located elsewhere within the system.

At this stage of questioning it is also possible to see how different life-cycle stages are being undertaken. For example, if a married couple were seen and they were in their mid-thirties after being married for ten years, it was useful to ask if they had any children. Although this is seemingly normative, it does gain secondary information about the current problem. The procreation of children may not be an issue but if one spouse wants a child and the other does not, this will have a bearing on a systemic understanding of the problem.

Life-cycle stages are not seen as discrete categories that have to be gone through, as in the metamorphosis of the cabbage white butterfly from egg to imago. They are heuristic devices for describing change in individuals and families. We, as therapists, should have enough knowledge of human expectations from our own cultures to be able to ask questions of those with whom we come in contact. That is not to say that we must have normative expectations about the way in which they should behave. Normative expectations can sometimes obscure the resilience of the people we see (Wilbraham 1996) and the problematisation of their predicament can subjugate them further (Soal and Kottler 1996).

Life events

Recent life events are collected for two reasons. First, life events are useful indicators of family transitions and a guide to what an individual and family count as important. Second, the previous literature on deliberate self-harm (Eggert, Thompson and Herting 1994; Isometsa *et al.* 1995a; Myers, Jacobs and Pepper 1972; O'Brien and Farmer 1980; Paykel, Prusoff and Myers 1975) has always included life events data. I am concerned that bridges are built between research efforts to see their grounds of commonality rather than disparity. Alienating other researchers and practitioners is not helpful in the larger systemic context of psychotherapy and community practice. Life events are a common ground for discussion. It is how these events are built into a narrative structure that is important.

By asking questions about life events it is possible to learn how the family construes the world. If a patient gives a life history of chronic pain and a recent event of dissatisfied attempted relief, this is a useful profile to consider for a possible treatment regime based on an understanding of 'pain relief'. Pain, or suffering, must be addressed therapeutically. It is also an indicator that an overtly psychological approach must be made carefully. If the recent life events are presented as those of escalating marital conflict, this will propose an avenue for the future resolution of distress that no amount of individual medication will resolve in the long term.

As has been mentioned in Chapters Four and Five, patients and their families develop rules for construing and regulating their distress and for construing and regulating change. The understanding of what counts as a life event in their terms is an important consideration in the management of distress (Suh, Diener and Fujita 1996). All too often, previous life events research has been concerned with imposing the researcher's idea of what counts as a life event. Although we can propose certain gross cultural indicators, it is an unfortunate oversight to ignore what the patient proposes as a significant life event. It is also important to consider that the two positions go hand-in-hand; neither is true by itself. The community at large will have understandings that the individual or family should behave in certain ways when faced with certain events. However, if we look back at the letters of the women in the previous chapter, something as simple as being invited out for a meal is seen as a significant life event for a person who is lonely. Buying new curtains is a significant life event indicating a commitment to the future but such an item will not appear on any life events rating scale. Patients have as many resources as practitioners when it comes to generating appropriate solutions. The role of the practitioner is to assist in the generation of those solutions. As we saw in Figure 5.4 (p.85), the solution itself becomes a life event that must also be accommodated.

Details of the episode

The episode of deliberate self-harm is reconstructed with the patient and specific concrete details are requested about 'what happened', 'who was present', 'what was said' and 'then what happened'.

Such questions bring valuable information about those instrumentally involved with the patient. They divert attention away from the individual and seek to discover how messages are handled by those involved. Problems are seen from a different perspective by shifting the nature of the questions. We asked what happened between different people and what they did rather than about individual feelings. These questions also propose a different time-frame from that used by the patient and the family. Instead of the episode being located in a frame of a crisis precipitated by psychopathology, and ascriptions made of impulsivity, the episode is located in a time-frame of escalating attempts to resolve an interactive problem. While it is important to ask how people feel, it is, perhaps, more important to ask about what people do when they feel. Suicidal behaviour is about feeling but the act itself is something that is done.

If I ask the question 'When did all this start?', I am asking about how that person sees the problem. If I then ask 'What was it like before these things started to happen?', I have shifted the persons thoughts to a different period of their lives. If I asked 'Who was suffering the most before things started to go wrong for you?', I have shifted the focus to a broader relational picture. If the episode is recent, it is possible to ask if the person has seen their doctor recently and what did they go to see her for. By asking these interactive questions and changing the time-frame as a punctuation of events, the family are faced with the emergence of the problem in different terms. This emergence may itself propose its own resolution. For example, in

Chapter Seven, instead of seeing impulsive overdose attempts by manipulative patients, a biographical time-scale proposed an understanding of patients who were trying to resolve a situation of escalating distress.

The elicitation of the specific episode of suicidal behaviour is necessary as it gives some indication of suicidal intent and that is an important part of any initial procedure (Hawton and Catalan 1982).

The problem as presented

Previous chapters have suggested that attempted suicide may be another attempt to resolve a recurring problem. When patients in hospital emergency rooms are asked, they give clear indications of what the problems are, who is involved in maintaining the problem, the duration of the problem, how it affects others and what it prevents the patient from doing. This assessment itself puts additional information into the family system. It seems that the process of hospitalisation, and crisis, temporarily crystallises the process and focuses on the problem. For a while it is as if there is an openness of communication which allows an overt statement about the problem

(Black 1981)). Rather than seeing these events totally negatively, we can see that such events are another episode where the individual and his family are trying to articulate their distress. Our skill as therapists lies in being able to interpret that distress and promote its articulation such that we can begin to understand it together. If expression is something that is done, the symptoms themselves, and the episode itself, is an articulation of distress. Our challenge is to provide such a situation that non-verbal articulacy can be overtly stated and understood. Perhaps it is here that the therapeutic seeds are sown in the establishment of a common language for the facilitation of distress, and that language is dependent upon relationship.

Attempted solutions

Before an episode of suicidal behaviour occurs there have been numerous previous attempts to resolve distress. We made an exhaustive effort to discover the attempted solutions to the problem by asking for a detailed concrete description of what had been tried. The answers were concise. For example, 'I have been to my doctor over and over again until he could do nothing for me and then he sent me to a specialist' or 'We tried to work it out by talking about it, but that didn't help and my friend suggested we tried marriage guidance'. This gives an indication of how the problem has been construed by the family, that is medical or marital. By knowing what has been tried before, it is possible to avoid the trap of falling into repeating previously failed solutions. It is also possible to propose at a later stage a therapeutic management strategy which offers an alternative to the family that has not been previously tried and recognises their construing of the problem. A further medical referral in a sequence of failed medical referrals, for example, is not helpful unless the nature of the referral and the reasons are negotiated. Similarly, a referral to a psychologist after a series of failed medical initiatives for the treatment of chronic pain is a recipe for an overdose of pain-killing medication.

The expected change

Once a problem has been elicited it is possible to discover a possible direction for change. This gives an indication of a future profile, which the patient and the patient's family construct for themselves. We concentrated on small indications of expected change. This process, apart from placing the expected change within the realm of the perception of the patient, also uses the patient's ways of seeing the world. Rather than a therapist imposing changes upon an individual or family, the patient and family propose their own change. A part of this process is to involve all present to participate in negotiating such change. When several members of a family sit down to consider what could change, what that change would look like, when it could happen and who would be involved, a powerful intervention has been made. This gives an opportunity to observe concrete negotiated indices of change.

As is seen in Chapters Six and Seven, a public commitment to concrete action is considered to be therapeutic. I suggest that this is best done under the meta-framework of 'information gathering' rather than therapy. By doing this the responsibility for change is firmly located within the boundary of the family and within their repertoire of distress management. A family is allowed to become autonomous and self-referential rather than reliant upon an external agent. By generating their own solutions, families don't become therapist dependent. It is also a powerful message that although something potentially tragic has occurred, the wherewithal to continue lies within their own capabilities. We encouraged families to try again generating ideas from within their own resources. Rather than seeing failed persons and incompetent families, we saw people that were trying to make sense of their lives and had the means to do this with sufficient help.

If no positive changes could be identified, or if the expected change was that the patient would die, then we knew that a situation of potential suicide was evident.

Observations

This section of the schedule is for any miscellaneous notes about the patient and the family which appear important at the time, particularly about individual and family styles of communication, how we felt about the situation and any hunches or intuitions that we might have had. Not very scientific perhaps, but clinically relevant.

Hypothesis

This section is a reflective section whereby the researcher considers the previous information and constructs hypotheses about how the behaviour is maintained within the family. For example, it appears that every time the parents begin to have a row and this row threatens to become violent, the middle daughter develops abdominal cramps and a doctor has to be called in. The hypothesis in this case would be that symptomatic behaviour by the daughter is a means of managing escalating distress in a context of marital conflict. Once a tentative hypothesis has been made, it will be used to inform the questions at next assessment interview and tested for validity by asking questions about other situations where distress has occurred.

Responses of significant others

By discovering who is willing to be involved in the recovery, treatment or support of the patient, it is possible to gain further information about who is involved in the family system. As the patient is often discharged back to the family context in which they have been involved, it is necessary to discover if those conditions are the same or have changed. To ignore this may well account for the high repetition rate within three months of discharge after an overdose (Hawton and Catalan 1982; Kreitman 1977; Morgan 1979; Runeson, Eklund and Wasserman 1996). All too often such repetition is seen as evidence of psychopathology within a deviant individual, rather than the failure to understand suicidal behaviour by practitioners as it occurs in an interactive context. Sending a teenager who has recovered from an overdose and exhibits no further suicidal intent back to a home where the father says that it would be better if his son had died is counter-therapeutic. It is necessary, then, to ask those living under the same roof what their responses are, or at least to discover these from the patient.

Future action

This section is involved with making a concrete description of the next steps to take. These steps are discussed with all present in terms of what will happen, who will do what and at what time. We also noted who should be contacted in the community and who was responsible for making that contact. A commitment to specific action is an important step for the individuals and families involved. While it may not be therapy, it is step that must ethically be made in terms of responsibility for the management of the problem. It must also be said that should there be evidence of extreme psychopathology or evident suicidal intent, the psychiatrist exercised her right as clinician and took the necessary formal steps under the Mental Health Act to protect the patient or society.

The research data

The results of this research will be presented in two sections. The first section will present data about the families and propose systemic hypotheses about the management of distress. The second section will be concerned with the effects of research on the process of therapy, recovery and community practice related to suicidal behaviour and is presented in the final chapter.

Age and marital status

No patients were seen under the age of sixteen years on the ward of the general hospital. All the patients included in this study were over eighteen years old. Approximately one-third were male and two-thirds were female (See Table 9.1). Sixteen patients were married, and of those sixteen, six were second marriages (See Table 9.2).

Table 9.1 Ages of the patients admitted to the hospital emergency ward after an episode of suicidal behaviour

Age	Females	Males	Both
18–19	2	1	3
20–25	6	2	8
26–49	4	6	10
50–58	4	2	6
59–76	1	–	1
Total	17	11	28

**Table 9.2 Marital status of patients admitted to the hospital
emergency ward after an episode of suicidal behaviour**

Marital status	Females	Males	Both
married	11	5	16
single	4	4	8
divorced	1	1	2
separated	1	1	2
Total	17	11	28

Life events

The life events were placed into four categories of transition, conflict, social and somatic or behavioural problems from the way in which the people being interviewed described those events (see Table 9.3). As the reader can see, each event is a part of a small story in its own right and contributes significantly to the larger narrative of family life.

The problems as presented

The problem presented after an episode of deliberate self-harm was rarely that the person felt suicidal (see Table 9.4). There was usually a clear description of a specific problem. These problems were arranged into five categories. As in the life events, we were concerned with what the subjects saw as a problem. If more than one problem was presented, we would ask the subject to indicate the principal problem by asking: 'On a scale of 1 to 10, how do you rank problem A'?

In Table 9.5, the problems presented are predominantly concerned with marital conflict and symptoms. These problems are located within a context of life events mainly concerned with either transition or further conflict.

For some families where life events involve a transition within the immediate nuclear family, the most common presenting problem is that involving behavioural symptoms. For example:

> A woman, aged 24, lived with her parents, a younger sister and an elder brother. She had taken an overdose of anti-depressant medication. She had complained of not being able to go out with people, nor to engage others in conversation. For this problem she

Table 9.3 Categorisation of reported events

Events of transition:	Death or dying; recent loss of a partner; leaving school, work, hostel or accommodation; moving or leaving home; remarriage in the immediate family, change in employment status; partner leaving.
Events of conflict:	A row or a series of rows; rows in the family, at work or with friends; asking for a divorce; threatening violence.
Social events:	A court appearance, threat of prison or debt.
Events associated with somatic and behavioural problems:	Continuing pain; medical investigations; hospitalisation; sterilisation/vasectomy; drinking.

Table 9.4 Problems as presented at interview

Familial conflict:	Rows with parents.
Marital conflict:	Row with partner; threat of violence; communication break-down; custody of, or access to, children; sexual difficulties.
Social problems:	Difficulties with money; nowhere to go; lonely; no work.
Death:	Death of a loved one.
Symptoms:	Loss of concentration or decision-making skills; lack of confidence; unable to cope; pain; depression; suicidal feelings; excessive drinking; anorexia; phobia.

Table 9.5 Problems as presented in the context of life events

Problems as presented

Life events	Familial conflict	Marital conflict	Symptoms	Social	Death	**Total**
Transition	2	1	8	1	1	13
Conflict	–	9	–	–	–	9
Social	–	–	–	1	–	1
Somatic/ Behavioural	1	1	3	–	–	5
Total	3	11	11	2	1	28

was treated by her general practitioner with medication, although the problems worsened.

The family presented the significant life event as that of the youngest daughter leaving home to go to New Zealand and work as a nurse. This daughter who was leaving had been highly favoured by the family, although she had continually caused them concern over her independent behaviour.

Focusing on treating the individual symptoms of the older sister had ignored the systemic location of the familial distress. The following examples reflect a similar process:

A 34-year-old woman came with her husband to a clinic in the psychiatric day hospital after taking an overdose of medication. She described a long list of recent deaths in the immediate family (her father-in-law, grandmother and two stillborn children). Her problem was presented as a burning sensation in the mouth. She had tried medication and a psychiatric hospitalisation for this condition. Her husband said he was reaching the end of his tether. The tension between the woman and her family of origin had become more frequent and intense.

A 56-year-old woman had taken an overdose of medication. She said that during the previous year she had reluctantly given up her job to move house and live in another part of the country. Her husband was about to sail his yacht around the world but he was not taking her. He had invited his secretary to go with him. This woman said that she had become 'depressed'. She had tried to alleviate her depression by taking medication prescribed by her general practitioner.

A 30-year-old-man overdosed with his prescribed medication and alcohol. His wife had petitioned for divorce. Three weeks before this she had taken their children and left him. He began to drink heavily. Drinking was the problem as described by his mother and the neighbours. He had contacted his general practitioner to help him cope with the loss of his wife and children. He was offered anti-depressant medication.

All these examples present individual symptoms located within a context of transitional life events and inter-personal problems. Significantly, all these people were offered medication to relieve their problems – medication that was subsequently misused. The message implicit in using such medication is: 'This will make you better'. The consequent logic is, if the original dose does not work, then more will.

Marital conflict as problem and event

In nine of the cases marital conflict was given as a problem and as the recent life event. For example:

> A 40-year-old woman was seen after an overdose. The significant life event for her was her husband asking for a divorce after an affair with another woman in the village. Although the man and wife still lived together, they lived in a context of disharmony and outbreaks of overt conflict. The woman expressed marital conflict as her principal problem. Interestingly, she had been treated for 'depression' by her general practitioner, although he knew of her marital difficulties.

I am not necessarily proposing a causal link between events and problems, rather a dynamic link that suggests that problems, when they are presented, must also be located in particular contexts. People do this in making a common-sense understanding of their predicament. It is only treatment agencies that describe these problems in individualised contexts. By and large, individuals understand that their problems are part of a bigger context and connected ecologically to the way in which they live, as we read in the last chapter. Unfortunately, primary care systems are organised around the recognition of individually presented distress. Even those who present their distress as individual symptoms locate their problems in a transitional context. Lay beliefs commonly locate mental disorders in psychosocial contexts too (Matschinger and Angermeyer 1996).

A previously attempted resolution of a current problem

Most of the patients seen had attempted to resolve their current problem by contacting an agency outside the family (see Table 9.6) and three-quarters had been in contact with a general practitioner.

Table 9.6 Previous contacts to resolve the problem

Contact	n
General practitioner	6
General practitioner + psychiatric treatment	11
General practitioner + social worker	1
General practitioner + solicitor	1
General practitioner + marriage guidance	2
Marriage guidance only	1
Talking to a friend and temporarily leaving home	5
No previously attempted solution	1

The family doctor is the primary community agent for contact in times of distress and this is reflected in the predominance of general practitioner contact for solving personal problems. In our culture, problems are presented to a doctor as symptoms and medication is expected to cure those symptoms. The questions asked by family doctors are concerned with personal constitution and with linear causal descriptions. This ignores the contextual nature of the presented problems, implies a position of deviance and individual pathology and fails to address the generation and maintenance of distress within a systemic context.

The maintenance of problems and community practice

From the descriptions of the suicidal episodes presented by patients in the general hospital, a common pattern emerge (see Figure 9.2). This is a variation on the model that was proposed in Chapter Five (see Figure 5.4, p.85).

Stage I

Families faced with a life event attempt to change to accommodate that life event. This change proves to be problematical and itself demands a strategy of management to resolve the problem. This is an attempted solution. If the problem is resolved and familial distress reduced, the family continues as a viable system. They successfully negotiate the 'change' that they are faced with and this confirms their strategy of resolving problems as being effective. This model also accepts that distress is a naturally occurring phenomenon and is not in itself negative but a normal part of human life. I am not using strategy in a 'thought-out' sense here. Change, and resolution, happens.

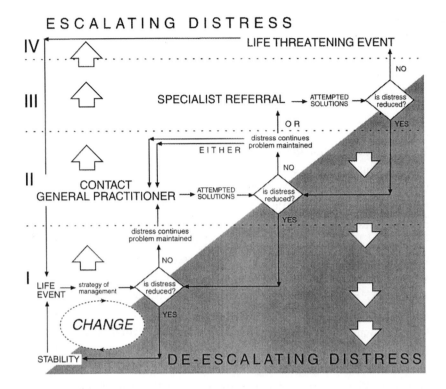

Figure 9.2 Stages in the escalation of distress and the referral to practitioners

Stage II

Occasionally, attempted solutions fail or problems persist. If problems persist, a general practitioner is contacted who implements a number of attempted solutions to manage the presented problem. These strategies of resolution are usually based upon a linear cause and effect understanding of the problem. When a relational understanding is made, it is often one that sees one of the members of the family as being deviant in some way.

Attempted solutions, often involving medication, are implemented by the general practitioner. Either these work, and become part of the repertoire for managing familial distress, or distress continues. The general practitioner can then try something else or consider referring on to a specialist practitioner.

Stage III

Should distress still continue, a specialist referral is made. As in the previous stage, strategies of management are implemented until either distress is reduced or the strategies are exhausted. Unfortunately, the strategies are predominantly concerned with resolving personal deviancy and ignore systemic contexts. These strategies may themselves become part of the families' repertoire of distress management, yet, at the same time, amplify the distress by locating the problem within an individual.

Stage IV

When treatment strategies are exhausted and distress escalates, an acute attack, or an overdose, or a rapid escalation of the symptoms occur. This, too, acts as a life event which must be managed by the family. Either the family changes or they settle into a pattern of continuing chronic problems and episodes of acute distress.

Suicidal behaviour is not an isolated act by a manipulative impulsive individual. It is an episode in a series of attempted solutions to resolve a systemic problem. Previously attempted solutions fail to reduce distress and unwittingly promote processes that maintain distress. What we need to understand are the ways in which change and distress are positively managed by individuals and families. It is distressing when our children grow up and leave home. It is also liberating for both children and parents when they do so and it is a life cycle change within our culture that is necessary and accepted. When marriages fail, that too is distressing. The whole process of divorcing is fraught with difficulties. However, the change too can be liberating and bring new personal perspectives. Losing work, becoming redundant or facing retirement are all transition phases in a working life that must also be accommodated. These also bring both joy and pain. Losing a valued position at work can be bitterly distressing. That too can change and the opportunities for change can be transforming, for some. For others, the opportunities are few and the distress is never overcome, as we read in the literature relating unemployment to suicidal behaviour (Chuang and Huang 1996a; Dooley, Fielding and Levi 1996; Fagin 1978; Maris and Silverman 1995; Mccrea 1996; Mulder *et al.* 1994; Saunderson and Langford 1996; Starrin *et al.* 1990; Viinamaki *et al.* 1995; Weyerer and Wiedenmann 1995). No amount of personal interventions from general practitioners is going to make a change in such a massive cultural influence. No amount of medication is going to ameliorate such distress.

How are we then to recognise the escalation of distress and the cycles of management that reduce that distress? Or, as importantly for practitioners, how are we to identify those cycles where strategies of management are only making things worse?

Three systemic hypotheses

There appear to be three main ways of interpreting how suicidal behaviour is generated based upon the data gathered from the assessment of families.

1. Systemic Transition: A family is faced with 'change' and the necessary adjustments to accommodate 'change' are not made. Suicidal behaviour in such families is a strategy of 'promotion'. Something has to be done to accommodate change and promote transition.

2. Rigid Homeostasis: A family is faced with 'change' and this 'change' is accommodated by repeating previously tried solutions. In such families there is usually a tradition of one member adopting the status 'sick'. Suicidal behaviour in such families is a strategy of 'restoration'. In some sense, for these families, there is too much change and the suicide attempt is to keep things how they were. In other words, their strategy is not to change.

3. Marital Conflict: Suicidal behaviour is a strategy in a pattern of escalating symmetrical or complementary relationship. This strategy can be an attempt to promote resolution or maintain conflict.

The reader will note that systemic transition and rigid homoeostasis are opposing poles of suicidal behaviour as a strategy of accommodating 'change'. In one, suicidal behaviour promotes a reorganisation of the family pattern of interaction to accommodate change. In the other, suicidal behaviour is an attempt to keep the family the same or to restore the family as it was in the face of change. We can see that a therapeutic intervention advocating change, when there is too much change, would only exacerbate the problem. For example:

> A woman of 43 years came to see me. Her husband had died three years ago and now she had a male lodger who was the same age as herself. In the same house as her and her lodger lived her 25-year-old son and her 20-year-old daughter. Her eldest daughter lived locally and was about to produce a first child. She was about to be divorced. There were open and concealed conflicts between her lodger and

her children, principally over financial matters and who had the right to interfere in family affairs.

Systemic transition

This hypothesis is made from the life events data (see Table 9.7). Although the presented problems vary, the changes being demanded of the system appear to be the same. The changes involve entrances or exits to the systems. Any reorganisation necessitates a strategy of management by those persons involved. This strategy of management may itself become problematical and the family becomes distressed further. At such a point, one member will attempt to 'promote' change by a seemingly drastic act. For example:

> Her lodger found her after her overdose on his return from the pub – he was concerned about her non-arrival. He organised what was to be done next and came to the interview at the day-hospital. During the interview he suggested things which could change and that they could do together. The episode of overdosing appeared to have precipitated a change whereby the lodger had occupied the role the woman wanted and she said that her children now realised how hard it had been for her.

> The whole family system had been accommodating a transition of leaving by death, entrance by relationship, entrance by future birth, a changing relationship *vis-à-vis* children and mother and by a change in the lodger's marital status.

For this family the incident of suicidal behaviour promoted a change in the family. It appeared that the family had been trying to keep the system as it was and resist adapting to the current situation. When this woman could no longer cope with managing the family distress she implemented a strategy which meant that all the family members had to be something differently.

The following examples also show how massive changes in family relationships are accommodated but can sometimes lead to problems.

> A woman of 37 was seen after an overdose. She had recently been married for a second time. She and her new husband had been living for the past seven months with his mother in his mother's home. The husband had lived in the same house for the past five years since the death of his father. They had recently had their honeymoon. They had not been able to have a honeymoon before because his mother had to be admitted to hospital. She was thought to be dying after a stroke.

During the post-honeymoon period, in the three weeks before the overdose, the woman's first husband had been seen in the area. A series of arguments began, involving the current husband and the ex-husband, concerning the woman's access to her children. The woman and her second husband were contacting a fertility clinic. The second husband was unemployed and the woman complained about his excessive drinking.

A man of 50 was seen in the general hospital after he had taken an overdose. His eldest son had recently died in a car accident. He used the tablets the general practitioner had given him to calm him down as a means of attempting suicide. Two months later the man's wife was referred to us. She was feeling suicidal about the death of her son. Her husband was also leaving her and having an affair with another woman.

An 18-year-old woman came to the psychiatric hospital with her parents. They said that the most significant events for them were the daughter's eighteenth birthday, the birth of a granddaughter and the loss of the daughter's long-standing boyfriend. Both parents had been expecting their youngest daughter to marry this boyfriend and that she would be 'off their hands' in the near future. They had become grandparents for the first time and wondered when their younger daughter would get married. Her father wanted her to leave home and become independent. Her mother said that it was not that easy as she had always been the 'baby' of the family and the time was not right for her to leave.

In such circumstances it appears that deliberate self-harm is a promotional strategy to implement necessary changes. We are all faced with the inevitability of change. How we manage such change is idiosyncratic to us as individuals and families. However, we are offered imperative alternatives by the cultures we live in for managing distress or bringing about systemic resolution, for example 'drown your sorrows', 'take these to calm you down', 'go out and enjoy yourself', 'do something about it', 'see your doctor'. When these solutions do not work, it is necessary to implement an alternative strategy. In this way, deliberate self-harm becomes a means of interrupting a sequence of failing attempted solutions to accommodate systemic change and itself may become positively framed as an attempted solution rather than attempted 'suicide'. From this perspective, individuals are not seen as weak or manipulative but part of a pattern of maintaining systemic viability. The behaviour can be positively connoted and becomes understandable within a developmental context.

One of the apparent difficulties for our current society is that when attempted solutions fail at the level of management by community practitioners where the problem is punctuated as individually pathogenic, the culture offers a repertoire of behaviours that signal escalating distress. These behaviours (overdosing, wrist-cutting, anorexia, depression, schizophrenia, delinquency, psychosomatic problems, alcoholism) are taken as further examples of individual pathology and become maintained within a family system as a pattern of accommodating change (see Chapter Five). This has a price for the individual but maintains the larger systemic unit.

Table 9.7 The Incidence of life events in the context of systemic hypotheses

Systemic hypotheses	Life events				
	Transition	Conflict	Somatic/ behavioural	Social	All
Systemic transition	5	–	1	1	7
Rigid homeostasis	6	–	3	–	9
Marital conflict	2	9	1	–	12
Total	**13**	**9**	**5**	**1**	**28**

Table 9.8 The incidence of presented problems in the context of systemic hypotheses

Systemic hypotheses	Problems					
	Familial	Marital	Somatic/ behavioural	Social	Death	All
Systemic transition	2	1	2	1	1	7
Rigid homeostasis	1	–	7	1	–	9
Marital conflict	–	10	2	–	–	12
Total	**3**	**11**	**11**	**2**	**1**	**28**

Rigid homoeostasis

The repetition of patterns of behaviour to manage change is described here as rigid homoeostasis. When a system is faced by changes, one member will repeat a previous strategy to manage change. This may mean an exacerbation of symptomatology or a repetition of self-harm. The hypothesis of rigid homoeostasis is made when life events of transition are recognised and contextualise the presentation of somatic and behavioural problems (See Tables 9.7 and 9.8).

When looking through the hospital notes of such patients it is usual to find a 'thick' file reflecting a history of medical contact. An interesting point is that during the course of the hospital medical history the notes begin to introduce comments suggesting that the patient's symptoms have psychological or social origins. These notes often suggest that physical symptoms, which persist despite treatment, are functions of interpersonal conflicts. For example:

> A young woman of 20 was seen with her husband after she had overdosed. Throughout her life she had had problems with a congenital deformation of her hip and, at 15, the suggestion was made by the medical staff that this was exaggerated. A year later she overdosed after an argument with her mother over school attendance. The idea was first raised that there were multiple marital disagreements. Two years later she was pregnant and had an abortion. Her father was not told. 'It would kill him', she is reported to have said. Her mother knew about the abortion. During this period, and throughout her life, she was admitted to hospital with acute attacks of asthma. When eventually she married she was allowed to have a house rather than a flat because of increasing disability in her hips. She was told that it was something she would 'have to live with '. She had one baby but refused to have another because of the asthma and her hips. She returned for a consultation at the hospital one month before her overdose and was told that she would have to (a) accept the pain in her hip for years and (b) that she was 'obviously much too fat'. Soon after, she argued with her husband in a series of escalating rows and her mother said that she did not know how he puts up with her.

It appears that this woman had presented quite legitimately over the years with pain from her hip. Yet, at the same time, it also appears that this pain could have been used to divert attention away from parental conflict. When her pain increased, or she had an asthmatic attack, her family became united in purpose and conflicts were set aside. This seems a crucial function of illness behaviour in many of the families seen. Illness brings unity. However, that illness has to be seen as legitimate by the treating agency. Once the presenting patient is seen as illegitimately occupying the status 'sick', problems arise. Another example:

> We saw a woman, Veronica, in hospital. She was 20 years old. Later, we saw her father and the following events were relayed. Two years ago her mother had died of stomach cancer. Since then she had been treated for recurrent stomach pains with no recognised organic cause. During that time her father had married his girlfriend and Veronica had left home. She and her father's new wife did not get on. When she argued, her step-mother developed a rash, so she had to go. Throughout her adolescent life she was described as a problem child who had at one time been fostered out. She had had numerous scrapes with the law and had gradually incurred a record of delinquency. She had been fostered out because her mother could not cope with her at home. It was suggested that there was a considerable amount of marital disharmony between her parents. Recently, she had continually tried to involve her father in her life once more by asking for money for transport to job interviews and for shelter. He had briefly accepted her when she had had severe stomach pains but this had stopped when his new wife developed a rash again. Once more it appears that a system was accommodating an inevitable change. However, a traditional means of stabilising this family had been Veronica's delinquent or deviant behaviour. When this strategy failed, illness behaviour was used and proved to be temporarily successful until she was deemed illegitimately ill.

The presentation of behavioural symptomatology as a means of regulating systemic change by restoring the *status quo* is described here as rigid homoeostasis. On further investigation of patients' notes, and at successive interview, I found that there is often a family history of maintaining family stability by illness behaviour. Brent *et al.* (1996), in a controlled study of adolescent suicide victims, found that rates of suicidal behaviour were higher in the relatives of the adolescent suicides than in a community control group. Such a situation may reflect considerations that some behaviours are transmitted genetically. It may be, however, that such behaviours are transmitted within the culture of the family and that the strategic management of change is learned. In such a way, what constitutes change, and how that change is regulated, will be subject to familial rules and construing (See Chapters Four and Five). Certainly, suicidal behaviour is a non-verbal means of signalling distress and all these patients have lived in a family milieu where non-verbal communication, such as rashes and increasing pain, is used to signal distress. When contact is made with caring agencies that base their approach on a predominantly verbal form of communication that demands the articulacy of what may be, for the patient, forbidden to be expressed, small wonder that such patients are not understood.

Livingston, Witt and Smith (1995), for example, investigated children of people with somatisation disorder and children of less severely affected somatisers and identified parental predictors of children's somatisation. Children in families with somatising children had more emergency room use, more suicidal behaviour and more disability. Children in families of somatisation disorder adults had 11.7 times as many emergency room visits as less severely affected somatisers. Parental somatisation, substance abuse and anti-social symptoms predicted children's somatisation.

Marital conflict

In two papers, Lester (1968; 1969) investigates attempted suicide as evidence of hostility and as evidence of resentment and dependency. Suicidal indi-viduals are characterised as demanding confirmation of their beliefs through hostility and as being resented by those on whom they are primarily dependent at times of crisis. I believe that these views can be restated in familial or marital terms. In the couples or families where a hypothesis of marital conflict is made, the life events and the problems presented are those of marital conflict (see Table 9.8, p.182). Within these relationships, hostility is present in both partners. The relationship is hostile; both partners demand confirmation of their beliefs. This appears as a symmetrical relationship, each partner demanding: 'Tell me I was right about you'.

Further to this, both partners resent each other yet are dependent upon each other in times of crisis. By the time an overdose has occurred, a pattern of action has been in operation which is usually a succession of rows which escalate in frequency and intensity. These rows are punctuated by attempts to resolve the conflict. This resolution is temporary and can itself lead to further rows. For example:

> A 39-year-old man had overdosed. His marriage was, he said, breaking up over the years. First his wife thought he was leaving and became sleepless. They then moved to separate beds. Later she said she had no love for him and he feared she would leave him. The episode occurred after his wife had contacted her solicitor that

morning to petition for divorce. He had sat down with her later to talk it over, where she told him the talking made it worse. He then took the tablets in the evening.

A 32-year-old was interviewed after an overdose of medication. She described how she had left her husband following an episode of violence. Whilst away, she had met a man and became pregnant. On returning to her husband she told him of her affair. He accepted her back home and she arranged an abortion. Following the abortion, further outbreaks of rowing and violence occurred. After one of these rows she overdosed.

A young woman of 21 overdosed after her husband had left home. She described, with her husband present, how they failed to communicate to her satisfaction and of a series of rows. These rows always followed attempts to resolve their different sexual needs and parental interference from both sets of in-laws by sitting down and talking to resolve the problem.

The literature about self-harm continually refers to such inter-personal rows and conflicts as occurring before an episode of deliberate self-harm. From the reports these patients made, the general practitioner was often brought in to resolve the individual distress and was presented with evidence of marital conflict. However, in a medical culture distress is presented as individual symptoms of 'anxiety', 'depression" or 'sleeplessness'. Although evidence of marital conflict is also presented, it is medication for individual symptomatology that is prescribed. This medication is often the means for the overdose (Wells 1981).

The way that distress is medicalised and treated is a reflection of a collective cultural epistemology regarding the causation and presentation of illness and the control of deviance in which we all participate – that distress can be handled by alcohol or drugs and that the problem is located in one person. However, a systemic understanding of change and conflict resolution and that symptoms are the expression of a distress that may be located elsewhere would lead to differences in practice and a reduction of the escalation of distress. There is a need for an improvement in the way that general practitioners are trained to recognise distress (Appleby *et al.* 1996; Marks, Goldberg and Hillier 1979; Rihmer, Rutz and Pihlgren 1995) and in the way that they are trained to manage such distress. While pain can be resolved with a pill, suffering cannot be solved pharmaceutically. Deliberate self-harm can be understood differently: as a strategy of promoting change, of restoring the *status quo* or as a strategy of conflict resolution. Distress must be understood in what it is signifying and what it hopes to achieve. This is an understanding of the constitution of distress that leads to a regulation of distress. If pain has a purpose, suffering has a purpose too. I am not advocating the active embrace of suffering but rather that suffering is not wasted when it is itself an impetus to resolve a systemic problem.

The next step, follow up

By actively calling members of a family together for the purpose of assessment, we were intervening in the family system of the individual. By the nature of the questions which were asked, we were placing the episode of suicidal behaviour within a nexus of relational events. I believe that research such as this cannot abdicate a responsibility to the patient. If we by gain information and make an understanding and then fail to act further, we have abdicated our responsibility to the patient. Such inaction itself would be discourteous and unethical. As a result of these considerations, we offered either a therapeutic contact or a referral to further therapy with other therapists. While this may blur the boundary of research, it makes research feasible in clinical practice by acknowledging ethical requirements. The next steps were as follows:

1. The general practitioner was informed, briefly, of the understanding that we had made at the hospital interview and if we were to follow up for further assessment, the general practitioner was informed. For the general practitioner, it was still her patient. It is vitally important to keep the system of other professional agencies informed. To ignore the presence of other treatment agencies is as much a mistake as it is to ignore the interactional nature of the symptoms within a family context. This also prevents the family from becoming overloaded or confused by conflicting advice. The practitioner is also given a chance to approve of the intervention and provide additional information. In practice, the general practitioners approved all the interventions made by the researchers. One reason for this may be that the general practitioners have come to the end of the road themselves with some of the patients and, as they say, have exhausted their own resources.

2. We offered a further appointment for assessment at a psychiatric day-hospital to review the situation. This is not a postponement of therapy but a strategy of holding off on direct change and seeing if the episode of deliberate self-harm itself brings any change. Beer

(1975) notes that all too often oscillation occurs when precipitate changes are made as interventions when change has begun to happen anyway. The label of 'therapy' is avoided as this proposes a responsibility by the researchers, whereas the responsibility for some change is with the patient and the patient's family. Notwithstanding, there were times when the psychiatrist must intervene in terms of the Mental Health Act or in cases of child abuse.

3. Benefits of this psycho-social assessment procedure were an increased co-operation by the general hospital staff to hold a patient overnight, so that we could see the family in the hospital, and a reduction in stigmatising of self-harming patients by the emergency ward staff. Patients were no longer treated in a hostile manner and this appeared to be a direct result of the researchers being able to visit soon after an admission. By talking to the hospital staff, and sharing our thoughts with them, we were taking part in changing the ecology of ideas in another systemic perspective, that of the hospital. Other researchers also recommend that the family treatment programme begins in the emergency treatment room (Rotheramborus *et al.* 1996) and that casualty officers and specialist mental health teams are involved as soon as possible (Pang, Catalan and Booth 1996).

There was a reduction in psychiatric admission to the psychiatric hospital. By concentrating on the solving of problems within an interactive framework, the incidence of mental illness rarely became an issue. When it did, there was the additional advantage of psychiatric screening being built into the assessment procedure. The reduction of admissions to psychiatric hospital further reduced the episodes of self-mutilation on the hospital ward. This re-iterated what we saw in Chapter Seven, where changes in one group lead to a broader change within the greater system. This is what I mean when I talk about a change in the ecology of practice.

We also developed a co-operative relationship with general practitioners in the immediate community. To offer alternatives to general practitioners means that they approach their patients from a different perspective. Rather than having manipulative hopeless cases, they are faced with individuals attempting to solve complex problems with concrete objectives. General practitioners were willing to refer earlier once they had established that a competent support service existed.

4. Once the assessments have been made, the following referral pattern took place.

    If we believed that we had an adequate understanding of the problem, therapeutic help was offered or the patient was discharged home. This choice was the responsibility of the patient and the patient's family if the psychiatrist judged that there was no immediate life-threatening danger. If a particular psychotherapist or social worker was already involved in treating the patient and the patient asked to be referred back to that therapist, the researchers did so, informing the therapist as they did with the general practitioners. We routinely informed the casualty officer in the general hospital where the initial emergency admissions were made. Pang, Catalan and Booth (1996) refer in their work to a such a need for improved co-ordination between hospital and community mental health services. If we failed to gain an satisfactory understanding, a referral was made to a Family Therapy clinic. Some patients and their families were discharged home and contact offered if needed in the future.

The referral on to a Family Therapy clinic proved to be a mistake. First, the referral was a precocious assessment of the problem and a punctuation by us that the problem was a 'family' problem. Second, there was too long a time lapse between referral and take-up that ignored the current nature of the problem. If distress is immediate, then the bureaucracy of referral is terminal. Third, some patients resented being passed on to other therapists. In the process of becoming suicidal, as we have seen earlier, patients go from one practitioner to another with ever-escalating distress and a problem that fails to be resolved. At this moment of crisis, to refer them on is understood as being another way of getting rid of them.

Table 9.9 Post-assessment referral for therapy or follow-up

Family therapy	4
Hypnotherapy	3
Return to psychiatric treatment	5
Direct discharge from hospital to home	3
Refer to researchers for follow up	13
Total	**28**

Table 9.10 Outcomes of therapy and assessment

Number of referrals	Number of times seen	Outcome
5	1	satisfactory*
1	2	satisfactory
2	3	satisfactory
1	4	satisfactory
2	5	(1) satisfactory
		(1) problem persists
2	did not arrive	non-attendance

*Satisfactory is a category which is based upon what the family see as satisfactory. This was usually a resolution of the problem they had presented.

Referral to therapy after assessment

The referral on to another therapist or the researchers (see Table 9.9) was accompanied by a brief resumé of the assessment stating the problem presented, expected changes, previously failed solutions and a systemic understanding tested out in the presence of the involved significant others. It may well be that this assessment was the therapeutic intervention. Of the twenty-eight patients and their families seen in this study, only two families have had an occurrence of suicidal behaviour in a twelve-month follow-up period (see Table 9.10). All family members interviewed were included in those follow-up figures, as were all patients seen by us in hospital, regardless of their post-assessment referral. The number of patients seen was too small to be compared statistically with the large-scale studies made by other researchers. It is an indicator, however, of how prevention strategies may be implemented and formulated.

Referral to the researchers

We saw families if clear cut problems were identified and concrete steps were expressed that represented desired change. The nature of the therapeutic contact centred on giving tasks to perform that involved all the family. In some cases where symptoms were involved, a daily chart of the symptoms was made. Where conflict was involved, a mutual solution was negotiated. The principles of therapy were those presented by the Brief Therapists at the Mental Research Institute (Fisch, Weakland and Segal 1982) and are presented elsewhere in the literature (Aldridge and Rossiter 1983; Aldridge and

Rossiter 1984). Although family therapy principles were used, we did not use the formal approach using a one-way mirror or external supervision. Neither of us were comfortable as therapists using this approach and the families that we saw found the room with the one-way mirror disturbing.

The two referrals who did not arrive both had social problems as their principal problems, had a wide array of social support agencies and were known as 'difficult cases'. No person was seen for more than five sessions. As soon as a problem was resolved and a goal reached, discharge from therapy was negotiated (see Table 9.10).

A number of patients were seen only once. Once patients recognised and negotiated mutual goals, they brought about those changes without any outside help. We often found at the single therapeutic contact that the individual or family goals set in the session of assessment were reached by the time 'therapy' began. For example, one married couple expressed communication as being their problem. At assessment we asked them what they wanted to communicate, how they could achieve that communication, what communication approaches they had tried before and what would be the outcome of a successful communication. By the time the appointment for further contact arrived, they had already achieved what they has set out to do.

Monitoring

When patients were discharged home directly, or after brief treatment, although their problems were resolved, we occasionally found that they and their general practitioner were anxious about such seemingly precipitate discharge, even though the identified and presented problem had been resolved. To overcome this we 'monitored' the patient and arranged a family interview after three months. This was a useful tool for follow-up studies. It allowed a contact to be made that was punctuated as assessment, not therapy, and allowed for a contact that was not precipitated by crisis. Those involved were reassured that they could obtain support and there was a finite arrangement for contact. Monitoring was used to reinforce progress and a situation of expected recovery. A similar set of questions were asked during the monitoring interview as in the assessment schedule. The questions were all concerned with current problems, who was involved and what solutions had been attempted. Any problems occurring after the therapeutic intervention were noted and the systemic nature of such problems, if any, were discovered. Monitoring, like assessment, is not about 'change' but about gathering information in a systemic manner.

Problem resolution

The successful resolution of suicidal behaviour appears to be concerned with legitimating the person and accepting the family as competent. Understanding the systemic context of individual behaviour and punctuating the behaviour of individuals as part of a circular causal sequence of interactive behaviour is also therapeutic. A development of this systemic perspective is that the significant variable associated with repetition proposed in Chapter Seven – the location of the problem within the individual – is modified by locating the problem within a causal nexus. The negative side of such a view can be that we not only have an individual problem now but we also have a family problem. As one patient so eloquently said, 'When I came here it was only a headache, now my marriage is in question.'

In Chapter Eight the women reported that someone objective to talk to, support and practical activities were helpful in recovery. This form of assessment used those principles, offering a neutral arena for discussion with those intimately concerned and concentrated on practical problem resolution. As in Chapter Seven, the divergence of abstract conflicting beliefs was countered by a convergence of practical steps leading to mutual agreement. These items of agreement and steps to further action were publicly stated with a vocal commitment by all parties.

Warning signs

From the descriptions that these families give about the escalation of distress, there are important stages to consider that are warning signs. The process of this escalation, or de-escalation, has been schematised in Figure 9.2 (p.177).

A family tradition of symptoms

The presentation of symptoms by more than one member of a family to a helping agency within close temporal proximity is a warning sign of an impending crisis. Many of these families had been to see their general practitioner with an assortment of ailments, differing in severity, within a period of one month before the suicide attempt. This reflects the work of earlier researchers in general practice (Hopkins 1959; Wells 1981). What some general practitioners may have not picked up is that several of the family members were visiting their general practitioner, or turning up to see different practitioners within the same practice, and these isolated individual visits were linked by a family context of continuing distress.

Similarly, in research into suicidal behaviour we may be better directed to look at the incidence of distress in the family milieu of the patient rather than solely at the identified patient.

Escalation of symptoms

The presented symptom escalates with greater severity and increased frequency. If this is a pain, the pain occurs more often, is disabling and restricts the activity of the patient and other members of the family.

Ascription of legitimacy

There are overt expressions of hostility and conflict made by the patient about the family or the family about the patient. If this is about pain, the family will complain that something should be done about 'it' and perhaps the patient is not co-operating with either treatment or family routine. The demand for a 'pain-killer' in such contexts has a certain significance.

Threat of imminent systemic dissolution

A threat of divorce or separation may be made between marital partners. Parents of an adolescent may threaten to throw him or her out of the home. Some member of a family will say that life is not worth living with those with whom they live and that the situation is hopeless. The same thing occurs in old peoples homes where a resident claims that she is not understood and will find somewhere new to live or the carers begin to claim that the resident is worse than they thought she would be when she was admitted.

I have used the word dissolution here as it means to separate into parts and is traditionally applied to the breaking down of a social organisation or assembly. And this is what we see with families in distress.

Further ascription of illegitimacy

Those agencies involved with helping the patient or family begin to express their frustration that no improvement occurs and intimate that the situation is hopeless, that they have exhausted their strategic resources and threaten to reject the patient. None of us really like to admit that we cannot do anything more but, even when unspoken, such an attitude gets conveyed to the patient. Hopelessness is a factor often associated with suicide and attributed to the individual patient. From my perspective, hopelessness is a valuable concept but it refers to the relational aspect. Not only is the patient hopeless but the carers are too. Like hostility and conflict, hopelessness is a relationship.

Change of status

There is often a precipitate change of treatment strategy whereby the treatment agency will change its treatment line from physical to psychological. This unilateral change of treatment perspective ignores the position of the patient and the patient's family on the problem. From being legitimately 'sick' through physical causes, the patient may become seen as illegitimately occupying the status 'sick' and is, thereby, manipulative. This is often the case for patients suffering with chronic pain that worsens. During the course of investigation the specialist decides, after exhaustive tests, that there is no physical cause and refers the patient on to a psychologist or psychiatrist. It is then that an overdose of pain tablets occurs. When this happens the family believes they have been tricked by the identified patient and their worst suspicions are confirmed. The patients biography is reconstrued in the light of further deviancy and the patient becomes seen as illegitimate.

Total negative connotation

Finally, any attempts to resolve distress, or any actions by the patient, are seen as further acts of deviancy. Any action becomes a confirmation of a deviant person from the family side or as family rejection from the patient's side. Both sides say 'NO' to the existence of the other. This can just as well apply to the treatment agencies as well as the families.

It is these warning signs which will be considered in the next two chapters.

CHAPTER TEN

Suicidal Behaviour and Adolescence in Family Contexts

> *It is possible to approach personal constructs through the analysis of spontaneous activities without depending upon the person's verbal explanations. The sequence of activities, and the situations in which they are carried out, indicate with some measure of clarity the personal constructions which underlie them... It may be as meaningful to find out when a person does certain things as it is to find out what he does and why he says he does them.* (Kelly 1955, p.739)

Families talking about their problems

A feature of this book is that suicidal behaviour is considered in a number of differing contexts to gain an eco-systemic understanding. The previous settings have ranged from the naturalistic (letters and conversations with persons) to the formalised (questionnaires and hospital interviews). The following chapters will investigate how those previous understandings appear when families talk about their problems in therapy.

In the last chapter an attempt is made to describe suicidal behaviour as a strategic move to maintain the viability of a family within an eco-systemic context. The features of the systemic context of suicidal behaviour appear to be: (a) an escalation of familial problems, represented by more than one family member, within a context of family change, (b) overt expressions of hostility, conflict and an immediate threat to the disruption of the viability of the system (divorce, separation, death or leaving home), (c) the presence of a negative connotation within a wider systemic context, by a treatment or support agency with ascriptions of further deviancy or illegitimacy and (d) any attempts at problem resolution by the individual or the family become seen as further evidence of deviance or pathology.

In this chapter I will investigate families further in the way in which they talk about distress.

The procedure for studying the families

Families were videotaped in a family therapy clinic. The first interview was generally concerned with gaining a systemic understanding of the problem being presented along the lines we have seen in the previous chapter – who was involved in the systemic management of the problem, what previous solutions had been attempted to resolve the problem and what therapeutic goals could be negotiated.

Family problems

The general orientation of family therapy has been to understand how problems are handled in the family. This fits in with the previous chapters that consider suicidal behaviour in inter-personal contexts. What differs in this chapter is that the data is gathered by directly observing the families in interaction. The family is observed in the presence of a family therapist and with the general orientation of therapy. It must continually be borne in mind that the family will be presenting information that is biased towards their problem and to their perception of therapy and treatment. Further to this, most families, prior to such an interview, are seen by a general medical practitioner, a psychiatrist and sometimes a social worker. This consultation for family therapy must be considered as part of a cycle of attempted problem resolution (or maintenance), as we saw in Figure 9.2 (p.177).

Problems as presented

In keeping with the previous data in this study, the families were assessed in the priority they gave to their problems and how these problems were voiced (see Table 10.1). The principal problem presented was that of behavioural psychological problems. The second group of referring problems were those concerning marital problems. Not surprisingly, within the context of a psychiatric day-hospital, psychological problems are prominent.

The presence of marital problems may be an artefact of the referral process. Those patients seeing the consultant psychiatrist and his assistant were generally referred to the family therapy clinic if a persistent marital problem was expressed. Two patients were referred with primarily physical symptoms. None of the categories are discrete in relation to the others. Rather, the categories reflect the way the family presented the problem. Thus the problem may have been presented as depression but this could be in the presence of a marital conflict. Two patients are included who had had problems with the law.

Table 10.1 The presentation of problems and the presence
of suicidal behaviour in the families

	Suicide attempt	Threatened attempt patient or family	Previous attempt in	Not discovered	n
Overt marital/ relational conflict	3	1	–	–	4
Psychological 7 behavioural problems	3	3	1	5	12
Physical symptoms	1	1	–	–	2
Problem with law	–	–	1	1	2
Total	7	5	2	6	20

Studying activity; the context of suicidal behaviour

In this section I will describe families with an adolescent who has attempted suicide or who has threatened suicide or where another family member has engaged in suicidal behaviour in the past or where no suicidal behaviour is known.

Chapter Eleven describes families where psychological problems are presented and where a suicide attempt has taken place or suicide is threatened or no known suicide has occurred. Relationships are presented where relational/marital conflict is evident and presented as the problem after a suicide attempt and after a threat of suicide.

The comparison between the groups gives an indication of possible processes whereby threats are converted into actual behaviour or to avert certain situations. What I will present is a series of extracts from family stories as narrated by the various family members.

Families with an adolescent patient

The Brighams: after an episode of attempted suicide
THE PROBLEM AS PRESENTED
This family is composed of a father, mother, a 17-year-old son (the identified patient), an elder daughter aged nineteen and a younger daughter aged ten. On being asked what the problem is the following events ensue:

Father: Well what brings us here now is that Peter a few months ago, er, which was, it's hard to say what it was brought on by, it was a lot of different problems, I think with Peter and his mummy were keyed up with Christmas coming round and things in general, we don't really know, what actually brought it on, it was just one of those things that, I think Peter was trying to feel his feet a bit, and we was trying to bring him down to understanding there is things he can and he can't bring do, and he was rebelling against it, and I think that's the reason we are here now, it came out of the circumstances that occurred.

From a family life cycle perspective, Peter, at the age of seventeen, is making a bid to become independent. His parents, however, are anxious to impress upon him that he is still part of the family and conspire to 'bring him down'. This introduces the boundary consideration in this family of 'in the family: out of the family'. A bid for independence is a potential area of conflict for Peter and his parents. His father refers to Peter's mother as his 'mummy'. His mother refers to his father as 'daddy'. Peter's mother takes over the narrative from her husband and elaborates the reason for the overdose.

Mother: Peter and I don't get on too bad, we do have our disagreements, because I was nagging him, and I knew this is true because he won't keep his room as clean as I'd like him to, he has a problem of wetting the bed still. I got to the point at Christmas where I couldn't stand it anymore, and if he was going to continue on the way he was continuing then it would be better if he moved out. I was very hateful to him, I must admit that. I think I've hurt him a lot by the things I've said, but daddy said he would take him over and I'll win his confidence and trust and he'll be alright, and, but, I know that, I know Peter very well, I found wet sheets hidden in his bedroom, and I took them because I've said he's deceiving you as he deceived me...

I think both of us were fed up with him, and I think he got so depressed, I think that he's depressed, I

> think that he's a child that he doesn't ever tell us
> what he's doing at work or things like that, we have
> got to drag it out of him, it's not so obvious with
> girls

Following on from the father's contextualising of the problem in terms of dependence / independence, the mother elaborates the parental construing of the problem further. Although both parents locate the problem within an inter-relational context, the specification of the problem revolves around the personal characteristics of Peter, who is seen as dirty, deceitful, depressed, wet 'boy' and still a child. His mother admits being hateful to him.

A difficulty faced by this family is that a move from being a wet child on the part of Peter will mean becoming a dry adult. The attainment of a dry adult status would promote an opportunity for Peter's independence and, as the parents say in the father's narrative, the gaining of independent stature for Peter is problematical for them. This is the first inkling that what appears to be problematical or dysfunctional behaviour, bed-wetting, at one level of understanding, becomes a means of maintaining *status quo* in a family and, at another level, of systemic organisation. It is also interesting to note that Peter's father is brought in to handle the problem when it appears to be worsening and the relationship between Peter and his mother becomes one of conflict.

PETER'S VIEW OF THE PROBLEM
When Peter is asked how he sees the problem, he locates the problem within the relationship between himself and his mother.

> Peter: Well, it seems like it was getting to the stage where
>   whatever I did it was wrong, that's what it seemed
>   to be, things gradually seemed to be getting worse
>   during the last three, four months worse and
>   worse… If I tried to do something right, say
>   unload the shopping and pack the stuff away
>   without being asked to do it, I'd put it in the wrong
>   place and everything what I did wrong.

From Peter's perspective any attempt to conform or help becomes construed as further evidence of deviant behaviour. Instead of being wrong some of the time, he occupies a worsening position of being wrong all of the time.

BED-WETTING

During the interview the continued bed-wetting of Peter is returned to time and time again and becomes the focal point of the family's explanation.

Mother:	I found that with the bed-wetting after he took that overdose, he went almost a month, the shock of him doing that has made him see he's got to improve. I know that if he wants to be dry he can be dry…constant wetting of the beds, I think was the problem more than anything else.
Therapist:	So that it's been a problem for quite a long time?
Mother:	Since the day he was born. Peter's never been dry.

This appears to be a conspicuous example of how a current, although persistent problem, is traced back to origins in the past, which are quite ambiguous yet are currently given a negative connotation. It might be reasonably inferred that a dry child, when first born, would be considered rather more of a problem. However, the seeming illogicality of the above passage begins to make sense when the parents are asked about their own history of bed-wetting and the toilet training of their other children.

THE FAMILY CONTEXT; THE DAUGHTERS

Diane, the 10-year-old, is rarely mentioned in the family discussion but Jane, who is nineteen, is brought into the discussion by the therapist. The parents are not too keen on this and indicate that they do not want her brought in as she would take sides and that would provoke a family argument which they, the parents, wish to avoid. Jane is, significantly, engaged to be married and about to leave home within the next few months. This leaving places a contextual frame around Peter's behaviour and his strivings for independence. Far from his behaviour being wholly negative, she distracts his parents from a preoccupation with the loss of a daughter and the disintegration of the family and he engages his father into the fold of the family in an active way and reassures the family that, at a time of change, some things will remain the same. A father is still needed in this family. The intractability of his bed-wetting is a necessary means of maintaining family stability. However, in terms of maintaining the coherence of Peter's personal development, bed-wetting is problematical. This is what I mean by a behaviour having differing functions at differing levels of understanding. For Peter, at the personal level, wetting the bed is uncomfortable and doesn't allow him to develop and is negative. However, at the family level, the behaviour functions to deflect distress from the imminent loss of the eldest daughter and is positive. At a cultural level, the suicidal behaviour and bed-wetting appear to be deviant and is negative.

Father:	This is where conflict can come, the wife being overloaded with work, extra washing and all this to do, especially in the winter when you can't dry the washing... Peter feels down because he's done it, you know its one of them things, his attitude of mind, or it was before, I think its improving now he's realising that there is a family to help him.

This attitude of mind is described earlier as wanting to be independent and is described in other passages as being 'private', 'withdrawn', 'out of the family', 'not sharing his troubles' and is equated with defiance.

When the therapist goes on to ask the parents about their daughters the following dialogue ensues.

Mother:	Jane and Peter are close together, there's twenty months between them...when Peter was born and Jane was twenty months old she was dry, day and night, no problem, a perfect child.
Peter:	She isn't (perfect) now!
Mother:	...and Jane's never had a problem that way. I think she was dry in the daytime by the time she was a year, and she was dry at night.
Diane:	I had a little bit.
Mother:	That's only when you were poorly. You got out of bed at the time.
Father:	You had a temperature.
Mother:	You've had a temperature, but you've never wet the bed since you were about fourteen months old.
Therapist:	Could you tell me just a little bit more about... How did you do it, was it straight from nappies?
Mother:	Jane used to be potted regular and she just came to it naturally, and I thought I'd try the same with Peter, but Peter was totally different...even with a wet bed he's happy to stay in it, but the girls if they had a wet nappy and that they used to tell me, they never used to like it, so they were different.

The examples show how Peter is compared to his sisters. His closest sibling is seen as a perfect, dry, natural girl while he becomes perceived as a wet, unnatural different boy. The natural lapses of his sister are seen as legitimate examples of bed-wetting caused by fever.

Throughout his life, Peter had been treated by a number of specialist consultants, both physical and psychological, for his enuresis. However, by not responding to treatment, Peter was seen not as legitimately sick but illegitimately deviant and responsible for his own actions. The issue of illegitimate behaviour and his personal responsibility for bed-wetting is also located within a familial matrix of construing.

THE PARENT'S PERSPECTIVE

To discover the family context of bed-wetting, the therapist asks both parents for their history of bed-wetting.

> Mother: I'm from a bad home, and I wet the bed right up
>   until I was about eleven and then I was taken in by
>   my brother…and looked after me and I knew from
>   that day that I went there I had to stop, and I did, I
>   didn't wet at all when I went to live with him, but
>   up to that point I did.

The mother, who had a bad home, wet the bed as a child but after leaving her bad home was able, in different circumstances and by the exercise of willpower, to stop. This passage gives a clue to the mother's perspective of Peter's bed-wetting. His bed-wetting is seen as a reflection on the home circumstances and as a lack of willpower. Leaving home and becoming dry are further emphasised in this passage, with staying home and being wet as the necessary opposites. Once more, as long as Peter remains wet, he remains dependent within the family fold. But bed-wetting is still about a bad home! And becoming dry is about leaving home. Peter's father also had a problem with bed-wetting:

> Father: I had a problem for a few years. When it was I
>   couldn't tell you.

Peter's mother can, however.

> Mother: With Roy, his mum said he was dry until his dad came out
>   of the Army. He never saw his dad very much and
>   he never got on and she thinks that's why he
>   started wetting the bed for a little while because of
>   it, it was the worry of having his father around.

Peter's father is not nearly as concerned with the details of the bed-wetting throughout the interview but concerned with avoiding conflict and keeping the peace. Thus when Peter and his mother argue to such a level that their distress escalates, Peter's father is called in to stabilise the situation.

Peter's mother, as monitor of the family construing about bed-wetting, elaborates bed-wetting as being related to parental influence and the presence of a father figure. Continued bed-wetting, in this family, is taken as an implicit criticism of the parental relationship. The only way to dispel such an implied criticism is to demand evidence of personal deviance. Either Peter is sick or the family is bad. Peter's parents had taken him through the endless round of child and adolescent specialist agencies to maintain this personal validation of his deviance. By taking an overdose, Peter tries to locate the individual nature of his symptoms within the causal context of family relationships, despite the maternal effort to propose a litany of his personal faults. These difficulties occur at a time of family change, when the parenting abilities are being questioned and when presence or absence is raising its head. The oldest daughter is preparing to leave.

DEFIANCE

One further episode highlights the construing of Peter's behaviour within the family context. After his mother describes her constant nagging him to wash himself and clean his teeth, and how she may have pushed him too far, she also says that a further reason was '...because we gave him a time to be in and he just defied me on that, and that upset me.'

THE FAMILY CONSTRUCTS

From the family discussion, a number of constructs emerge which are used repeatedly to describe the children and the parents. These are listed in Table 10.2.

The poles of the constructs on the left hand side of Table 10.2 all become subsumed in relation to Peter. The ascription of dependency begins to work at two different levels. Peter's dependence is promoted by his being wet, his independence would bring all the positively connoted poles of the family construing. Yet his search for privacy is seen not as independence but as 'not being with the family'. At the same time, there is an evident expectation of children to grow up and leave home, as long as they stay with the family. Peter is only twenty months younger than Jane who is leaving. The conflict would appear to be located somewhere in the family relationship where Peter's behaviour serves a function.

Table 10.2 The Brigham family constructs

illegitimate	:	legitimate
wrong	:	right
defiant	:	conforming
dirty	:	clean
child	:	adult, or grown-up
unnatural	:	natural
Peter	:	others
no willpower	:	willpower
withdrawn, private or detached	:	with the family
remaining dependent	:	becoming independent

The key to the necessary dependence of Peter upon his family lies in the oblique reference to the home situation and the implication of parental distance in his father's family of origin. Peter's father only becomes actively engaged in the family when Peter's relationship with Peter's mother gives cause for concern. Then the father is actively engaged with the mother to maintain a position of authority in the family hierarchy and to implement disciplinary procedures.

FAMILY RULES

From the descriptions and the elicitation of constructs, a number of rules can be inferred about how certain acts are construed (see Figure 10.1). In the context of this family, and their expectations of their children, bed-wetting is seen as defiant and unnatural, a deviation from an expected norm. The presence of a dry bed is seen as an example of conformity that is natural and evidence of having a perfect child.

Within the further historical context of the family, bed-wetting as a behaviour becomes elaborated as an example of a 'bad home' and 'poor parenting'. However, such poor parenting can be overcome by willpower and effort by the individual. This effectively displaces any direct implication of poor parenting on behalf of the parents that Peter's bed-wetting makes.

'EVERYTHING I DO IS WRONG'

Peter remarks that everything he does is wrong and further evidence of his deviance. This is acknowledged by his parents, particularly his mother, after the event. Prior to an episode of suicidal behaviour, everything that this young man tries to do is negatively connoted by his family. His staying out late is seen as unacceptable and a further example of the defiance shown by his intransigent bed-wetting. Even when he goes to his room to withdraw

expected child behaviour

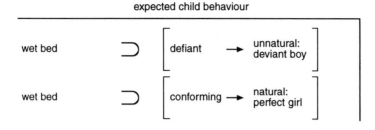

remembered family history

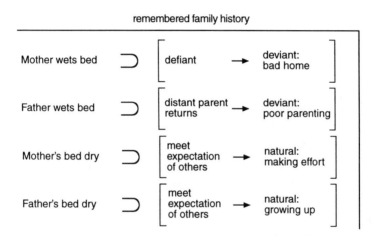

Figure 10.1 Constitutive rules relating to how bed-wetting is construed

from the arguments he is described as deviant in not wanting to be with the family. His attempts to help with the shopping are seen as wrong too.

All aspects of Peter's adolescent behaviour within the family context become framed negatively (see Figure 10.2).

This perception of an escalating number of unacceptable acts is regulated by appropriate sanctions and expectations on the parts of Peter and his parents. It must be stressed that Peter is not a hapless victim in this situation but participant in an interactional situation that will be revealed later.

The regulation of Peter's enuretic behaviour had a history of early physical treatments that were replaced by psychological and psychiatric

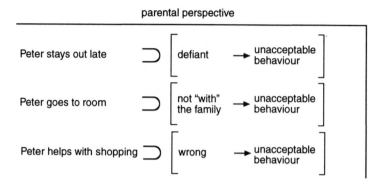

Figure 10.2 Parental constitutive rules regarding Peter's defiance

treatments. His parents steadfastly maintained that Peter must conform, and if he did not conform then he must have an individual problem. This was necessary to state as the alternative construing was that his problem was a reflection of a 'bad home'. When Peter's bed-wetting did not respond to any treatment, and he became defiant, it was necessary to 'bring him down'. The technique of bringing him down is then extended to a number of other unacceptable behaviours. However, it becomes important for Peter's mother that when she implements a strategy to 'bring Peter down', he does 'become down' and express the necessary contrition. If, instead, he argues back, this is seen as further evidence of defiance, necessitating a further strategy to bring him down (see Figure 10.3). To do this his mother brings in his father. Both parents become united in their efforts to impress upon their son the necessity to conform for the sake of family unity. The unfortunate corollary of these behaviours is that any dissent by Peter, albeit to express his own needs, is seen by his parents as unacceptable and defiant. To escape this field of an almost total negative frame he overdoses and temporarily opens up the arena of life and death issues. Being consistently brought down might be seen as a recipe for depression.

A DOUBLE BIND
Impressing on Peter that he must conform to parental wishes poses a double bind. On the one hand he is being told to grow up and become an adult and on the other, when he engages in those stages of growing up, he is brought

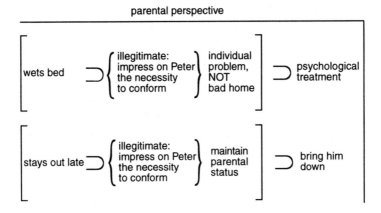

Figure 10.3 Parental regulative rules regarding Peter's defiance

down. Although required to be independent, he is told that he is incapable of rendering himself independent. Continuing dependence becomes his responsibility, his independence becomes a parental responsibility.

In controlling Peter's behaviour, rules can be inferred that give pointers to the regulation of the inter-personal distance between Peter's parents. The situation changes. Peter and his mother are actively engaged in conflict and Peter's father is peripheral. Peter's father then engages with Peter's mother and allows Peter to withdraw. In a system where a hierarchy is confused (see Chapter Eight), acting out behaviour will stabilise and temporarily reconcile such confusion. Peter and his mother arguing together engage his father in family affairs. Furthermore, this also occurs at a time when the eldest daughter is about to get married and the family will be disrupted. Peter maintains not only the involvement of his father but regulates the mainte-nance of the *status quo*. Peter's overdose may be seen as both a 'strategy of restoration' (keeping the family the same at a time of change) and as a 'strategy of promotion' (promoting new patterns of behaviour to allow him to grow up). This highlights the very duality of change and persistence, of restoration and promotion, and suggests attempted suicide is a bid to maintain systemic coherence at a time when a family is faced with a structural change.

THE CIRCULARITY OF INTERACTION

The first stage presented here is a punctuation of the circular causal train within the Brigham family (see Figures 10.4a and 10.5a). In figures 10. 4b and 10.5b, the regulative rules inferred for each stage are presented. For each stage in the circularity of interaction, the rules are presented from the parental perspective (Figure 10.4b) and from Peter's perspective (Figure 10.5b). Note that the stages are identical but the perceptions differ. These differences are united by the construing of legitimacy. Although Peter and his parents are seemingly poles apart, they are united in the commonality of the constructs being used.

This basic circularity is amplified in the situation leading to the overdose. However, the overdose meant that Peter's father stayed on to scrutinise Peter, leaving his mother free to withdraw and manage Jane's departure. This effectively maintains Peter's independence. Peter is not a hapless victim. The issue of dependence and independence is regulated between members of the

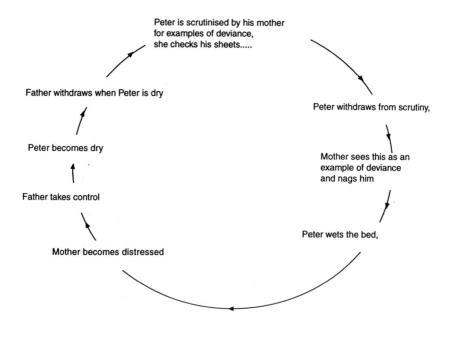

Figure 10.4a A cycle of interaction regarding Peter's bed-wetting

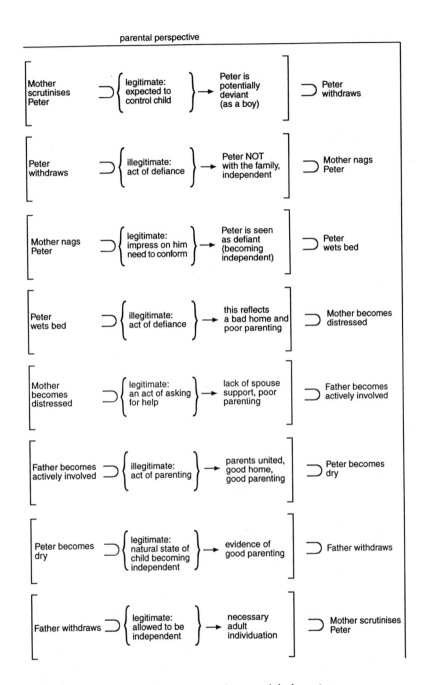

Figure 10.4b Parental regulative rules regarding Peter's bed-wetting

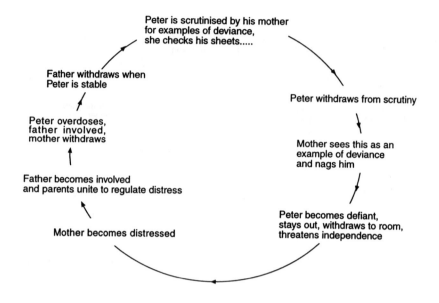

Figure 10.5a A family cycle of distress management

family. Peter can be seen as promoting his own dependence by overdosing and involving his father. A dangerous tactic for the son.

CONCLUSION

The homoeostatic cycle revolving around Peter's dependence regulates the distance between Peter and his parents and keeps Peter's father actively involved in the family (Figure 10.5a). This cycle maintains and regulates dependence and independence, marital distance and the family boundary. However, no human system is isolated or exempt from change whether they are life cycle changes or societal expectations.

In the Brigham family, suicidal behaviour is an attempt to manage change. The resolution uses the behaviours, construings and rules already present within the family repertoire. Here suicidal behaviour is a metaphorical communication about a system threatened with loss of viability. Within the family the core constructs of legitimacy, gender, dependency, boundary and

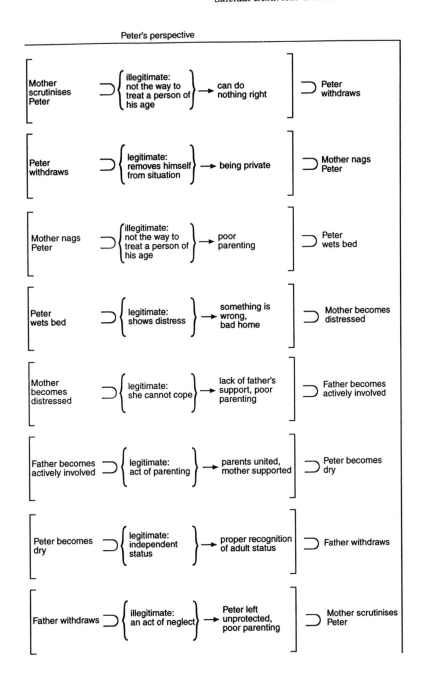

Figure 10.5b Regulative rules in a family cycle of distress management

distance are negotiated by one member adopting a 'sick role'. Peter could not amplify bed-wetting to any greater degree and accommodated the family by proposing further acts which could be termed deviant. In the face of a threat to his personal integrity, a total negative construing of him by his parents, he engages in suicidal behaviour (see Figure 10.4a). For a while this functions to placate the problem within the contextual understanding of his parents that it is something to do with the way they treat each other. By relocating the source of distress from a personal perspective to an interactive perspective, Peter is allowed some opportunity to change. In a family context, distress is presented physically. Someone wets the bed. When this no longer works, and the distress escalates, another form of physical presentation is made. This time as deliberate self-harm. The representation of distress presentation in this family is physical. The danger is that the extreme of this physicality is death.

For a while, during therapy, his bed-wetting ceases. A confirmation of the hypothesis of parental involvement is that when Peter's father begins to withdraw from an involvement with Peter, his bed-wetting begins again.

The Greens; a threat of suicidal behaviour

This family were referred for treatment by their general practitioner because their daughter, Elizabeth, had steadily lost weight and her periods had ceased. Officially described as suffering from anorexia nervosa, Elizabeth attended with her parents for family treatment. The interview below presents the parents together in the absence of Elizabeth and gives their perspective on the problem. The incident is raised because the parents believe that Elizabeth may become suicidal. A further reason for presenting this family is that the behaviour of self-starvation can be regarded as belonging to a class of deliberately self-harming behaviours. In Chapter Seven the issue is raised of self-starvation being a political act to gain status concessions. Like self-starvation, suicidal behaviour, or its threat, is a matter of regulating relationships. In addition, the threat of suicidal behaviour, even as a hint, is an important marker for indicating crisis treatment.

The parents are asked in the family therapy session about typical times where their daughter poses a problem for them. Like the Brighams before, the central construct of this family is that of dependence and independence. Everything that Elizabeth does is construed as illegitimate in the way that Peter's behaviour had been construed previously. However, Elizabeth is only 13 years old when first referred to the clinic. There are no siblings and no one is about to leave the family. An important transition is her father's intrusion into the home environment when he is made redundant from work.

The parents also see the transition of Elizabeth from primary to secondary school as an important landmark in what they refer to as 'her career as a juvenile delinquent'.

By the time this interview takes place Elizabeth's weight is not seen as the paramount problem. Her behaviour in terms of being amenable to parental control is an important issue.

LEAVING THE CHOIR
Elizabeth is described by her parents as being 'moody'. Evidence of such moodiness is given by them to illustrate the events surrounding Elizabeth leaving the church choir. Leaving the choir is a decision with which the parents do not agree.

Mother:	And she said: 'I told her I'm not going to choir any more'. I said: 'Did you tell her why?' She said: 'Yes, due to circumstances'. I think that was the wording (looks at husband).
Father:	Mm...
Mother:	So I said: 'Oh, I think you're being silly, that you'll miss going and other things will be involved, it makes things very awkward for your mum and dad. Still, you've done it now'. So we didn't say no more, Did we? (to husband), and then she cried the whole afternoon. We thought she was doing her homework, we went upstairs with a cup of tea about four o'clock and there she was crying her eyes out, so I think she really regretted doing it. Well, that was that, that got over that bit.

In this episode Elizabeth decides independently to leave the choir. She tells her parents of her decision. This decision is seen as both 'silly' and 'awkward'. There is an acceptance of the inevitability of such a decision and the parents appear to be satisfied by Elizabeth's crying as an act of contrition for taking such a pre-emptive decision. A move for independence, then, (by Elizabeth) within a system, also proposes a counter definition by others (the parents) to promote and reassure dependence at the same time (see Figure 10.6). Sluzki and Veron (1971) suggest that this is a statement by parents to a child of 'be independent, although you are incapable of it'. We saw the same process in the Brighams earlier. For both families there is a repetitive cycle of continuing physical symptoms and a negotiation of dependence/ independence. Any moves for elaborating either pole of the dependency

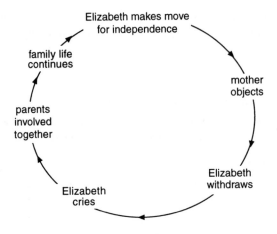

Figure 10.6 A cycle of independence, withdrawal and involvement

construct invoke a counter move. Elizabeth proposes independence but only to a level which is safe. She then proposes dependence.

As with Peter in the last example, this is not a one-sided negotiation or the victimising of an adolescent. Elizabeth is proposing not only a change for herself as a girl growing up to be a woman but a change for her parents in their development. This growth means their accommodating each other within their marriage, ready to spend a life together with an independent daughter. The issue of dependency is raised systemically. It is not necessarily a question of dependence or independence but the regulation of maintaining dependency and becoming independent.

A pattern begins to emerge where Elizabeth proposes independence and withdraws from her family but somehow manages to maintain her dependence and involve both her parents in caring for her (see Figure 10.6). Although the mother takes Elizabeth her tea, she refers to the 'we' of both her and her husband.

Although the construct of dependence/independence is used here, it is important to point out that it is my description. The constructs used by the parents in this situation are concerned with specific behaviours. These constructs are shown in Table 10.3.

Table 10.3 The Green family constructs

Elizabeth	:	us
disturb others	:	not disturb others
silly	:	sensible
awkward	:	conforming, easy to get on with

The implications in this episode are that, left to her own devices, Elizabeth will get into a terrible state but with her mother's help she will become trouble-free and normal. This leaves out the vital position of the father. It is he who is involved when Elizabeth gets into trouble and he who unites with his wife to sort out their daughters' problems (see Figure 10.7a). This parental unity, while seemingly proposed by Elizabeth, has other implications when proposed by the parents to Elizabeth, as will be shown below. Elizabeth's behaviour is a systemic move in the regulation of inter-personal distance between herself and her parents and between the parents (see Figure 10.7b).

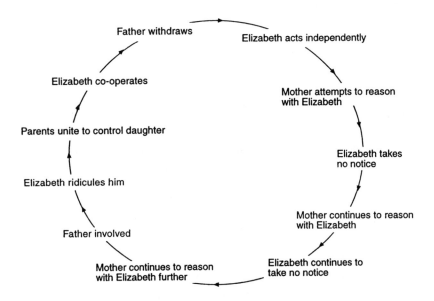

Figure 10.7a A family cycle to maintain coherence

parental view of Elizabeth

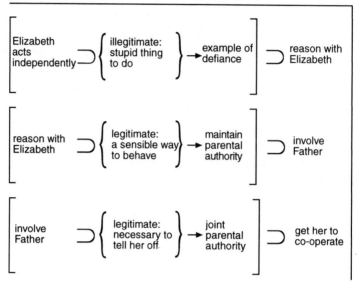

Figure 10.7b Regulative rules in a cycle to maintain coherence

GROWING UP

Elizabeth is growing up and making some moves to develop her own autonomy. Her father is redundant from his job and closer to home. This change is accommodated gradually as it offers a necessary personal negotiation between all family members. At the same time, Elizabeth's father is having problems with his eyes and eventually has a cataract removed. His loss of a job and health mean that he has little opportunity to exert any personal control and expertise in his own life. Furthermore, he has to spend long periods at home. A consequence of this is that all three become enmeshed in each other's lives. Elizabeth's father has to fit in with Elizabeth's mother at home.

Elizabeth's behaviour, like Peter's before, brings about a parental unity. For a while this temporary parental unity invades all regulation of Elizabeth's life. During the process of therapy the parents are encouraged to find areas of unity in promoting their daughter's welfare. Their unity becomes a by-product of their marital autonomy rather than a response to Elizabeth's provocation. This leaves Elizabeth free to develop, her symptoms disappear and she regains her periods. Elizabeth stopped attending the family therapy sessions. She said quite openly that her parents had the problem not her. Her parents continued to attend and concentrated on negotiating a common policy of handling their daughter. The focus of the therapy became the husband's redundancy, his declining health and what he did around the house.

It was the parents who had escalated the problems in that they were concerned about possible suicidal behaviour on the part of their daughter. For me, the interesting part if this narrative is that within the culture there is an expectation that escalating distress in adolescents can result in suicidal behaviour. Elizabeth's problems of dieting and exercise did eventually gain concessions and, in the politics of the family, those concessions were negotiated in therapy. Yet, the distress was located elsewhere. In this family, no one was leaving, the change that had to be accommodated was that the father needed to be more involved and that the parents must change their relationship.

The Jones: where another family member has engaged in suicidal behaviour in the past.

The Jones family were videotaped originally because they mentioned a previous history of attempted suicide and because Pam, the identified patient in the sequences below, was currently feeling suicidal. This had been a primary factor in her referral to the family therapy clinic. During this time I saw the family in the context of the general medical hospital after their adolescent daughter Maria (aged 17 years) had taken an overdose. The episode gave one of the few opportunities to view current family interaction before a suicidal episode.

The basic family unit consists of Maria (17 years old) and Evelyn (9 and a half years old) who are daughters of Mark and Pam. When they attend for therapy the couple bring along Pam's mother, who is a regular visitor to the house.

Therapist:	I'd like you to tell me what your problem is, why you are here.
Pam:	Well, because I'm very very depressed.
Therapist:	How do you know you are depressed?
Pam:	By the way I'm crying all the time. Well, I can't look after my family properly.
Therapist:	And how do you see this Mark?

Mark:	Well, it's a recurring thing, I've got used to it now, I just get uptight about it 'cos for years, since the last baby really, for the past nine years.
Therapist:	You were depressed after the last baby was born...
Pam:	Yes.
Therapist:	...and you've been depressed ever since?
Pam:	No, for about three years.
Mark:	This has been a long spell really. I don't get any reason for her in her environment. I used to think it was me, that we had a problem, in the end it turned out to be her problem, because it caused the problem. I got very uptight, and in fact I had a breakdown over it three years ago, but now I know it's not us and I think there's another reason for it. I'm not sure what it is.

Pam's problem is located within her as an unreasonable depression that is worsening and interfering with her ability to look after the house (see Figure 10.8a). As Pam says, the depression began about three years ago at the time when Mark had his nervous breakdown. Mark used to believe that it was a marital problem. Now he believes it is her problem but is not able to give a reason for Pam's depression. Whatever it is, he maintains, it is not their marriage.

We see here a similar pattern as before. An escalation of relational distress that becomes personified.

IT'S NOT A PROBLEM

When asked how the depression is a problem for Mark, he says it is not a problem at the moment.

Mark:	It's not a problem at the (pause) no problem.
Therapist:	So, who is it a problem for?
Mark:	(points to wife) Her problem.
Pam:	Yes, but Mark could get a problem if it went on much longer.
Mark:	No, no, not unless you get... I'm a lot easier going than I was. I haven't said anything to you about it, I haven't pressurised you into...

Pam:*(to therapist)* He has.

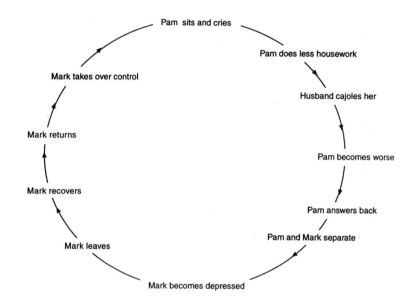

Figure 10.8a A cycle of interaction between Mark and Pam

The threat of an escalation in the symptoms is ever present. If Pam gets worse, Mark could be in for a hard time. If Mark pressurises his wife to conform, she will get worse. The politics of symptoms within the marriage are slowly revealed (see Figure 10.8b).

Therapist: So, no matter how depressed Pam gets you are going to be OK about her?

Mark: Yes, that's the only way to be. I've accepted the way that she is. We've got back together, we've... I love her and, I mean we, this is not good now. Whatever happens, a lot of things have happened in the past, if I was going to I'd be gone, we would have split, we even sort of separated for a year but we've got that together and there's no way we are going to

Mark's construing of Pam's problem

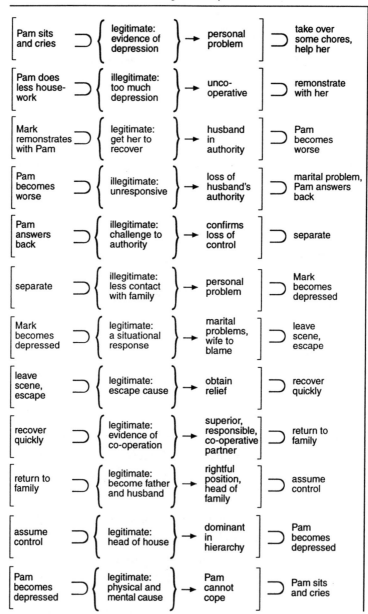

Figure 10.8b Regulative rules in a cycle of interaction between Mark and Pam

split. So you've just got to accept that, I've accepted what she is, and she's going to get over it.

Mark accepts Pam as 'depressed'. In a way it keeps him in a position of dominance. However, this position is precarious, for Pam can (as she threatens) become 'very very depressed'. This switches the hierarchy whereby should Pam become 'very very depressed' and less able to cope, this will have ramifications for Mark's mental health and the marriage (see Figure 10.8a). Furthermore, when things get really difficult, Pam's mother intervenes (see Figure 10.9a). This serves further to invalidate Pam in what she does (Figure 10.9b).

As was demonstrated in Chapter Five, family systems can accommodate a strategy of distress management within a repertoire of manoeuvres which calibrates the system to live at a continued raised level of distress (see Figures 5.4, p.85 and 9.2, p.177).

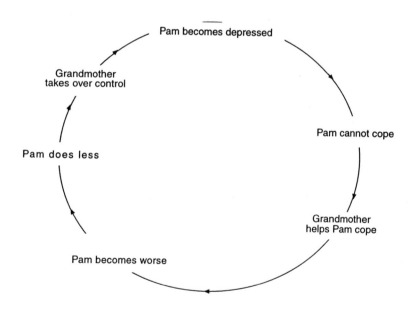

Figure 10.9a A cycle of coping interaction between Grandmother and Pam

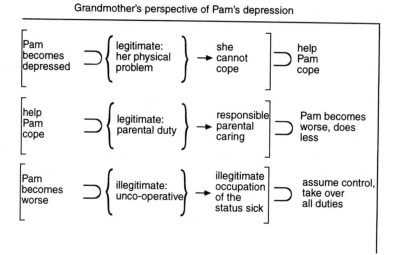

Grandmother's perspective of Pam's depression

Figure 10.9b Regulative rules in a cycle of coping interaction

For some families, the strategy of distress management, in this family 'depression', becomes an event in itself to be managed. However, the use of depressive symptomatology appears to be an ever present element in the pattern of marital conflict. Depression is also used as a means of regulating the marital distance. When Mark and Pam separate, he becomes depressed; as they become closer, she becomes depressed. Depression becomes an ever present entity that only becomes problematical when used politically to bring about a change in the hierarchy. Pam can threaten to control by becoming 'more depressed' or 'more demanding', whereupon Mark becomes depressed. Unfortunately, this inter-personal balance of power has to be exhibited materially and this is in the form of her continuing distress.

The couple stay together by her having a problem. To stay together and avoid him having a problem, Mark has to be less domineering. The danger of escalating depression is that culturally it brings the sufferer into the realm of suicidal behaviour, as one of the available behaviours from a repertoire of intense distress. As with Peter's bed-wetting, once the symptoms are intensified they threaten a threshold of distress that, once transgressed, threatens the viability of that persons existence. Suicidal behaviour is expressive of a life-threatening situation where distress has escalated to the extreme.

MARIA

Maria was seen in hospital after taking an overdose. She had argued with her mother on the morning of the overdose. Maria said she took the tablets to show her mother she was sorry for upsetting her. When asked what the problem was, Pam said that it was life with Maria. Mark said it was Pam's illness that was the problem but he thought that if Maria was 'out of the way', relationships would improve. Mark had tried to do everything for Maria. He had done all he could for her but nothing he did worked. However, he was not surprised as she was like him – 'wild'.

In the family interview a picture emerges that elaborates this perspective of who has the problem.

Therapist:	Can you tell me about the problems with Maria?
Pam:	Well she's 16 and a half, which I accept is a difficult age anyway, she's been very cheeky and she seems to take things out on me.
Therapist:	And how does she take things out on you?
Pam:	By being very cheeky to me, shouting and going upstairs slamming the door, and that.

Pam describes the problem with Maria but accepts such a problem as age-appropriate and intimates that Maria is taking something out on her. Mark, the husband and father, is far more explicit about the problem (see Figure 10.10).

Mark:	It's a sore point with me, Maria, at the moment, she's a pain, God.
Therapist:	So how do you react when Maria behaves like this to her mummy?
Mark:	She doesn't do it very often when I'm there because when I'm there she doesn't do it. You know, she doesn't do it with me because she knows I'd jump down on her straight away. I've nearly sent her to (pause) a few times, it nearly always ends in a big row, you just can't tell her she's like it, you know, it ends up in one big screaming match.
Therapist:	So you come down on her?
Mark:	The thing that annoys me most is that she won't do anything properly, no matter what it is, you name it

> she doesn't do it properly…everything she does, it
> can get you down…it doesn't matter what it is…

Pam: She's going through a very lazy stage at home.

A similar pattern of escalating negative connotation of all behaviour by the parents of the adolescent family member, as seen with Peter and Elizabeth, is reflected here. Everything Maria does is seen as not being done properly (see Figure 10.10). Ironically, this is the same veiled criticism of Maria which is made by Mark, that she is not doing the housework properly. Pam is also not disciplining their daughter properly. Whereas before he argued with Pam, which led to separation and his potential distress, now the marital conflict is detoured by Maria. Maria becomes subject to Mark's wrath and responds with overt and open conflict. When pushed to an extreme, she overdoses. This message of a threat to the 'life' of the family temporarily brings about a cessation of hostilities.

Within the tradition of this family, and from its repertoire of strategies for the management of distress, depression is a legitimate means of coping and a means of promoting unity, help and caring. But depression has a range of convenience. Its parameters are calibrated, there can be too much depression at one pole and not enough depression at the other pole. Either pole leads to conflict and challenge to the family hierarchy. The only way that Pam can be kept in her place is by maintaining a family pattern where her depression does not exceed the polar thresholds of depression. These poles, however, are not fixed and are negotiated when they are approached. This negotiation is promoted by the natural life cycle and developmental changes necessary within the family as the children grow up.

GROWING UP

The Jones family is faced with the transitional stage of a daughter growing up. Similarly, the parents are involved in negotiating their marital/parental relationships. Depression is used to accommodate change and maintain stability. Suicidal behaviour indicates a threat to the viability of the system. For the husband, he overdosed when divorce was imminent. For Maria, she overdosed when both parents were thinking that they would be better off without her.

At the same time, Maria's mother, Pam, is recovering from a period of depression and uniting with Maria's father, Mark. Suicidal behaviour is part of the family tradition. Change is accommodated by a family member becoming depressed but the adoption of the legitimate status of being 'sick' is questioned. What is important is that in this example Maria's behaviour

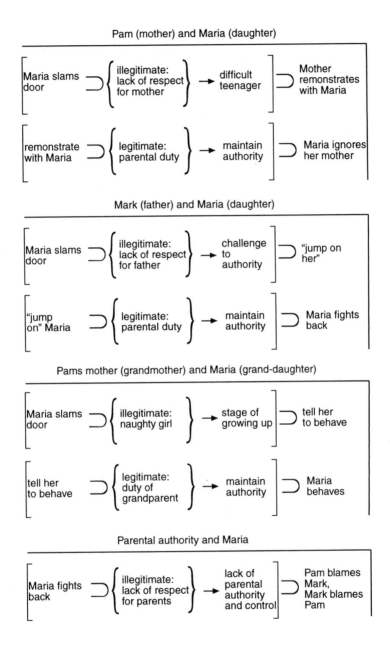

Figure 10.10 Comparative regulative rules for construing what happens when Maria slams the door

brings about the necessary parental distance. Whereas in the previous families adolescent behaviour had brought about family unity, here Maria is part of a pattern of relationships where the parents blame each other.

For all three examples the sick person becomes perceived as illegitimate in their occupation of that status. Although Maria was not perceived as 'sick', she was considered deviant and illegitimate in her demands. As an aside, part of growing up for adolescents appears to be that they storm out of the room, go upstairs and bang the door. In these families it is indicative of a problem, whereas most of us accept is as part and parcel of the stages of growing up. How we construe particular behaviours is important. They can be perceived of as normal, albeit naughty and as a subject for discussion, or they are evidence of a pathology.

The Grahams: where no suicidal behaviour is known

The parents of two teenage boys (aged 19 and 16) and a nine-year-old girl came to a clinic. The presenting problem is Mike, the 16-year-old son, who has just left school. Andrew, the elder son, has gained employment and is described as a 'lodger'. Although a problem in the past, Andrew has settled down and rarely comes into contact with his parents. Mike, however, is unemployed and hangs around at home. Amy, the nine-year-old, is the treasure of the family and different to her brothers.

Therapist:	And there's Amy, is that right? *(Both parents nod.)* She's nine and still at school. What's she like?
Husband:	Bright, isn't she. She is bright, you've only got to say it once and that's it. You just can't speak too highly of her, she's one apart.
Therapist:	Is she like her brothers?
Wife:	No…it was all the opposite, when you sort of went to school, their reports said they were glad to see the back of them you know (laughs).
Therapist:	So Andrew's got a job, Amy is doing well at school and Mike is trying hard!
Husband:	'Trying' is the word
Wife:	*(Laughs and nods.)*
Therapist:	So what's the problem?
Wife:	Well, it's difficult, I dunno what, just can't make him out…he'll sort of start talking and going on and

on, and I'll say 'Now look, would you talk properly please'. He'll say 'I'm talking properly' and I'll say 'I don't understand one word you are saying...'. When we ask him what he's talking about he'll just flare up and that's it, he won't say anymore.

Therapist: How does he manage to get himself understood?

Husband: He's not like it all the time.

Wife: Oh no.

Husband: Only when he gets excited over something.

Therapist: What sort of things would these be?

Husband: For instance, perhaps the prospect is he's got a job, anything out of the ordinary.

Therapist: So there would be the prospect of a job and he'd get really excited, and he'd try and tell you.

Husband and Wife: Yes, yes.

Therapist: And you'd say 'I can't hear a word you are saying'.

Husband and Wife: Yes, yes.

Therapist: And then what would he do?

Wife: He'd flare up and that would be it.

Husband: Or the other extreme, most probably he would overemphasise the slowness of his speech. He's taking the mickey out of us.

Amy is a bright obedient girl who is accepted at school. The boys, however, are challenging their parents and have to be nagged to conform. The presenting problem is that of both parents not being able to understand their son. When Mike becomes excited his speech becomes faster. His parents attempt to control him, he then alters his speech. This response on his part is regarded as excessively slow and insolent or he flares up. The issue appears to surround the issue of parental control of Mike, who is at an age where he is changing from a schoolboy dependent upon his parents to that of an independent man like his brother, Andrew. Andrew, who is now employed, is regarded as a 'lodger'. A critical point is that although Mike is problematical, he is 'not like it all the time'.

ANY OTHER PROBLEMS?

The issue of parental control is voiced in the following responses.

Therapist: Are there any other problems?

Husband: Well, behaviour in general. I've got very little control over him.

Therapist: What sort of things?

Husband: If I tell him to be quiet he'll make an excessive noise, or the other night I say 'Off to bed' and he slammed the front door and went off down the road, didn't he.

This issue is further elaborated when the father tells the son, Mike, what to do. Mike's response is to do the opposite, which promotes further confrontation. Mike walks off and this upsets Mike's mother too. The issue of control over acceptable levels of noise is negotiated between father and son (see Figure 10.11). When the argument escalates, the son threatens to leave, which will disrupt the family systems and this upsets his mother.

Figure 10.11 Withdrawal and involvement; a cycle of interaction in the Graham family

This whole argument appears to centre around achieving independence and making the transition from what is legitimate dependence as a child and legitimate independence as an adult.

When asked about how long the problem has been a problem, the parents place the problem within the context of a persistent problem.

Therapist:	How long has he been a problem then?
Wife:	Oh, years really, isn't it?
Husband:	Since he was a boy.
Wife:	We've always had it haven't we?
Therapist:	What, he's never co-operated?
Wife:	Well.
Husband:	Em, well, I don't think co-operate is the word but his behaviour pattern is a little different from what I remember other children have been through from that age.
Therapist:	He's been different from Andrew and Amy?

Wife and Husband: Yes *(nod)*.

Husband:	He's always been small and undersize, all kinds of silly things, like he'd never sleep in a cot, that was, he slept with us until he was nearly four years old.
Therapist:	What's made it more of a problem now?
Husband:	It's not so much of a problem now, but we thought, you're coming to the age of 16 and it's your last chance if we can do anything for him because we've got no more control.

The principal issue is one of parental control and becoming independent. Mike's father protects Mike and defends himself by intimating that Mike does not refuse to co-operate but has a behaviour problem. As with Peter, his life story is interpreted as a series of events that become indicative of his deviance. Mike, then, is to be treated rather than negotiated with. As Mike has not turned up to the interview, it appears that the parents have the problem in that they have relinquished any control over their son.

When Mike was asked to attend the family therapy clinic by his parents, he refused to attend.

| Wife: | It was mentioned back a while but he said that he wouldn't. No way. But he's been good today and been really busy at the back and if I'd have mentioned it that would have been it. You're frightened to death really...if I'd have mentioned it he would have gone into a temper and he'd have blown up. He could have gone off anyway. |

Mike had been to see his general practitioner.

Husband:	It started when me and Mike had a set to and I gave him a really good hiding 3 or 4 months ago.
Therapist:	So you went to see the social worker.
Husband:	Her did. She works with a social worker.

In asserting authority over Mike the husband uses an illegitimate amount of force according to his wife. Such a situation reflects the two-generation conflict described by Haley (1976, p.115):

1. One parent is usually in an intense relationship with the child where the relationship is both positive and negative. The involved parent, in this case the mother, attempts to deal with the child with a mixture of affection and exasperation.

2. The symptomatic behaviour becomes more extreme. Mike becomes abusive or changes his style of speech.

3. The mother asks the father for help.

4. The father steps in to take charge and deal with the child. He either gets very angry and orders Mike to bed (as if he were a child) or hits him.

5. Mother complains that the father is mishandling the situation and goes to see an external agent, the social worker.

6. The father withdraws to let the mother get on with it and relinquishes control.

7. The mother and child, Mike, carry on as usual with a mixture of affection and exasperation until they meet an impasse.

Haley suggests that the behaviour exhibited by the symptomatic child is a metaphorical communication which makes explicit the marital problem. In this case it could be speculated that the symptoms stabilise the parental relationship around the issue of control and independence. Mike's behaviour can be seen as part of an attempt to clarify a confused hierarchy in the organisation of the family. Mike is making that transition from child to adult. Dependence and independence become major issues that are confused with control. Although Mrs Graham tells her son to behave, she also treats him as if he were a peer when he refuses to comply. She then tells her husband to sort it out, but when he does she implies he has done it wrong. What differentiates this family from the other families with a problem adolescent is that independence is seen as a legitimate status. Independence is expected, the means of achieving it and the rate it is achieved are yet to be negotiated but the goal is legitimate.

Furthermore, all Mike's behaviours are not negatively connotated. When pressed, the parents say he's not bad all the time and that he does try to help, is looking for a job and wants to be of assistance. And, Mike refuses the sick role. He refuses to attend the clinic for therapy. His behaviour can be seen as an attempt to bring about change and clarify the family hierarchy. The symptomatic communication would not appear immediately to be about the threat of dissolution of the system, although his leaving home might be an escalation of the symptoms that have called for a therapeutic intervention. Within this family there had not been a history of sickness. Mike had been seen by child guidance but his problems were seen as behavioural.

This problem never reached the stage where an attempt was made to medicate or treat Mike, although he visited his general practitioner. All along the therapeutic strategy of management was concerned with the relationship in the family. Little further was said about Andrew, the lodger, who was the elder brother and seemingly distant from his parents and their control. Mike had traditionally played the role of the smaller boy that needed protection.

Families in transition

All these families are faced with adolescents in stages of transition. The stages are not necessarily about leaving home but about growing up and personal autonomy. This personal autonomy has ramifications for those others involved in the family. A core construct is dependent/independent. Although challenged critically at the time of leaving home, the negotiation of such an important familial construct has been a focus for family relationships in the ramifications it has for the parenting. What are 'mummy' and 'daddy' to do when the children grow up?

The construing of dependence has implications for a further core construct of legitimacy. The behaviour of family members is framed either negatively or positively with regard to legitimacy and dependency. Being dependent and legitimate become crucial issues for persons and persons within families in terms of relationship. The construing of self and others in terms of legitimacy validates the behaviour of others. In this way, the persons and the family reflexively negotiate personal and familial boundaries: the person becomes either in or out of the family. The family construe themselves as separate or united.

Within this family nexus of the validation of dependency and legitimacy there is the political negotiation of control. Personal autonomous independence is an issue of hierarchical control. For the adolescent who demands personal autonomy, this autonomy is regulated by the parents. However, this hierarchical control requires validation by the adolescent and by a united parental hierarchy. If a split should occur between parents, the issue of personal autonomy becomes a confused issue of control in relationships that cross generation boundaries. The negotiation of control becomes a circular means of negotiating the issues of dependence, hierarchy and inter-personal distance.

Although symptoms can be seen as a means of clarifying a confused family hierarchy, this position gives no clue as to why suicidal behaviour is any different to other symptoms of distress. One feature that distinguishes the suicidal families from the non-suicidal family is that all behaviour by one member becomes construed as illegitimate. As Peter says, 'Everything I do is wrong'. In the non-suicidal family parental control is an issue but Mike is seen as having positive features. Another distinguishing feature is that suicidal behaviour appears to be a metaphorical communication about a relationship system under immediate threat of breaking down or falling apart. In addition, change, in families where suicidal behaviour is present, appears to be managed by a history of someone adopting the 'sick' role. Suicidal behaviour appears to be the extreme of distress, indicating that the upper threshold of distress has been reached such that the individual is in a life-threatening situation.

The hypothesis of suicidal behaviour as an attempt to bring about a systemic resolution to accommodate change does not distinguish the families from each other.

CHAPTER ELEVEN

The Politics of Symptoms and Marital Conflict

> *Clinical observations are primarily judgmental or interpretative rather than strictly and simply statements identifying concrete phenomena. Whether such observations can be legitimately used and replicated is a matter of great interest to researchers wishing to assist clinicians directly.* (Warren Kinston, Family Therapy Research Day, Department of Psychology Great Ormond Street, London, 21 January 1984)

We have read in the previous chapters about a number of clinical situations where clinicians and families have tried to make sense of adolescent suicidal behaviour. A number of recurring core family construings are proposed. These construings have ramifications for each other and are concerned with the legitimacy of behaviour, autonomy of actions, parental authority and relational dominance or control and boundary (in the family or out of the family).

The ascription of total deviance whereby one family member is construed as illegitimate in all spheres of interaction appears to be a distinguishing feature of the families where suicidal behaviour has occurred so far. In addition, the role of one family member presenting him or her self as being sick when distress occurs appeared to be a distinguishing feature too. When such a sick, potentially deviant family member is treated medically and then this treatment fails to work, resulting in an escalation of distress as sickness behaviour, we have the potential for suicide. Furthermore, this escalation of distress occurs in a context where the threat of family breakdown is imminent.

As in the last chapter, I shall review a number of family interviews, comparing them for the presence or absence of suicidal behaviour. These families all have a history, in their words, of psychological problems.

The Jacks: after an episode of attempted suicide

Mr Jacks and his wife were originally seen in the general hospital after an episode of attempted suicide. He had taken an overdose of his pain medication. When matters failed to improve, the couple came to the family therapy clinic at the insistence of his wife. The couple had two teenage daughters.

The immediate precipitating problem is when Mr Jacks goes to see his general practitioner about noises in the head. His general practitioner is on holiday and the locum practitioner suggests that Mr Jacks returns to work. Although work is a source of stress for Mr Jacks, in that he perceives himself as redundant, staying at home is also stressful. The lack of money by being 'off sick' means that he is increasingly dependent upon his wife. This shift of dependency, and increasing redundancy, with its political implication of loss of control and loss of personal autonomy, becomes a major issue in the life of the family.

Therapist:	You've gone back to work and everything is all right, is it?
Husband:	I wouldn't say everything is all right. I just live day by day, and I get a lot of noises in my head, which becomes a problem. I'm still on drugs.
Therapist:	That's still a problem for you, is it, noises in the head?
Husband:	Yes, especially if there's any stress causation. It's there all the time anyway.

From this brief interlude it becomes apparent that an existential issue is raised for Mr Jacks. A perspective of 'living day by day' is an important clue in working with suicidal behaviour as it proposes an indication of suicidal ideation. It also implies an element of control, long-term plans are held in abeyance and personal autonomy maintained within the realm of temporal immediacy. It must be emphasised that the context of suicidal behaviour is important here for understanding the concept of living day by day. Living day by day may be a perfectly legitimate philosophy of life in other circumstances. For those of us who have worked in hospice settings, or with the dying, this concept has its parallels. Long-term goals are abandoned and the perspective of hope is changed and curtailed.

The persistent problem of noise has failed to be controlled by medication and an array of therapeutic strategies. Mr Jacks sees the causation of his problem as stress. Stress is ever present and he now has the problem of noise all the time. His whole life becomes contextualised by the problem rather than the problem being one area of a his functioning.

NOISES IN THE HEAD

The problem of noises in the head is not isolated to Mr Jacks. Mrs Jacks is involved in the management of these noises and implementing help. However, despite her help, the noises have worsened. But, as we will see, in the last resort the noises in the head belong to Mr Jacks alone and only he can say if they are there or not. While his wife may the breadwinner, he has total control over his own noises.

Therapist: Do you notice when he has these noises, Mrs Jacks?

Wife: Well, he tells me this is what is happening, that he's got noises in the head. When he says they are particularly loud I can always link with that he's been, perhaps, very low, so that his depression activates the noise, or vice versa, you know, whichever.

Therapist: So you say *(to husband)* there's noises in your head, but you *(to wife)* recognise that its...

Wife: It's usually if he's uptight, or stress, or particularly if uncommunicative. When he's very quiet he might say to me, perhaps hours later, 'I've had these shocking noises in my head' and I think 'Oh, that was due to the fact you weren't communicating, you were so busy with this, uptight and stressed'.

A constitutive rule becomes apparent. When Mr Jacks sits quietly, Mrs Jacks sees this as evidence of Mr Jacks being involved with the noises in his head and he must, therefore, be uptight and under stress (see Figure 11.1).

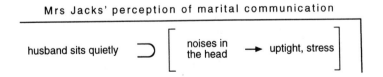

Figure 11.1 A constitutive rule about the construing of sitting quietly

When there are no noises in Mr Jacks' head he appears to his wife to be relaxed, communicative and not so depressed. The noises become part of a pattern of interaction between husband and wife, which, although seen as pathological in origin, regulates communication between husband and wife. Control over communication can be instigated by either partner, but Mr Jacks can regulate the communicational interaction by the amount of noise in his head. Rather than engaging in an overt statement of not wanting to communicate, he can say that he cannot communicate because of a personal problem. He has noises in the head that he is busy with. This may be seen as an avoidance of conflict in the ways that in some relationships a headache also serves to preclude further contact.

'I DON'T SEE IT THAT WAY'
One of the hazards about occupying the status sick, particularly that status which is involved with being depressed and incompetent, is that plans and ideas are dismissed.

Mr Jacks is asked about his view of his future.

Husband:	It would be five months on half pay, then retirement, then sell the cottage, then find a council house, then go on to social security, it's as clear as those steps.
Wife:	I don't see it in the same light as he does. Probably because I see it more positively rather than negatively. The area he was talking about, selling the cottage and getting a council house, that doesn't exist in my mind. *(To husband)* What you've done is created a problem in your mind about having to sell the cottage. Probably because it would realise money to keep you, but it would soon be eaten up in keeping you, but it's foolish to look at it like that.

Mr Jacks, then, is seen by his wife to be foolish in this thoughts. His negative picture of the future is seen as something which has built up in his mind. His view does not exist in her mind. As the breadwinner, she has the say in what is to happen to their house. In earlier sections Mr Jacks complains that he is ignored and that he is not listened to. His opinions do not exist. For him, the presentation of symptoms means that he can withdraw from the arena of disconfirmation by his wife (see Figure 11.2). By having noises in his head he diverts from the conflict between him and his wife, on whom he relies for support.

In this family the wielding of power as head of the household is a significant issue. Mr Jacks is considered as illegitimate by being totally invalidated. Throughout the years he has adopted the sick role that maintains the marital distance between him and his wife and attempts to resolve the conflict in the hierarchy. In his hospital notes he is found to have a pattern of similar instances of bouts of depression and hospitalisation (particularly at the time when he left his first wife). Prior to the recent complaints of noises in the head, he had been in pain with an arthritic hip, which was replaced. The onset of his noises in his head began after his successful hip replacement operation.

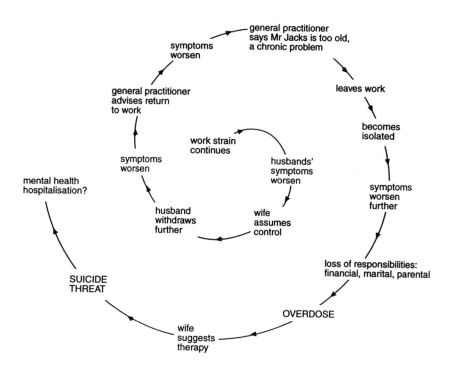

Figure 11.2 A spiral of escalation

The family has a problem which is perceived as resident in the former head of the household. That problem has proved to be intractable. Attempts to resolve the problem strategically by the wife, as new head of the household, and the general practitioner maintain the problem and fail to resolve the situation. In fact, the situation worsens. In this complex matrix of interaction the former head of household is now dependent upon his wife, who demands her say in marital affairs.

This man took a repeat overdose at a later date. When interviewed after the episode, the important issue was raised of the husband threatening to leave home and his wife being tired of his continuing problems. Although not mentioned in the videotape extract, this threat of a dissolution of the family and the loss of viability for the system reflects a crucial factor seen in previous cases. His overdose is another, albeit extreme, example of leaving the situation. Indeed, at a later interview the matter of mental health hospitalisation is seriously considered and his wife says that such an intervention would relieve her of the burden of him. As she says, in a later interview, she doesn't want to return home from work, or her daughter from school, to find a body hanging behind the door.

The Howarths: with the presence of a threat of suicide

This couple have two married children. A third son is living with them at home. He is 16 years old and has left school but has no work. The husband says that the son was not brought to the session as he did not want him to become involved. As the interview reveals, this son is very much involved in the marital conflict.

THE PROBLEMS

After a disastrous attempt to set up a business in Australia on the part of an eager husband and a reluctant wife, the couple return to England. Their savings are depleted and their situation is one of mutual dissatisfaction.

> Therapist: So what brings you here now?
>
> Husband: What's known as tension, anxiety. My main
>   problem is that I can't write, I've got a nervous
>   thing about writing. I can't write. If I go for an
>   application form I pick up a pen and I just start
>   and I can't write.

Mr Howarth, who cannot fill in his job application form, has always considered himself as an entrepreneur and a businessman. His major achievement in life had been to set up his own in business. Faced by financial difficulties, his wife is pressing him to get a job, any job. His symptoms can be considered from a functional perspective. He is refusing to comply with the demands of his wife. This conflict is covert. Rather than say no, the husband says that he cannot help it, he is 'sick' and not responsible. Furthermore, as the entrepreneur and boss, he faces a loss of status by becoming an employee.

Therapist: So what happens when you go for a job?

Husband: Well, I just shake. There is an odd occasion on which I can write!

Therapist: At some times can you control it?

Husband: Well, it's not a matter of me controlling it, it's just that I'm not thinking of it and I seem to be able to do it all right.

Before the children arrived this couple describe themselves as having a great deal of difficulty and as a 'right pair' together. Significantly, their son, aged 16, is entering that period of his life when he is preparing to leave home and leave his parents together in what they perceive as a situation of difficulty.

SYMMETRICAL CONFLICT
Bateson (1973) describes a symmetrical relationship between two people as one in which both persons' behaviours are similar. Their behaviours are linked in such a way that the given behaviour in one person stimulates more of it in the other person and vice versa. The relationship is 'symmetrical' in regard to these behaviours. Common examples of symmetrical relationships are 'armament races, keeping up with the Jones, athletic emulation, boxing matches and the like' (p.294).

This symmetrical relationship appears between Mr and Mrs Howarth in their presentation of symptoms. Combined with this presentation of symptoms, each partner disqualifies the opinions of the other.

Therapist: Who would you say was the more anxious?

Wife: Me, I should say.

Husband: It's a difficult question to answer. I should say I get tired and tense and when I get tired and tense I get a twitch in my eye.

In this escalation of symptoms the opinion of the other partner is disqualified. Such a pattern is dangerous. The escalation of symptoms to maintain a position of authority has serious manifestations for any recovery to health.

This couple have different perspectives on their mutual problem. Mrs Howarth is primarily concerned with finances but her husband is concerned with their relationship in terms of togetherness. When he raises the issue of sexual contact, Mrs Howarth dismisses the issue. As she says, she never thinks about it.

Any change for this couple concerned with their staying together, or obtaining a divorce, involves several implicatory construings, the contrasting poles of which are occupied by husband and wife. To avoid divorce he believes they should become closer, be more involved, talk about his hobbies, have sex and be better off financially. In contrast, she believes a divorce can be avoided only if they stay apart, have less involvement, he desists from his hobby, they have no sex and become better off financially.

The only item of mutual agreement is their financial position. Unfortunately, the activities which give Mr Howarth his only validation, as prestigious and competent, are the hobby activities which deplete the family finances. His previous business activities are seen as the cause of their current demise and, as Mrs Howarth is the 'breadwinner', she demands the position of executive authority. As in the family before, the breadwinner wants a say in the way that decisions are made. And as before, the role of the breadwinner has been taken over by a woman.

The Howarths appear to be characterised by a symmetrical conflict of mutual invalidation. The invalidation centres around occupation of the position of executive hierarchy. To counter Mrs Howarth's position of 'breadwinner', Mr Howarth adopts the status of 'sick' (see Figure 11.3). He becomes 'not responsible' for his predicament. Its not his fault that he is sick, he maintains, and part of the legitimate sick role is that the person is not blamed for being so. By being sick he can legitimately not comply with his wife's demands rather than confront her with open conflict. To maintain this position he amplifies his status of sick when confronted by his wife. Her insistence that he becomes 'the breadwinner' is seen by him as illegitimate. For his wife to 'demand' is to place her in a dominant position. To work for someone else is seen by Mr Howarth as illegitimate and fails to validate his personal construing of being a self-employed entrepreneur.

The sick role is then used as a means of validating a personal position, he cannot be self-employed as he is too sick and, within the marital

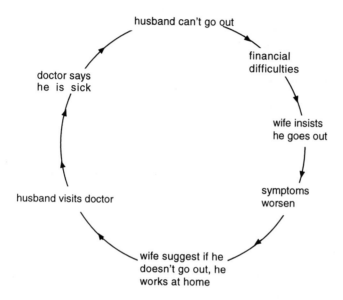

Figure 11.3 A cycle of interaction relating to symptoms and the status 'sick'

relationship, as maintaining his position of non-compliance. The crux of the issue is that the sick role is, in turn, construed as illegitimate by Mrs Howarth.

In a later interview Mr Howarth says that he had contemplated suicide when the situation became intolerable and he thought his wife was going to leave. The threat of systemic dissolution is significant. Any previous attempts to treat Mr Howarth's symptoms had consistently failed. These treatments had ignored the inter-personal context of his symptoms.

For this family, hierarchical authority is an issue. Symptoms are used as a strategy in the continuing conflict. The marital situation is complicated by the impending independence of the remaining son that throws the couple back to an unresolved situation from a previous stage in the marriage and for Mr Howarth to become dependent upon his wife. The family organisation is threatened with immediate change and a loss of viability when Mr Howarth's symptoms escalate and divorce is threatened.

The Brandts: where no suicidal behaviour is known

Mrs Brandt had a course of tests and treatment for her depression, which had proved to be intractable. The previous descriptions of her depression are concerned with physical causes but the primary cause is now seen by her general practitioner as psychological. After being referred to a psychiatrist, both Mr and Mrs Brandt attend for therapy.

Mrs Brandt is a nurse. While at work, her problem is less evident and she improves. Once she returns home her depression worsens.

Therapist:	What are the problems right now.
Wife:	I just wish I was the person I was four years ago. I've had a completely different personality change.
Therapist:	So you say you get depressed. What actually happens to you?
Wife:	(*to husband*) Can you explain it, how it starts, more than I can?

The wife shifts the questioning to her husband. When questioning shifts in this way and a partner is asked to give the information, it may be assumed that the partner, in this case the husband, is the complainant. The symptoms become an important part of the marital negotiations. Four years ago, when she became a changed woman, was the time when they were first married.

Husband:	Well you keep saying you've got arthritis.
Wife:	Yes, I know that.
Husband:	Personality's changed hell of a lot.
Therapist:	Can you give me an idea of, you said, bouts of depression?
Wife:	Well, it just happens, I can suddenly feel myself going down, suddenly getting miserable.
Husband:	Well you are completely tired aren't you.
Wife:	Well I think if you had 10 mg of Ativan a day...
Husband:	She's always flaked out or tired.

An apparent description of symptoms embedded within this dialogue is a clue to the political nature of these symptoms. When Mr Brandt says it is a change in personality, and implies mental problems and personal deviance, Mrs Brandt refutes this by saying she has arthritis. Paradoxically, when Mrs Brandt says she is 'going down' and feels miserable, Mr Brandt suggests that she is tired. Each partner disqualifies the other partner's construing, although they are both united by the same shared construct of physical/mental causation.

A ramification of this is that Mr Brandt, who is the complainant, sees his wife's tiredness as a result of going to work. He would prefer her not to work outside the home and carry out her duties as a housewife. Mrs Brandt says her tiredness is because of the medication she takes for her depression. Her depression and her tiredness are not something for which she is responsible. Her husband disagrees. If she did not work at the hospital, she would not be so tired. If she were not so tired, then she would be willing to have sex with him like before they were married.

WIFELY DUTIES
Mr Brandt says that his wife is more amicable when she is not depressed and that she does more things in the house.

> Wife: I can still cope. I still cope with the housework and you never want for clean socks or a clean shirt, or things do you? I suppose there's a lot I don't do.

Mrs Brandt goes on to tell how she maintains the home, although tired and depressed. It appears that Mrs Brandt is not satisfying her husband over and above maintaining her role as housekeeper.

> Wife: I work five half-days. I do three days from a quarter to eight to quarter to one and two days from four until nine. I do what I can. If I come home and I'm tired, what else can I do?

This statement reflects Mrs Brandt's position. She will do whatever is necessary to keep up the legitimate position of wife. For her, her depression is the source of tiredness. To remove this source of tiredness would imply that she could do more than just her housekeeping duties (see Figure 11.4). She is not responsible for her tiredness as her depression is spontaneous and something that happens to her.

The sick role is used as a strategy in the negotiation of hierarchy and inter-personal distance in the marriage. Instead of the sick role keeping the partners close together in this family, the sick role keeps the partners apart. Being sick maintains a marital distance. Like the previous families, the issue of who is 'breadwinner' is significant but does not distinguish the suicidal from the non-suicidal families.

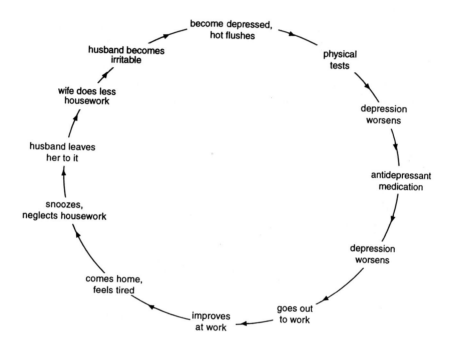

Figure 11.4 A relational cycle of depression and autonomy

Mutual validation is, however, a significant issue. Although neither partner construes each other as totally illegitimate, the couple seem to be engaged in a cycle of escalating and worsening symptoms. Eventually Mrs Brandt is hospitalised. Her depression worsens. It appears that in the non-suicidal couple symptoms are the means of maintaining marital separation rather than for the suicidal couples where symptoms maintain marital closeness. In the suicidal families there is a threat of an immediate dissolution of the relationship, which escalates distress. In the Brandt's marriage, the separation by hospitalisation relieves Mrs Brandt's distress. In all three families the husband's perception of what is to change, particularly an intensified sexual involvement, is invalidated by the wives' perceptions. The wives don't even think about it. For the families where there are psychological problems, sexual activity maintains male dominance and keeps the couples together.

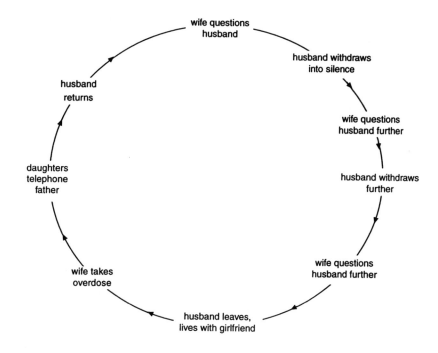

Figure 11.5 A cycle of family interaction involving withdrawal

Families presenting overt marital conflict

The Yeats: after an attempt at suicide

Mrs Yeats took an overdose of medication and was seen in the general hospital. She said straightforwardly that she had taken an overdose after her husband petitioned for divorce (see Figure 11.5).

When asked in the videotaped session with the husband present, he says:

> Husband: Yes, she said when we got up that she would, if I went back to work, she would take these tablets. She was in bed, then she came down and said that she wanted to stay home because I'd told her that I wanted to divorce her.

This is a straightforward threat of an imminent dissolution of the family system. Although their two teenage daughters are living at home, and obviously involved, the principal agents are the wife and husband. The wife does not want a divorce and the suicide attempt appears to be a strategy to maintain some marital involvement of the husband with her and her daughters. When asked about where the daughters will live, the wife replies:

Wife:	It's up to them to decide, I think they are old enough. I do not want to hold on them, it's not fair.
Therapist:	Who do you think they would choose to live with?
Husband:	I feel the same way as my wife about that, I think they would live with her.

REASONS FOR LEAVING

The reason the husband gives for wanting to leave is the reason we have seen in other families where suicidal behaviour has occurred. Everything that one person does is construed as wrong. Both partners see each other's behaviour as illegitimate.

Husband:	They are not reasons really. I'm leaving because I'm fed up, really.
Therapist:	Fed up?
Husband:	That's putting it mildly.
Therapist:	Fed up with what?
Husband:	Nagging. Getting on to me all the time. Anything that comes into her head.
Therapist:	So what do you say?
Husband:	Sit and listen.
Therapist:	And then what happens?
Husband:	She eventually calms down.
Therapist:	And Mrs Yeats, do you see that as a problem?
Wife:	No, I don't think so... I don't demand him to do anything. I just ask him. Ask him if he could do this, this weekend, or do that at the weekend, and he might not do that. He might go off for the day. He'd rather go off with his mates than stay at home with me.

The issue appears to be about a husband erring and leaving his wife at home to look after the house and children while he goes out to play golf. This is not quite the whole picture.

Husband: I don't go out very often.

Wife: Yes, but you want to all the time though.

Husband: Well, if the weather's good. You have to go if you can.

Wife: Yes, but you don't think about us.

Husband: I do.

Wife: No, you don't.

Husband: When was the last time I went out then?

Wife: I can't remember.

Husband: There you are.

Wife: You know I can't remember things.

(Silence.)

Although the overdose and threat of death keeps the husband at home, his presence is maintained by the activity of his daughters.

Therapist: If you want a divorce, what's keeping you.

Husband: Nothing now, really, just habit I suppose. Children really. I did leave before you see but they came over, this was about eighteen months ago. When I left, they phoned me up.

Wife: We talked about it. I said I'd go away for a week because it was too hot at home.

The marital distance between the partners has been an issue of negotiation. When Mr Yeats left the first time it was to live with another woman. He eventually returned. Despite his return, he worked away during the week and only came home at weekends. For this couple, anything either of them did was wrong. The episode of attempted suicide seems to be a last-ditch stand to restore the former marital *status quo*. In this state of open conflict neither partner will validate the other. The suicide attempt is a strategy to maintain the family as a coherent system when threatened with imminent dissolution.

At a later date the couple come to the family therapy clinic because Mrs Yeats is experiencing suicidal thoughts. When asked if he has a current girlfriend, Mr Yeats admits to living with another woman while he is away from home at work. It appears that the threat of suicide has maintained the husband at home part of the time, yet secretly he has developed a parallel life with a new partner.

The Embers: where a member of the family has threatened suicide

A similar story emerges in this next family (see Figure 11.6). This time it is the husband that presents the problem and he is the one who leaves home. He intimates that he is suicidal and during the interview the wife proposes that the marriage has deteriorated. She has had enough. She has been considering living without her husband. Once more there is an immediate threat to the viability of the family. This threat occurs in a sequence of escalating problems that include Mr Embers having problems with his eyesight, his continuing problem finding employment and the arrival of twin daughters.

THE NEGOTIATION; HOME OR AWAY?

The threat of suicide, and the husband running away, has a powerful effect on the marital relationship. Not only does it communicate that if things continue in the same way the system will cease, but one of the parties will be responsible and is to blame. If he attempts suicide, it will be her fault. This is the manipulatory element that makes some suicidal attempts difficult for practitioners involved in the management of such problems.

Husband:	I think the outcome of it is that it's had more of an effect on Sheila and her state of mind than it has on me. She obviously feels I could do it again. Although I might tell her that I'm not going to do this or I'm not going to do that, I've put the doubt in her mind.
Therapist:	Is that right?
Wife:	Yes, it's not as bad as it was.
Husband:	It is pretty well over now.
Wife:	My first reaction was it was really going to happen again because I just couldn't face it. I suppose somehow I wanted to get rid of Don so I didn't have to face it again. I could sort of choose to make things not happen again.

In the latter part of this episode we see the other side of this argument. She can indeed get rid of him. The suicidal metaphor is 'to get rid of'. What appears to be a manipulation on the part of the husband can easily tip over into control by the wife. As she says, if he so chooses to react to her, she can choose to make things happen. This is the reason why it is important not to take sides in such a marital process and understand suicidal behaviour as an interaction in a relationship. Both partners consider their own possible opportunities for exerting personal autonomy. The incident also serves to impress that no matter what Mrs Embers does, Mr Embers is able to choose and exert some personal autonomy. This appears to restore some equality in the marital hierarchy and improve their mutual situation.

For this family, marital distance is a matter of emotional and physical distance. Mrs Embers is urging her husband to take whatever steps he wishes. The very act of telling him to choose places her in a dominant position. At the same time, when he does take his own initiatives in business, he brings about family misfortune. Both of them are faced with looking after children in a difficult financial situation, a situation which is seen negatively as a result of Mr Ember's ineptitude. To resolve the situation both partners have threatened to leave. The suicidal episode can also be seen as an attempt to get things right and bring about resolution and coherence. By appearing together in therapy, the complete issue is brought into the open. While privately they have withdrawn from each other as a means of coping, a strategy used by several couples, this proves to be dysfunctional. Suicide is the ultimate withdrawal from a relationship. This couple recognise the threat of such coping and, through such an incident, attempt to resolve their problem using another strategy.

A complicating feature of this relationship is that when the couple met, Mr Embers was living with his divorced sister-in-law. Since the Embers married, and he left the home of his sister-in-law, she found a partner and had recently married. The marriage of the Embers, the marriage of the sister-in-law, the arrival of the twins, the threatened loss of eyesight and the debacle of his employment are all important events to be negotiated in terms of their implications for the construings of Mr and Mrs Embers.

Separating the suicidal from the non-suicidal

Of the twenty families studied, six were found to be 'free' of suicidal behaviour or suicidal intentions as far as I could discover by going through the medical and psychiatric hospital notes. Fourteen families presented with some instance of threatened or actual suicidal behaviour. The recent chapters have suggested a number of possible hypotheses about what contributes to promoting suicidal behaviour. These contributory factors are:

- the presence of marital or relational conflict

- a situation which appears to escalate over time, that is things get worse, the symptoms and conflict increase

- one member becomes construed as totally deviant

- there is a confused family hierarchy, or a struggle for control between marital partners

- within the family context of suicidal behaviour there is a family history of change being managed by a family adopting the status 'sick'

- the family/marital system is faced with imminent dissolution where one member is leaving, has left, or is being asked to leave

- symptoms are a means of maintaining familial and marital distance between members.

Relationship conflict

All the families considered in this chapter exhibited relationship conflict. This is not surprising as the persons involved had been initially referred by a psychiatrist to a family therapy clinic. To justify the referral, the psychiatrist would have sought evidence of marital, or familial, conflict either as a direct admission from the patient or as a clinical judgement. Conflict appears to be evident in the organisation of a relationship where both individuals demand of each other 'see it my way, my way is the only way'.

Escalation over time, an interaction

Relationship conflict, as a pattern of organised behaviour, appears to worsen over time. In Chapter Nine we read that a feature of suicidal families, or a feature of 'crisis' development, is an escalation of the problem which has persistently failed to be resolved. In these families a situation occurs where the family attempts the same patterns of problem resolution over and over again. However, the problematic behaviour is amplified. More of behaviour A leads to more of behaviour B, which leads to more of behaviour A in a cycle of escalating interaction. Bateson (1973) refers to this as a process of schizmogenesis, where a pattern of behaviour which attempts to promote stability leads to 'runaway'. And, in some instances, this literally occurs, one person runs away. The interaction escalates and the situation worsens. In the families described, the more one person does to convince, cajole, influence, direct bargain or demand, the more the other demurs, rejects, fights back, withdraws or refuses. The more one refuses, the more the other demands. This is a cycle of escalating interaction. The conflict lies in the pattern of organised interaction, it is not resident in one person.

Escalation did not distinguish the families as suicidal or non-suicidal. All the families showed a pattern of worsening symptoms, attempted solutions, more symptoms, more solutions, referral to outside agents, more symptoms, more complaints and further referral or a continued therapeutic contact.

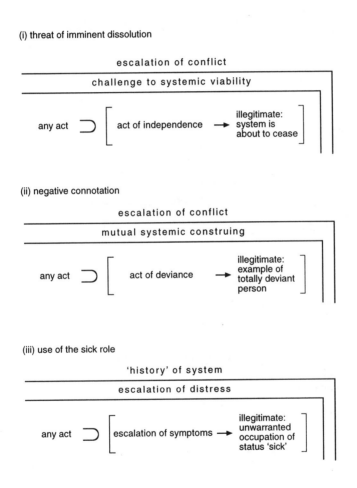

Figure 11.6 Constitutive rules regarding the construing of behaviour in three systemic contexts: threat of imminent dissolution, negative connotation and use of the sick role

Table 11.1 Factors distinguishing the families where suicidal behaviour had occurred from those families where no suicidal behaviour had occurred.

(i) threat of imminent dissolution

	the threat of imminent dissolution	no threat
suicidal	14	-
non-suicidal	-	6

* p <.005 Fisher-Yates   N=20

(ii) negative connotation

	a negative connotation of all behaviour	partial deviance
suicidal	14	-
non-suicidal	1	5

* p <.005 Fisher-Yates   N=20

(iii) a tradition of conflict management by adopting the 'sick' role

	tradition of sickness	no tradition
suicidal	13	1
non-suicidal	2	4

* p <.05 Fisher-Yates   N=20

* Fisher-Yates test of significance in 2 x 2 contingency tables.
Finney,D. (1948) Biometrika, vol. XXXV, parts I and II.

A threat of imminent dissolution

The factor which clearly demarcates the suicidal from the non-suicidal families is the threat of a complete breakdown of the family system (see Figure 11.6 (i) and Table 11.1 (i)). One member is about to leave, has left or is being told to leave. This situation arises after the previous processes of continuing escalating conflict and a mutual negative construing which encompasses all behaviours. I have called this imminent systemic dissolution as we can see the possibility of suicidal behaviour occurring in settings other than family systems.

Previous researchers into suicidal behaviour have noted the presence of a breakdown of a relationship but have not located this in a sequence of interactions. This 'breakdown' of relationship is seen by those researchers as impulsive. I propose that human behaviour only appears impulsive if viewed in a narrow individualistic context. In a wider context of interaction and relationship, within a cultural context, suicidal behaviour becomes understandable. Rather than being an example of continued deviance by a deviant person, the behaviour can be seen as part of a pattern of recurring behaviours. Suicidal behaviour at the time of a threat of systemic dissolution is a strategy of maintaining relationship. In Chapter Seven the behaviour is seen as resolving conflict, albeit temporarily. In Chapters Ten and Eleven suicidal behaviour is seen as part of a process of maintaining relationships. For some relationships, suicidal behaviour temporarily resolves conflict.

In all the cases, suicidal behaviour is a metaphoric communication about the life or death issue of the system. The current system is about to cease. This occurs when, after a process of escalation, the systemic thresholds of distress are threatened to excess. Suicidal behaviour, in attempting to maintain the system, is a strategy to recalibrate those thresholds of distress. While seemingly punctuating an 'end process' where a relationship ends, the presence of suicidal behaviour can be seen as a continuing process of negotiating relationships. Again, Bateson (1973) proposes that in some circumstances there is a positive feedback loop to increase the behaviour which precedes the discomfort. This feedback loop might increase the discomfort to some threshold level at which change becomes possible. It is this process which is reflected in these families. A feedback loop of escalation occurs until the discomfort increases and change occurs. However, Bateson does point out that sometimes the feedback loop continues beyond the systemic threshold of distress and even death: '…the possible existence of such a positive feedback loop, which will cause a runaway in the direction of increasing discomfort up to some threshold (which might be on the other side of death)' (p.299).

Total negative connotation

In Figure 11.6 (ii) and Table 11.1 (ii) a negative connotation of all behaviours by the suicidal person is seen as an important factor in distinguishing the suicidal from the non-suicidal. In the process of escalating conflict, the suicidal person is seen as totally deviant as a person rather than exhibiting deviant behaviours.

In Chapter Seven the women that were mutilating themselves on the hospital ward became construed by the staff as illegitimate, demanding, manipulative and totally deviant. Similarly, in the suicidal families everything one person does is seen as illegitimate. This is reciprocated in that the suicidal person sees the key involved others as illegitimate in their treatment. The negative connotation, like the conflict, is resident in the pattern of interaction.

In the families of adolescents the adolescent comes to be construed as deviant. As Peter says: 'Everything I do is wrong'.

The negative case in Table 11.1 (ii) is interesting in that it refines the factor of 'total deviance'. What distinguishes this family is that although the adolescent daughter is construed as deviant and not being able to do anything right, there is no threat of the daughter leaving or of being thrown out of the house (imminent systemic dissolution), nor is there any evidence of the daughter having a history of sickness. Significantly, it is the parents who are the complainants and the mother is the identified patient. The behaviour of the adolescent daughter functions to involve the father. It is the father who 'sorts out' the family and it can be argued that the daughter's behaviour keeps him in ultimate authority. During the family interview the father says that he is reluctant to involve the family in therapy and prefers to sort out the situation himself.

Hierarchy and control

For all the families, the issues of conflict appeared to centre around who was in control. This is the political negotiation of power within the family. People who have a history and a future together continually negotiate their ways of behaving with one another.

In the families described here, particular issues are raised. These issues are not discrete, they have ramifications for each other. Similarly, these issues are part of a process within a developmental context. The issues raised for negotiation are those of dependency, autonomy, legitimacy and boundary. As the reader can see, the negotiation of these construings is at the core of the 'conflict'.

Haley (1976) writes that when we look at family relationships in terms of hierarchy, the power often resides with the parents who nurture and discipline the children. As families grow up, so must the hierarchical relationships, and family organisation, change. When an individual shows symptoms, the hierarchical arrangement is confused. It is confused by being ambiguous. Nobody knows who is a peer and who is superior. A source of this confusion can be that one member of a family forms a coalition against a peer with a member at another level of family organisation.

Evidence of such confusion is presented in Chapter Seven, where the ward hierarchy was confused. Suicidal behaviour is seen as an attempt to clarify the hierarchy of the ward organisation of staff and patients. Similarly, in these families suicidal behaviour can be understood as a bid to clarify the family organisation.

A tradition of distress management

In the suicidal families there is a family repertoire of distress management by someone becoming sick. This presentation of symptoms appears to be a means of regulating conflict and stabilising confusion within a family hierarchy. In the hospital ward the presentation of a cut wrist temporarily brought about a resolution of other problems and each person knew what to do according to their pre-ordained roles.

For the non-suicidal families there does not appear to be a family tradition of conflict management using the sick role. However, in two cases this did not hold true (see Table 11.1(iii)). For these two cases symptoms of depression appeared to keep the partners separate rather than together. This is an example of negative cases refining a previous hypothesis. Where a family tradition of symptoms keeps a family together, and resolves conflict, suicidal behaviour may occur at the threat of separation. When sickness in a relationship keeps partners separate, separation is not a critical issue. Togetherness becomes problematical.

Wrong, sick and about to go

For these families the presence of suicidal behaviour occurs when three variables are present (see Figure 11.6 and Table 11.1). The presence of suicidal behaviour is seen in a developmental process where hierarchy is challenged and that challenge is experienced as conflict. During this process those involved construe each other as illegitimate in their demands or in their behaviour. Although traditionally such relationships have been regulated by one member becoming sick, that person now becomes construed as illegitimate in the role of 'sick person'. The message in these families appears to be that 'You can be sick as long as you do not leave'. If that person threatens to become independent and insists on occupying the status 'sick', mutual validation is denied. A family member then leaves or threatens to leave the system.

The status sick is a temporary status and has particular cultural obligations, that is that the person is not seen as responsible for their condition and co-operates with treatment. Although conflict may be reduced temporarily by one person becoming 'sick', the continuation of symptoms, and the refusal to validate their legitimacy, promotes further conflict. More symptoms are then used to regulate this conflict and a cycle of escalating distress begins. We have seen this in the escalation of depression in marital relationships and it is also a common feature of attempted suicides where pain management fails.

Becoming suicidal is a process in the political management of family power and inter-personal relationships. The issues raised in this political management are those of autonomy (who is dependent or independent and when), legitimacy (who is validated and by whom), boundary (who is in the system, who is out of the system, how close the members are) and power (who is in authority and control). Suicidal behaviour is a metaphoric communication about a relational system under threat of imminent dissolution. Within this relational context there is a tradition of change being accommodated by a family member becoming sick to keep the family together.

This method allows for an expression of quantitative data as qualitatively expressed rules. In such a way, we can see how statistical data can be interpreted and applied to understanding narrative data collected from family interviews.

CHAPTER TWELVE

The Dialectical Process
of Negotiating Distress

*People require social life, and therefore social regulation and the other
elements of culture. In extreme situations, their insufficiency leads to
suicide: 'egoistic' suicide, if the individuals feel isolated and
abandoned, or 'anomic' suicide, if individuals feel bereft of reliable
orientation to guide their choices of actions.'* (Eckstein 1996, p.482)

*Meaning-systems provide actors with what Weber called
Sichverhalten: they relate the self to the situations that confront them
and in which they are forced to act. They orient people to situations,
such as maps orient travellers.* (Eckstein 1996, p.483)

*Personal misfortune is increasingly experienced through a medical
lens which encourages us to understand and shape our troubles in a
clinical way: as something like a disease which suddenly constrains us
from outside our intentions, with its particular cause and
characteristic patterns, and for which doctors possess essential
treatments.* (Littlewood 1996, p.245)

Culture and the politic of meaning

The descriptions of suicidal behaviour presented so far are concerned with
how we understand the world. It is about both freedom and constraint; how
we are free to choose but within a range of constrained choices. This is a
stochastic process and reflects the discussion throughout the literature
contrasting the individual and her social relations, autonomy and determi-
nation. Stochastic is defined by Gregory Bateson (1979) from the Greek,
stochazein, as 'to shoot with a bow at a target; that is, to scatter events in a
partially random manner, some of which achieve a preferred outcome. If a
sequence of events combines a random component with a selective process
so that only certain outcomes of the random are allowed to endure, that
sequence is said to be stochastic' (p.245).

In our culture we have a repertoire of roles. These roles are available to us as persons under certain constrained circumstances. We have ways of assigning structure and meaning to our activities, to the activities of others and to our mutual interaction. That ceaseless stream of events which we actively perceive is organised, construed, constructed and punctuated into certain imputations of meaning and courses of action. Such a process is not one of determining or being determined, rather a dialectical process of negotiation. This negotiation is a political activity. The imputation of meaning, the regulation of action, the manifestation and resolution of conflict, the maintenance of stability, the promotion and labelling of deviance, the formation of opinion and the formal, or informal, constitution of systems at varying levels is political. Within personal relationships this is the politic of the family. Within the doctor–patient relationship this is the politic of health.

The use of the word politic is deliberate. It is a metaphor which emphasises the vital interactive processes of behaviour. It is concerned with debate, negotiation, coercion, conflict, dissent and co-operation within the person, between persons and within organisations, as we have seen in the family, the hospital ward, the hospital emergency room and the family therapy clinic. The regulation of conflict, the government of family affairs, the negotiation of power and hierarchy and the struggle for autonomy are part of the politics of personal behaviour. The politic of the family is concerned with membership, rules, dependence, control and legitimation. The use of strategies of personal agency is a political move within a community of intimate others. As we saw in Chapters Seven and Eight, the attribution of legitimacy to an act is a political move. We are, according to the context we are in, heroes or villains. We are free to choose but the choice is limited by culture. Sick or sane are labels that are negotiated, the ramifications of which are salutary.

Similarly with the use of 'culture'. I am using culture to mean a set of orientations towards social objects. Thus we may have a family culture and a ward culture as well as a medical culture and a community culture. Culture will offer the individual role obligations and norms of interaction that regulate subjectivity. And those subjectivities too will comprise and dynamically influence culture. Culture, then, will have its own constitutive and regulative rules about what is proscribed and prescribed behaviour in particular settings. Social phenomena have meanings for the individual participant and those meanings have to be negotiated and interpreted. Actions have meaning for the actor, but not absolutely.

Meaning is based on rules of communication

The thesis of this book is that people invest meaning in what they do, and I have tried to objectify those meanings as if they are rules based. Interpretation and negotiation are constitution and regulation, meaning and action. Meanings and their consequent actions are woven into episodes as narratives that explain daily life. Stories are the basic explanatory medium for conveying meaning. Patients try to use them when they encounter their practitioner and it is stories that we scientists tell each other to illustrate our own ideas and theories away from the lecture platform. Yet meanings have to be tested in further action, they are open to challenge. 'Why did he pull the trigger?' is a basic dramaturgical question and at the core of a thousand stories. Each story will be different but within each culture there will be rules for articulating that story and to whom it can be told. Therefore, if culture is that which underlies shared behaviour and is based on meanings and rules that are negotiated, it is a process that is active and subjective to change. In this way, science, as doing knowledge (in the German *Wissenschaft: wissen* = knowledge, *schaffen* = doing), is an activity that is performed in practice. We may have to reorganise our knowledge of what human health activity is as something that is done, as an activity in practice, not solely as thought in practice. Thus we move from the concept of *cogito ergo sum* – I think therefore I am – to that of *ago ergo sum* – I do therefore I am. Thus meanings are coupled with their actions and consequences, as constitution and regulation.

A note on the research approach

Human nature cannot be understood from one point of view. Within the total repertoire of science it is necessary to have different approaches to understanding the world. In this book I have woven differing perspectives together, a thick description (Geertz 1973), to make a fabric that reconstructs suicidal behaviour in an eco-systemic context. It is up to each reader to cut that fabric to make a personal fit.

In the preceding chapters suicidal behaviour is described in differing contexts. The familial situation of the person is the prime analytical device. Within the situational context, the meaning of personal and inter-personal behaviour is discussed. In the discussion of meaning it is reports of the persons, the actors themselves, that are seen as the best source of information. Douglas (1967) also proposes that suicidal behaviour is best understood by locating particular meanings in their relevant contexts and that such an understanding is often neglected in descriptions of suicidal behaviour. Traditional studies of suicidal behaviour have proposed either studies of large populations, or of the individual, and sometimes of families. However, it is not just the individual or her family or society separately but the individual in the context of her intimates within a particular cultural setting. Inevitably, as social scientists, we have to make a choice of where to cut that descriptive boundary and present a description. To do this we must at least mention that we have made such a cut and, at best, offer an understanding of the relationship of the part to the whole. In this book I have tried to present different settings as contexts and then see what those contexts have in common.

As researchers, we are not separate from influence or, by recreating understandings, from influencing. The very nature of research itself contributes to how behaviour is understood, directing away from and steering towards particular understandings. The process of research becomes an element in the political process of constructing understandings of behaviour and an element in negotiating what meanings are maintained and validated within the culture. The concept of illness itself is culture bound (Littlewood 1996) in that there are socially prescribed responses to symptoms and as to how distress is to be manifested.

In Chapter One one of the aims of understanding suicidal behaviour is to formulate strategic interventions to guide the therapeutic management of suicidal persons. As soon as research enters this arena of guiding therapists and clinicians (the traditional stance of medical research), it is part of a political process. The politics of medicine and psychotherapy will be discussed later in this chapter. Similarly, the collection of data for research has implications for the way in which persons construe their relationships.

The researcher cannot stay neutrally outside the collection of data and the formulation of understandings. Research itself belongs to the culture and the researcher is not outside of that culture but part of it. By being part of that culture the researcher influences and is influenced by what happens. Although this reflexive process appears to limit personal autonomy, the understanding of such influence frees the researcher from the constraint of ignorance. We may be constrained by structure but we are no longer determined by it (Sapsford 1983). However, we cannot pretend, as researchers, to be neutral. By asking the very questions that we do we are intervening. Indeed, taking an interest in what a patient has to say about himself, with a willingness to discover another's point of view, appears to be an important strategy in potential therapy. But there is also a fundamental issue at stake here. As academics, we are concerned with all that is possible to verbally articulate. Our knowledge of health care dialogues is restricted to the words that we use, as indeed the latter chapters have been. Yet the patients that we encounter in our clinical contacts are articulate in a much broader sense than simply lexical meanings. As practitioners, we are trained to stand back, to think and then respond. However, this abstraction loses an immediacy and contact with the patient that is congruent with the way in which they communicate. Our patients understand us in the way in which we respond non-verbally, as well as verbally, and in the immediacy of our response.

In addition, we cannot help but be touched by the stories of those that we hear. How do we deal with hopelessness in our own lives? Ignoring the question only builds a distance between ourselves and the people we may be supposed to be helping. Indeed, it is the existential question of life's meaning and the effectiveness of our own agency that is, perhaps, central to the treatment dilemma in suicidal behaviour. Patients contact practitioners, yet they fail to discuss their suicidal feelings. Rather than categorise this as a feature of those who come to us in distress, perhaps we may have to reflect upon how we conspire not to discuss such matters. Given the incidence of suicidal behaviour among members of the medical profession, there may be indeed a common question that both patient and doctor are asking that neither can answer.

Culture and psychology

The repercussion for psychology itself is that as a study it develops within a context of contemporary Western culture. Within this culture a high premium is placed upon knowledge that can be used to change, control, manipulate and order both nature and society. The emphasis on control, of personal agency, of individual freedom and the disposal of commodities influence psychological theories. The neglect of communion, inter-personal influence and the contribution of ecology has led to the promotion of individualistic causal trains, partial descriptions of sequences of events and the maintenance of the *status quo*. Yet in the previous chapters we see that when people talk about their problems, and the ensuing distress, causality is relational, events are located within episodes and sequences and changes are being sought. Indeed, the language of distress is varied and has implications for intimate relationships.

Attempts to resolve distress, when it occurs as conflict between individuals, without changing the systemic context within which they are located is a political and ideological strategy. Trying to resolve conflict without an understanding of social context may mean that some persons are asked to live with raised thresholds of distress. The use of psychotherapy, psychotropic medication, counselling and welfare by concentrating on the individual, without directing understanding to the context of the interaction, is a political act. By ignoring the political process of describing conflict and distress, and the place of the describer in context, we, as researchers and practitioners, become purveyors of a divisive ideology which denies legitimacy to certain groups in the population.

Liazos (1972), in a paper entitled 'The poverty of the sociology of deviance: nuts, sluts and perverts', proposes that the emphasis on deviant and personal problems, rather than larger social and political problems, directs away from institutional deviance. In attempts to humanise and normalise the deviant, the study of deviance itself confirms that the person as deviant is an appropriate subject for study and ignores the political activity of the person. For deviance to become a social fact, deviance must be perceived and an understanding must be resident within the culture that a particular act counts as deviant (Becker 1963). Jadhav (1996) makes a similar statement concerning the understanding of distress and the use of the category 'depression', emphasising that each culture generates a local psychiatry '...that constitutes and articulates the moral values and health concerns of that particular culture' (p.271).

Deviance from a particular state is negotiated with others and is a confirmation of a social definition (Dentler and Erikson 1959). By studying particular definition of what is deviant, we are involved in a political process by maintaining what issues are worthy of attention and what causal trains are to be invoked. This recognition of deviance occurs at a number of differing levels. By research into individuals, concentrating solely on individual deviance, we can only be concerned with individual internal causal trains. The move to a group perspective does not necessarily lead to an interactive perspective if it consistently refers to either one individual deviant member within a collective of persons or a deviant group. An understanding must be made of how behaviours are organised and co-ordinated such that one member becomes construed as deviant and how that behaviour is induced and sustained in interaction.

Even this group perspective fails to alert us to the politics of deviance unless we locate that perspective within an understanding of the range of possibilities which the culture makes available to us. The move from descriptions of personal deviance to group deviance may merely be a re-location of normative description unless we are careful to reflexively understand our part as social scientists in describing what counts as deviant behaviour (Pfohl 1977).

What we have experienced in recent times is that organised self-help groups concerned with the sufferers of AIDS and breast cancer have successfully challenged medical hegemony regarding research and treatment and the allocation of funding. Rather than remaining sick, separate and deviant, they have become united, active and accepted as a lobby for their rights.

At a time of limited resources, to focus on some areas for treatment and not others is a political decision. When suicidal behaviour is such a serious public and mental health problem in many countries, ranking among the top ten causes of death and with, perhaps, ten times as many non-fatal suicides (Diekstra 1996), the allocation of health care budgets and lack of public outcry, as there is over other health care problems, is a matter of political will.

Medicine and social control

Much of our daily living has become medicalised and the labels of health and illness are increasingly part of human existence (Zola 1972). We are continually exhorted to beware of what we smoke, how and what we drink, how and what we eat, how we should conduct our relationships and how to regulate our intimate activities (Aldridge 1997). The history of public health began as a commitment to change social aspects of life and used the arm of the state to change social conditions. Psychiatry developed to rehabilitate those legitimate deviants in society who are not criminal. The choice of whom to treat, and what means of treatment to use, is a form of discrimination.

The medico-psychiatric model has had the superficial impact of lifting moral condemnation from the individual (Szasz 1986). Sloth and guilt are no longer sins but have been transformed into symptoms of depression (Jadhav 1996). While the criminal is thought to be responsible or punishable for his act, the sick person is not so condemned. Ironically, the judgement of such personal responsibility is removed from deviant women. Women are likely to be judged sick and not responsible rather than criminal and, thereby, responsible (Heidersohn 1968). However, the criticism of Szasz that the medicalisation removes the notion of the sinner from the act is questionable. As we saw in the newspaper reporting and the hospital ward (Chapters Six and Seven), the lifting of the condemnation of women is temporary. The sick are scrutinised as to what they do about their demise. The person, rather than the context, is scrutinised for her role in her own personal inadequacy and process of recovery. Medicine retains the power of the doctor and the priest. The suspension of the judgement sin is dependent upon the recovery of the patient. Co-operation, or compliance to give it a more common medical term, is seen as being the responsibility of the patient. The good doctor does what she can, pity the poor sinner that does not comply.

When we ask the questions about 'Why at this time?' or 'Who is involved?', the rational veneer of science is soon split. Illness is concerned with the judgement of individual responsibility, accountability and moral judgement. This sphere of influence by medical personnel extends further than the solution of physical problems. Medical professionals advise on prevention and how to avoid certain conditions with the implications of self-neglect when such advice is ignored. Indeed, as we saw in Chapter One, the definition of suicide is that of personal intention. A definition that should exclude the consideration of suicidal behaviour from medical gaze.

Physicians are in a powerful position to judge and regulate the moods of their patients by the prescription of psychotropic drugs. Little credence is given by such professionals to the interactive nature of mood shifts or their own labelling of such states. The labelling of an internal state varies according to context (Schachter and Singer 1962). Furthermore, the politics of symptoms are ignored in the location of individual pathology. Not surprisingly, those who engage in suicidal behaviour have been offered treatment by their general practitioner, which they do not follow. General practitioner treatment is often in the form of medication (Wells 1981). To fail to comply with this treatment regime is rarely construed by the practitioner as an example of an inappropriate treatment regime. Rather, non-compliance is seen as further evidence of deviance and recalcitrance by a resistant manipulative patient. Even areas of social concern that are overtly dependent upon social or cultural factors – ageing, pregnancy, alcoholism and drug addiction – have come under the aegis of medical speciality.

The types of intervention in these arenas are designed to return sick individuals to a state of health or into a conventional social role. If not, persons are expected to adjust to an impaired role (the deviant, delinquent, the schizophrenic) or become comfortable with a condition (the chronic sick, post-natal depression). Interventions are made from the basis of an ideology that locates a deviant pathology within the individual. These interventions are designed to eliminate, modify, isolate or regulate behaviour socially defined as deviant. This is a political process.

The physician may argue that only a technical perspective of applied knowledge is being used. This denies the construing of the social group to which the physician belongs. The values of that group are latent within the practice of the techniques. The labels of personal behaviour are increasingly medicalised and such labels depoliticise personal issues. The label of hyperactive, for example, when applied to a child, or anorexic, to a young woman, depoliticises and diverts from the interactive issues. The ascription of depression in women ignores the interactive component in the politics of a marriage. By locating the source and treatment of problems in an individual, other levels of intervention are ignored. Similarly, the recognition of a specific undesirable state as an illness leads to decisions about the 'how' and 'when' of treatment but seldom is the decision whether to treat at all, or a decision made about the label, given to that condition. Even when a shift is made from the individual to the familial it is possible to 'treat' difficult or deviant families rather than understand the ecological significance of such behaviour.

Illich (1977) is concerned with the way in which the public norms of health are decided and about what is to be treated. The professions of the various helping agencies not only say what is good but what is right and thereby legitimise behaviour. The withholding or application of legitimacy is, as the previous chapter shows, a powerful factor in describing and regulating suicidal behaviour. By ignoring general health needs, persons become seen as, at best, foolish and, at worst, illegitimate. The correction of transgressors becomes the domain of the medical profession. Furthermore, those behaviours that are legitimate at one level (familial) may be illegitimate at another level (communal).

Psychotherapy and social control

By concentrating on treating individuals and fostering an ideology of intrapsychic conflicts and dynamic forces, psychotherapy is concerned with changing individuals. Individuals are treated to promote their accommodation within society. The whole psychodynamic ideology makes personal problems of political issues (Hurvitz 1973) and this is precisely what has happened in the traditional psychiatric study of suicidal behaviour. Even the large epidemiological studies that take account of ecological and demographic data return to the episode of suicidal behaviour as an impulsive individual act. The notion of Western society that equates personal worth and failure with a person's inherent limitations contributes to the belief that failure of the poor is their own fault. Psychotherapy fosters the belief that persons can live fulfilling lives without basic social changes. The labelling of mental illness or maladjustment is a political decision that stresses some aspects of behaviour above others.

When psychotherapy concentrates on changing an individual patient's perspective, the social causes of that behaviour, and the social position of being a patient, are ignored. By accommodating the conditions which give rise to complaints, the psychotherapist is an agent of social control. This is evident in the way that women are medicated, cajoled and induced to accommodate their political objections into medico-psychiatric frames of post-natal depression, anxiety, phobias and pre-menstrual tension.

A difficulty for the psychotherapist, to which Szasz (1967) alerts us, is that the psychotherapist is a double agent. While overtly claiming to serve the patient, the psychotherapist also serves society reflecting societal concerns and diverting from threatening construings. In Chapter Six we see the furore which followed the coroner's description of the suicide of the two unemployed men. In the current climate of community psychiatric practice, and an increasing interest by general medical practitioners in psychiatric problems, problems presented by individuals with a possible social genesis are treated as resident within individuals. A complication of this is that even though enlightened practitioners understand social causal factors, their perceived effective treatment strategies are organised to treat individuals. While recognising social or interactive problems, it is still the individual that gets the treatment.

A critique of family systems theory

The way in which a problem is defined and the means invoked to resolve that becomes a cultural issue. The locating of individual distress within a person is seen as maintaining a problem and promoting the escalation of distress. To relocate the problem within a familial organisational perspective can fall into the trap of defining deviant or problem families. Any endeavours to resolve distress as presented by persons must be aware of the shifts in legitimacy which are made by the therapeutic agent. Therapists are part of therapeutic agencies and these agencies are part of maintaining the *status quo*. Such an approach means that networks must be considered within a community of all those involved in the formulation, identification and the management of problems.

To adopt a network, or eco-systemic, approach offers a number of differing perspectives and a number of different places for intervention. Furthermore, a network approach promotes a contextual analysis of problematic behaviour that moves the location of deviance from individual persons. We can see how in Chapter Six the descriptions offered of the two boys as martyrs or villains has powerful implications for the legitimacy of actions which question the *status quo*. To legitimise the description of 'no hope' as a cause for suicide, and as a corollary of unemployment, would have ramifications for governmental approaches to unemployment and to suicide prevention.

Ecological solutions; the resolution of a dilemma

A difficulty of this approach is that once we move from an individualistic stance to an interactive position, all problems can be defined within an economic or cultural frame. Such problems are resolved not by therapeutic strategies but by political moves and revolutionary changes. The therapist or practitioner must become, in this view, revolutionary. Meanwhile, clients wait in personal distress, and a distress that inhibits their activity as personal and collective agents of change.

To deal solely with the familial consequences of unemployment is to ignore the wider politics of employment, commodity fetishism, the status of women and the distribution of capital. To concentrate on political lobbying is to ignore the obvious manifestation of personal and familial distress. An eco-systemic approach, which concentrates on multiple dimensions of meaning, the involvement of a network of involved others and the systemic nature of political process, resolves this false dilemma.

I have tried in these pages to locate suicidal behaviour and personal distress immediately within an organisational frame of a community of intimates while accepting that the political dilemma still exists. Rather than depoliticise and invalidate individuals and families by describing them as illegitimate and deviant, I propose that the resolution of distress, by ascribing legitimacy, frees the individual and family to actively engage within the community. By becoming sick, individuals are divided from one another. By promoting health, individuals can unite in their legitimate grievance.

> As a society we construct the social world according to our interests and beliefs; and as individuals we construct our beliefs to make sense of our own particular experiences of the world. So shared experience and beliefs support each other – at least for a good deal of the time. (Fransella and Frost 1977, p.24).

To understand suicidal behaviour the researcher should discover concrete descriptions in particular contexts. Instead of asking the question 'Why', I have asked the participants 'What happens'. To ask the question 'Why' generates understandings that are already resident in culture and ignores the social relationship between who is asking and who is being asked. To discover patterns of interaction, and the way in which interaction is described, generates an alternative description by the observer and elicits a processual description from the subject. This processual description, as regulative rules, is not generally used in eliciting descriptions of personal behaviour. To evoke a processual description of circular interaction between involved others removes the labels of personal, deviant, manipulative agency and suggests cyclical patterns of repeated interaction. Suicidal behaviour no longer becomes the act of an impulsive, weak, non-coping stigmatised person but an interactional strategy to regulate relational or familial coherence. To reduce distress, then, we must understand the construing of those who are distressed and the ramifications of their, and our, actions. What we have to face up to is that the tactics of distress management, as they are simply formulated as interventions with pre-suicidal and suicidal patients, may contribute to the escalation of distress. This means that the blind prescription of interventions based on group probabilities according to medical theories is a hit-and-miss affair that may contribute to further distress, that is iatrogenic (see Figure 9.2, p.177).

CHAPTER THIRTEEN

The Politics of Prevention

Over the last two decades motor traffic mortality rates have been decreasing while at the same time suicide rates, particularly among adolescents and young adults, have been sharply increasing. But in all countries, without any single exception, the resources being made for preventive interventions in the case of suicidal behaviour constitute only a tiny fraction of what is available for the prevention of motor traffic deaths' (Diekstra 1996, p.2)

The construction of social knowledge

Throughout this book the emphasis has been that knowledge is constructed at a number of differing levels. At the personal level this knowledge is negotiated and maintained with those whom we are intimate. The parameters and norms for the construction of reality and the management of a shared reality are proposed as constitutive and regulative rules. Change, regularity, agreement, disagreement, order and instability are negotiated at a number of levels that provide meaning and continuity to interaction.

In the case of the family, interactions are understood within particular family construings. A family member gains definition by belonging within the family boundary, by sharing and actively participating in the familial way of organising reality. This provides identity at one level but also constrains individual behaviour at the personal level.

At the societal level there are gross cultural understandings that are less accessible to negotiation and change. These understandings are conservative and persist. We know that the earth circles the sun yet still in our language we persist in talking about how the sun rises in the morning and sets at night as if the sun circled the earth. In the same way, cultural descriptions of personal behaviour persist using linear trains of cause and effect that we know from personal experience are inappropriate. These cultural descriptions offer explanations of behaviour at times of disagreement, ambiguity or when a common interpersonal understanding is not negotiated satisfactorily. At such times cultural understandings are invoked to validate personal and familial behaviour. When people exhibit distress and suicidal behaviour, the reasons for that distress are articulated by observers. Either patients, or their families, are potential deviants threatening the very fabric of society by their fatal intentions or victims of an uncaring state that is dedicated to the values of consumerism and success as measured by attainment and income.

The variety of possible explanations for suicidal behaviour are reflected in the plethora of possibilities for intervention and prevention.

Approaches to prevention and intervention.

Most of the authors writing about prevention attempt to identify risk factors (Garland and Zigler 1993) while accepting that prediction of suicide is difficult (Tanney 1995), although there appears to be a process of development involving predisposing factors, perpetuating conditions, precipitating conditions and preventive measures (Diekstra 1992) with some sort of ranking of targets for change (Gunnell 1994; Silverman and Felner 1995). A central issue is how we, as a society, decide to allocate our preventive resources if the individuals or groups that we should target are elusive to identification (Maris and Silverman 1995).

The public health model, based on a medical understanding of suicidal behaviour, favours clear signs and symptoms and bases its interventions on statistics for prevalence and incidence (Silverman and Maris 1995). A natural history of the process is sought and then possible interventions are made along a pathological trajectory. Identifying decision points appears to be a critical part of this process and is relevant to other models too. As we saw in Chapter Nine, there is an identifiable process of escalation in terms of human distress but there is no single suicidal path making prediction difficult but not impossible. As suicidal behaviour is not a disease, we should not expect that there is a pathogen and a disease trajectory, however neat this would be for medical practice.

The operational model is not based on aetiology or causality and aims to identify individuals at greater risk. As definitive risk factors are difficult to find, other than a previous history of attempted suicide, such screening programs are expensive and inefficient. The risk factors associated with suicidal behaviour are the presence of a psychiatric disorder (Rihmer 1996; Whitfield and Southern 1996) such as depression or schizophrenia (Appleby 1992), anti-social behaviour (Johnsson Fridell, Öjehagen and Träskman-Bendz 1996) or alcohol and substance abuse problems (Garland and Zigler 1993). As we have seen in the previous chapters, psychiatric illness plays a role in the development of escalating distress. However, the labelling of the patient as psychiatrically ill may itself may be a part of the developing process. When a patient becomes labelled as psychiatrically ill, they have access to an available repertoire of suicidal behaviours from the milieu in which they find themselves. As we saw in Chapter Seven, suicidal behaviour was part of the behavioural repertoire on a psychiatric ward. As a risk factor in psychiatry, suicidal behaviour is expected, thus closing the circle of a self-fulfilling prophecy.

Some authors consider secondary risk factors and tertiary risk factors such as early parental loss, isolation following separation, divorce or widowhood, unemployment or major financial problems and severe negative life events (Rihmer 1996). If we consider the factors in Chapter Eleven of imminent systemic dissolution, total negative connotation and a history of illness presentation, we see that what are considered by some authors to be secondary factors are here considered as primary. The difficulty of the factor approach beloved by epidemiologists and medical practitioners is that the developmental process is left out and the meaning of events is not even considered. For a middle-aged academic in Germany, for example, the loss of hair and middle-age spread is no major tragedy but for my Mediterranean neighbour it would be a catastrophe in terms of his identity. It is not the event that counts but the way the event is perceived and that makes a mockery of the specific risk factor approach. Only when a developmental view is considered, can we begin to compare common processes.

Recent work with deliberate self-harm in adolescents (McLaughlin, Miller, and Warwick 1996) has highlighted the role of hopelessness as negative expectancies concerning the near future in the generation of suicidal behaviour. Many parents were not aware of the extent of their childrens' concerns or feelings of hopelessness prior to a suicide attempt. Linked to hopelessness was the problems that adolescents felt hopeless about, and these were related to family, friends and school. While some authors seem willing to consider age, either adolescence or old age, as a risk factor for suicidal behaviour, it is the studies relating hopelessness to particular ages that contain a key to understanding the process of escalating distress and isolation. If adolescents in our society are lacking in hope, and their parents are not aware of the depth of their feelings, then maybe we should be tackling the matter of our own insensitivity, as adults, as the target for prevention. Stack (1996) reminds us that being adolescent means belonging to an 'at risk' group and market economies have a weak social safety net for the poor and the unemployed.

Similarly, if the aged are choosing no longer to live with us by killing themselves, we must reflect upon the society that we have produced such that they no longer feel at home. If being old is to belong to a suicidal risk group, and the numbers of elderly committing suicide has increased significantly over the last few years, then we may have to look further than the simple factor of age and begin to understand what it means to be old in a modern industrialised society.

Old people are losing their will to live because life holds no meaning for them and they are alienated from their families and from all that had meaning for them. Labelling this as depression, in the hope that it can be treated, is to put a medical gloss upon an existential problem that is at the heart of our post-modern dilemma.

If the financial burden of caring for the elderly is emphasised, and many of them think their lives are meaningless, then we run the risk of colluding with the belief of many elderly people that they are worthless because no longer productive, and that the cost of supporting them is too much. This is a dangerous liaison of ideas that can too easily find political expedience. We then begin to talk of assisted suicide rather than supported life.

Who, then, is to be an advocate on behalf of the poor, hopeless and handicapped – those people who are expensive to support and, in a modern world, can only be seen as non-productive? The fatal cycle is that these very people, when isolated, come to the conclusion that they really are worthless and that their lives are no longer worth living. That is the scenario for hopelessness and alienation, two precursors of suicide.

Finally, it is not the simple factor of age that must be considered in our research studies but how we relate to people at particular stages of their life cycle.

Therapeutic procedure

In Chapter Seven a description is made of how conflict and distress on a hospital ward is resolved. A similar pattern of management is used in the therapy of those who are seen after an episode of attempted suicide and those who present with suicidal feelings (see Chapter Nine). Throughout this process different contextual levels of meaning are borne in mind: the personal, the familial and the cultural (Aldridge 1985; Aldridge and Rossiter 1983; Aldridge and Rossiter 1984).

A systemic description

Instead of considering personal deviance alone, an understanding of the suicidal individual is sought within an interactive nexus of significant others. All involved persons are asked about what they do in managing their collective behaviour concerning a commonly identified problem (Aldridge and Rossiter 1983; Aldridge and Rossiter 1984). Instead of imposing a therapist's view upon the family, the family are encouraged to reconstruct their reality in the presence of the therapist. The concerns are directed from the individual to the collective, from feeling to action. Feelings are important but it is when they occur and what is done about them that is relevant for suicidal behaviour.

Negotiation

All involved members, including the therapist, are involved in negotiating a common goal and means of attaining that goal. The procedure is one of recognising and implementing discrete steps to attain that goal that do not repeat previously attempted solutions but utilise the rules and construings resident within the family. This approach is concerned with understanding the family within the terms of the family (Dallos and Aldridge 1987). The onus is on the therapist to understand the problem, not for the therapist to teach the family what the problem is.

The therapist takes a position of being a neutral adviser. A stance of being involved, but not being in an executive position, allows the organisation of those involved to remain self-regulating. Rather than see a therapist to resolve problems, the family are encouraged to use their own problem-solving resources. This is a useful antidote to the feeling of being manipulated that some practitioners feel, or controlled or dominated as some patients feel. As soon as patients and practitioners become co-operative partners negotiating what is, or can, be done as consensus, no one is imposing on the other. Indeed, the idea of consensus, a common sensing and joint feeling (Eckstein 1996), is appropriate and evokes the *filial* sense in family where each works for the benefit of the other (Bourdieu 1996).

There is a rider to this stance and that is in those cases where overt threats of suicidal behaviour occur. Then it is the responsibility of the therapist, nurse, psychiatrist or general practitioner to implement whatever legal steps are necessary to ensure the immediate safety of the patient. In Chapter Nine we saw that, when necessary, the psychiatrist at the initial interview in the hospital after an episode of deliberate self-harm would respond according to the answers she received.

Positive connotation

Instead of damning the family as deviant, incompetent and illegitimate, the family are encouraged to see themselves as legitimate, resourceful and attempting to resolve a situation of complexity and difficulty. The suicidal individual is construed as legitimate and pursuing a sacrificial course of keeping the family together at the personal expense of individual distress and legitimacy. By proposing a positive understanding, without denying the severity of the situation, to the family, the therapist offers an opportunity at a time of heightened distress for a new understanding to be made and a new process brought into action.

Conflict

Rather than seeing conflict as being resident in warring factions that are failing to agree and, by implication, are failing in their relationships, conflict can be seen as an attempt to resolve a situation. Conflict is a description of the way in which the systemic behaviour is organised. Once conflict is seen as resident in the interactional sequence, it can be negotiated by focusing on a goal common to all participants. Therapy becomes not a remedial phenomenon of fixing what is wrong but a generative phenomenon of inventing new capabilities. By taking this tack the therapist becomes concerned with evolutionary change from a basis of competence, rather than remedial change to accommodate pathology and deviance. The therapist becomes a facilitator who offers choices which the family can utilise. To do this the therapist must understand the rules and construing, the language of the family and make choices available in this language rather than coach the family in the language of the therapist.

Again there is a rider to this situation. Where violence occurs, or a child is abused, such positive reframing can effectively dismiss a very real problem of physical abuse by one partner of another. As in the example of life threatening behaviour above, the therapist may have to take statutory steps first for the protection of the patient. This in itself is an event that must be accommodated and can exacerbate the situation of suicidality.

Concrete action

The process of therapy is concerned with understanding patterns and meaning and offering acceptable alternatives. These alternatives are converted into concrete steps to achieve negotiated goals. Instead of proposing abstract solutions to global goals, therapists can negotiate particularised solutions. Instead of medicating to relieve depression, this approach concentrates on how relief is recognised in particular situations where depression occurs and what particular steps are taken to obtain relief with those concerned. When depression is related to marital harmony, this approach concentrates depression and harmony are related. Indeed, as one woman said in her letter in Chapter Eight, harmony was achieved when she became divorced. In this case therapy may have to do with negotiating marital separation rather than marital counselling to bring people together. In a political climate where marriage and the family are emphasised as traditional values, the maintenance of marital relationships may condemn some people to a prolonged misery and undue distress.

The process of obtaining relief or harmony has implications for those others involved in the wider community of systemic involvement. Marital harmony may be negotiated, but at the risk of ignoring the ramifications for the step-children or in-laws. To ignore these implications for maintaining systemic coherence is a mistake that compounds the previous strategies made by other agencies that have failed to resolve the distress.

No change

No attempt is made to stop the suicidal behaviour immediately, as we saw in Chapters Seven and Nine. Rather than coerce the individual into conforming, the family or group are exhorted to respect individual autonomy. Similarly, the process of assessment is not one of change or therapy but of gathering information. If suicidal behaviour is anything to do with accommodating change, assessment of the situation does not compound the situation by proposing further changes. A critical step in the therapeutic process is understanding whether distress is a result of too much change or not enough change (see Chapter Nine).

Death

Death is more than a medical event and is not exhausted by medical meanings (Wildes 1996). Different cultures will understand death differently, and this applies to families too. Death can be openly discussed as an issue as a cultural, moral and religious event (Aldridge 1988; Aldridge 1991). The discussion of death, if suicidal behaviour is a metaphor for the death of a system, raises the inevitability of certain actions. Those concerns can be raised that reflect an imminent breakdown of the system and the consequences of a family or relational split planned. The possible dissolution of one system, a change in the family system, can be seen as being a stage for the emergence of a new system. We must negotiate the architecture of living, even in the presence of dying. The organisation of the new is negotiated with those who are to be involved and in the presence of those who are threatening to leave (Aldridge 1987).

In the case of the dying, it is important that family matters are discussed. Unfortunately, we often live in communities where dying is not talked about, yet the distress of dying is articulated by a family member to a doctor as somatic symptoms. Lester (1993) found that people who were dying from cancer and who had attempted suicide were the recipients of more prejudice than ethnic or religious groups. Talking about a mother who is dying within a family context may relieve the presented distress of the eldest daughter and bring comfort to the mother too. As suicide is such a high risk in the elderly over 75 years of age, and, in particular, men, we may have to consider how older men present their distress as physical complaints to their general practitioners, and the relational contexts of where they are living, to make any substantial change in reducing deaths by suicide.

Death will occur no matter what we do. The means of how dying is achieved is, however, open to our influence. If we begin to consider euthanasia and assisted suicide, we also introduce into our communities the idea that there is such a thing as a 'good death'. While a good death is pertinent within the context of the hospice movement, it is a dangerous concept within a climate where health savings have to be made. We have to consider for whom the death is 'good'. The impetus for most health care practitioners is to heal, and so are they trained. Part of the problem that they face in dealing with the dying and chronically sick is that those healing endeavours are severely challenged. Yet that does not qualify them alone to participate in assisting death.

A different frame

By concentrating on repeated sequences of interaction, the episode of suicidal behaviour can be construed not as impulsive but as belonging within an extended time-frame. Rather than punctuate reality into a short arc of critical disturbance, it is possible to see the episode as belonging to a cyclical pattern of escalating interaction. The understanding of a social reality on a longer time-scale of circular causality also leads to considering deviant acts in an alternative way. Rather than malicious delinquent acts that are negatively connoted, it is possible to see positively connoted acts of problem resolution (see Chapter Six). Instead of seeing senseless acts of personal inadequacy, it is possible to see meaningful acts of social significance. By considering different punctuations of social reality, individuals become construed as legitimate in their intention.

A strategy of prevention

Preventive strategies are politically difficult. They can mean intervening in processes before crises occur. As Szasz (1986) comments, this is a direct affront to personal autonomy, the resolution of which is still open to a debate that is not easily reconciled (Lester and Leenaars 1996). Medicine already offers a whole series of advice and propositions for avoiding disease entities that invade areas of personal freedom and choice. As I have suggested in the previous chapter, the wilful ignoring of such advice has implications for personal validity and responsibility, personal legitimacy and access to treatment. If unemployment, poverty, poor education and disenfranchisement are causal in the train of suicide, as they are for poor health generally, then political solutions are one of the means for improvement. That is a macrosocial intervention.

However, a preventive strategy for suicidal behaviour can be implemented at other levels. The first of these is that a change in understandings of personal distress must be made in primary care by general practitioners. Individual problems must not only be understood as they occur in relational contexts but treatment initiatives must take this into account. While some practitioners may already recognise the relational component, it is the insistence on individualised solutions that are problematic.

It is important that the general practitioner recognises a process where distress is escalating (see Figures 5.4, p.85, and 9.2, p.177). Prescribing psychotropic medication to alleviate overtly described interactive problems is ineffective in the long term. However, it is important to offer the general practitioner professional support from mental health and social services that makes a systemic understanding of the problem and offers alternative strategies of problem resolution. Moving the focus from individual medical strategies to individual psycho-therapeutic strategies itself is no great change in understanding and, as Hawton and Catalan (1982) propose, is of little use. However, the continuing training of medical practitioners in emergency medical units and the availability of mental health teams to those practitioners is a relevant strategy in bringing about change (Pang, Catalan and Booth 1996).

Any approach must utilise the resources of the persons immediately involved and be based upon discrete concrete actions, as we saw in Chapter Nine. The location of distress management must be made from the individual being treated to one of organisational change and the promotion of alternatives. This approach will involve changes in treatment approaches that means health care professionals working together as a team. As each specialisation in a mental health care team becomes more complex, we must find a way to pool our varying resources as effective teams. However, what we must not forget is the resources that the patient and his family bring. Rather than be faced with socially inept deviants, both patients and practitioners, we perhaps have to recognise that all of us bring a variety of resources together that we can share.

One of the benefits of working with families in Chapter Nine was that by involving the general practitioner there appeared to be fewer episodes of deliberate self-harm in the community, although more suicidal persons were referred for help. Prevention occurred using a community solution involving a network of practitioners rather than on individualistic therapeutic endeavours. The same family-based approach was used in a South African study, with even better results, based on a community perspective that focused on the general hospital setting (Wassenaar 1987).

Suicidal persons are trying to make sense of themselves and the world in which they live. Their actions belong in a reciprocal ecology of interacting persons. As far as suicidal behaviour is an attempt at resolving a problem located in an interactional nexus, the continued management of the individual as patient is a political move which ignores systemic understanding. Our continual ignoring of the problem of suicide in terms of fiscal measures to implement change reflects the paucity of our understanding of human distress and the poverty of political will that denies the sufferer relief. We are facing the next century with an escalating rate for youth suicide within the industrialised nations. How are we to explain to the next generation that we do not find their plight worthy of consideration? At the other end of the age spectrum old people are killing themselves. Their lives no longer have any meaning for them and dying itself appears to have a social expediency. We are the architects of distress and it appears that at the same time as we are stopping up the windows of hope, we are also opening up the doors of despair.

For the person who is suicidal, then, distress has escalated beyond the thresholds of their toleration. They have no more resources to sustain themselves. This is the process of desertification. Those resources are not simply personal but relational, familial and social. Distress lies within a network of interactions. Once people become isolated they are cut of from potential sources of help. Young people, unemployed and homeless, living in centres of urban decay are vulnerable. So too for the elderly, isolated in inappropriate accommodation and welfare support that is stretched beyond its means. But there are others too in our society who lack social support, where their personal lives are perceived to be failing and their relational support is disintegrating. Suddenly, the challenge is too great for the resources at hand. The next century faces us with the challenge of how to hear distress when it is articulated and to respond adequately. If we fail to meet this demand, all our technological endeavours will be of nought. We must ask ourselves why people are choosing not to live among us. How is it that civilised communities in the late-twentieth century have evolved that people choose death rather than life and that for one group, the elderly, some practitioners are wondering how the quality of living can be improved while, simultaneously, another group in the community are actively seeking ways to bring about death?

Coda

So what do I tell my daughter about her friend, Ruth? From what we have read, we can expect that all was not well at home, something was about to happen. Indeed, Ruth's parents were living together under the same roof but her father was having an affair with another woman. Ruth had returned from university for the vacation. She was, however, having a hard time. Always a brilliant student at school, university life had pitched her into a milieu of equally brilliant students. Personally, she was struggling to maintain an identity and at home that family identity was being threatened. The world was not as it was and she could not see how to change it. In addition, Ruth had suffered previously with an eating disorder, she had rigorously control-led her weight and had been treated for anorexia nervosa. All the signs were indeed there, but only if you knew what to look for. And, often, the factors are well concealed.

If we return to the suicide of Bruno Bettelheim, we find that his friend and colleague, who knew that Bettelheim was suicidal, was also shocked when the event actually took place (Fisher 1992). Somehow the message of distress has its own circuit in which it is communicated. Outside of that system, everything appears to be in order. For Emily's friend Ruth, she could go shopping with her and drink coffee together quite freely and socially. The distress was not in their relationship. The suicide itself was intended to communicate distress in another set of relationships, in a system where it would have its own function.

Finally, we must not forget those who remain after a family member has committed suicide; the survivors, as they are sometimes referred to (Mauk and Rodgers 1994; Seguin, Lesage and Kiely 1995; Silverman, Range and Overholser 1995). For Ruth's parents, they were devastated at the loss of a daughter who had showed so much promise. And like all of us as parents, when our children suffer, they too had asked the question: 'Where did they go wrong?' It is a question that echoes through the years afterwards. Similar questions are asked by friends: 'What did they miss?' or 'What could they have done differently?'

We know from the literature that bereavement from suicide demands a difficult and complex adjustment for the surviving friends and family members. Suicide survivors are likely to experience more intense grief reactions and may suffer from social rejection and alienation. Silverman, Range and Overholser (1995) found in college students that bereavement from suicide was associated with more intense grief reactions than the other bereaved groups. It is yet another reflection upon our ways of handling distress that we have neglected the survivors of suicide. Perhaps because survivors remind us of our own failure, we find it difficult to support them.

The hand of suicide seems to reach from beyond the grave and touch those who remain with its tragic finger. While time heals, the power of suicide is the potent effect that it has upon the survivors. But as we have seen in Figure 5.4 (p.85), the threshold of recovery has been transgressed. There is no going back. I have used the term 'desertification' earlier because this reflects that all the personal resources have been used up. For those of us remaining, it is a challenge to our future civilised communities that we can convince other individuals that we are part of their resources. To do so we must establish contact with those who suffer, to listen to and to tolerate distress, even when it reflects our own adversity. As I have proposed earlier, hopelessness is a relationship. Hope, too, is a relationship that we build with others, but we must build that hope upon the foundations of those with whom we live together.

References

Adamek, M.E. and Kaplan, M.S. (1996a) 'Firearm suicide among older men.' *Psychiatric Services 47*, 3, 304–306.

Adamek, M.E. and Kaplan, M.S. (1996b) 'The growing use of firearms by suicidal older women, 1979–1992: A research note.' *Suicide and Life – Threatening Behavior 26*, 1, 71–78.

Adler, A. (1958) 'Suicide.' *Journal of Individual Psychology 14*, 57–62.

Alderson, M. (1974) 'Self-poisoning – what is the future?' *Lancet, 1040–1043.*

Aldridge, D. (1984) 'Family interaction and suicidal behavior: a brief review.' *Journal of Family Therapy 6*, 309–322.

Aldridge, D. (1985) 'Suicidal behaviour: an ecosystemic approach.' Ph.D, The Open University, Milton Keynes, England.

Aldridge, D. (1987) *One Body: a Guide to Healing in the Church.* London: S.P.C.K.

Aldridge, D. (1988) 'Families, cancer and dying.' *Journal of the Institute of Religion and Medicine 3*, 312–322.

Aldridge, D. (1990) 'Making and taking health care decisions.' *Journal of the Royal Society of Medicine 83*, 720–723.

Aldridge, D. (1991) 'Healing and medicine.' *Journal of the Royal Society of Medicine 84*, 516–518.

Aldridge, D. (1992) 'Suicidal behavior: a continuing cause for concern.' *British Journal of General Practice 42*, 482–485.

Aldridge, D. (1997) 'Lifestyle, charismatic ideology and a praxis aesthetic.' In S. Olesen, B. Eikaard, P. Gad and E. Høg (eds) *Studies in Alternative Therapy 4. Lifestyle and Medical Paradigms.* Odense: Odense University Press.

Aldridge, D. and Dallos, R. (1986) 'Distinguishing families where suicidal behavior is present from families where suicidal behavior is absent.' *Journal of Family Therapy 8*, 243–252.

Aldridge, D. and Rossiter, J. (1983) 'A strategic approach to suicidal behaviour.' *Journal of Systemic and Strategic Therapies 2*, 4, 49–62.

Aldridge, D. and Rossiter, J. (1984) 'A strategic assessment of deliberate self harm.' *Journal of Family Therapy 6*, 113–125.

Andersen, J.Ø. (1995) 'Lifestyles, consumption and alternative therapies.' In S. Olesen, B. Eikard, P. Gad and E. Høg (eds), *Studies in Alternative Therapy 4.* Odense: Odense University Press.

Andersen, M. and Lobel, M. (1995) 'Predictors of health self-appraisal: what's involved in feeling healthy?' *Basic and Applied Social Psychology 16*, 1 and 2, 121–136.

Andrews, G. (1981) 'A prospective study of life events and psychological symptoms.' *Psychological Medicine 11*, 795–801.

Appleby, L. (1992) 'Suicide in psychiatric patients – risk and prevention.' *British Journal of Psychiatry 161*, 749–758.

Appleby, L., Amos, T., Doyle, U., Tomenson, B., and Woodman, M. (1996) 'General practitioners and young suicides. A preventive role for primary care.' *British Journal of Psychiatry 168*, 3, 330–333.

Arensman, E. and Kerkhof, A. (1996) 'Classification of attempted suicide: a review of empirical studies, 1963–1993.' *Suicide and Life – Threatening Behavior 26*, 1, 46–67.

Arnold, E. (1911) *Roman stoicism.* Cambridge: Cambridge University Press.

Asch, S. (1971) 'Wrist scratching as a symptom of anhedonia: a prodepressive state.' *Psychoanalytic Quarterly 40*, 603–613.

Ashby, W. (1960) *Design for a Brain.* 2nd ed. London: Chapman and Hall.

Atkinson, J. (1978) *Discovering Suicide: Studies in the Social Organization of Sudden Death.* London: Macmillan.

Auerswald, E. (1968) 'Interdisciplinary v. ecological approach.' *Family Process 7*, 202–215.

Bach-Y-Rita, G. (1974) 'Habitual violence and self-mutilation.' *American Journal of Psychiatry 131*, 1018–1020.

Baerveldt, C. and Voestermans, P. (1996) 'The body as selfing device. The case of anorexia nervosa.' *Theory and Psychology 6*, 4, 693–713.

Ballinger, B. (1971) 'Minor self-injury.' *British Journal of Psychiatry 118*, 535–538.

Bancroft, J., Skrimshire, A., Reynolds, F., Simkin, S. and Smith, J. (1975) 'Self-poisoning and self-injury in the Oxford area: epidemiological aspects 1969–1973.' *British Journal of Preventive and Social Medicine 29*, 170–177.

Bancroft, J., Skrimshire, A. and Simkin, S. (1976) 'The reasons people give for taking overdoses.' *British Journal of Psychiatry 128*, 538–548.

Bancroft, J., Skrimshire, A., Casson, J., Harvard-Watts, D., and Reynolds, F. (1977a) 'People who deliberately poison or injure themselves: their problems and their contacts with helping agencies.' *Psychological Medicine 7*, 289–303.

Bancroft, J. and Marsack, P. (1977b) 'The repetitiveness of self-poisoning and self-injury.' *British Journal of Psychiatry 131*, 394–399.

Bancroft, J., Skrimshire, A., and Simkin, S. (1979) 'The reasons people give for taking overdoses: a further enquiry.' *British Journal of Medical Psychology 52*, 353–365.

Bannister, D. and Fransella, F. (1971) *Inquiring Man.* Harmondsworth: Penguin.

Barter, J. (1968) 'Adolescent suicide attempts: a follow-up study of hospitalised patients.' *Archives of General Psychiatry 12*, 213.

Bateson, G. (1973) *Steps to an Ecology of Mind.* London: Granada.

Bateson, G. (1978) 'Afterword.' In J. Brockman (ed) *About Bateson.* London: Wildwood House.

Bateson, G. (1979) *Mind and Nature.* Glasgow: Fontana.

Beautrais, A., Joyce, P. and Mulder, R. (1996) 'Risk factors for serious suicide attempts among youths aged 13 through 24 years.' *Journal of American Academic Child and Adolescent Psychiatry 35*, 9, 1174–1182.

Becker, H. (1963) *Outsiders.* New York: The Free Press.

Beer, S. (1975) *Platform for Change.* London: John Wiley.

Bergner, R. (1978) 'The marital system of the hysterical individual.' *Family Process 16*, 85–95.

Berman, A.L. and Jobes, D.A. (1995) 'Suicide prevention in adolescents (age 12–18).' *Suicide and Life – Threatening Behavior 25*, 1, 143–154.

Bille-Brahe, U. (1993) 'The role of sex and age in suicidal behavior.' *Acta Psychiatrica Scandinavica 87*, Suppl. 371, 21–27.

Birtchnell, J. (1973) 'The Special Place of Psychotherapy in the Treatment of Attempted Suicide, and the Special Type of Psychotherapy Required.' In *What is Psychotherapy?* Proceedings of the Ninth International Congress of Psychotherapy, Oslo, 316–318.

Black, D. (1981) 'Children and parasuicide.' *British Medical Journal 283*, 337–338.

Blumer, H. (1972) 'Society as symbolic interaction.' In J. Manis and B. Metyler (eds) *Symbolic Interaction: a Reader in Social Psychology.* Boston: Allyn and Bacon.

Bogue, H. and Power, K. (1995) 'Suicide in Scottish prisons, 1976–93.' *Journal of Forensic Psychiatry 6*, 3, 527–540.

Bostic, R. (1973) 'Self-immolation: a survey of the last decade.' *Life Threatening Behaviour 3*, 66–74.

Bostock, F. and Williams, C. (1974) 'Attempted suicide as an operant behaviour.' *Archives of General Psychiatry 31*, 482–486.

Bourdieu, P. (1996) 'On the family as realized category.' *Theory, Culture and Society 13*, 3, 19–26.

Bowlby, J. (1973) *Attachment and Loss. Vol.2 'Separation: Anxiety and Anger.* London: Hogarth.

Bowling, A. and Windsor, J. (1995) 'Death after widow(er)hood – An analysis of mortality rates up to 13 years after bereavement.' *Omega – Journal of Death and Dying 31*, 1, 35–49.

Brenman, M. (1952) 'On teasing and being teased: the problem of moral masochism.' *Psychoanalytic study of the Child 7*, 264–285.

Brent, D., Bridge, J., Johnson, B. and Connolly, J. (1996) 'Suicidal behavior runs in families.' *Archives of General Psychiatry 53*, 1145–1152.

Brent, D. and Perper, J. (1995) 'Research in adolescent suicide: Implications for training, service delivery, and public policy.' *Suicide and Life – Threatening Behavior 25*, 2, 222–230.

Brewster Smith, M. (1994) 'Selfhood at risk: postmodern perils and the perils of postmodernism.' *American Psychologist 49*, 5, 405–411.

Bronisch, T. (1996) 'Suicidality in German concentration camps.' *Archives of Suicide Research 2*, 129–144.

Brown, B. , Nolan, P., Crawford, P. and Lewis, A. (1996) 'Interaction, language and the 'narrative turn' in psychotherapy and psychiatry.' *Social Science and Medicine 43*, 11, 1569–1578.

Brown, G., Bhrolchain, M. and Harris, T. (1975) 'Social class and psychiatric disturbance among women in an urban population.' *Sociology 9*, 225–254.

Brown, G., Harris, T. and Peto, J. (1973) 'Life events and psychiatric disorders. Part 2: nature of causal link.' *Psychological Medicine 3*, 159–176.

Brown, L., Overholser, J., Spirito, A. and Fritz, G. (1991) 'The correlates of planning in adolescent suicide attempts.' *Journal of the American Academy of Child and Adolescent Psychiatry 30*, 1, 95–9.

Brown, R. and Lenneberg, E. (1965) 'Studies in linguistic relativity.' In H. Proshansky and B. Seidenberg (eds) *Basic Studies in Social Psychology.* New York: Holt Reinhart and Wilson.

Buckley, W. (1967) *Sociology and Modern Systems Theory.* Englewood Cuffs, NJ: P. Hall.

Bursten, B. (1965) 'Family dynamics, the sick role and medical hospital admissions.' *Family Process 4*, 206–216.

Bursten, B. and D'Escopo, R. (1965) 'The obligation to remain sick.' *Archives of General Psychiatry 12*, 402–407.

Burvill, E. (1981) 'Suicide in Western Australia, 1967. Analysis of coroners' records.' *Australia and New Zealand Journal of Psychiatry 5*, 37–44.

Butterworth, C. and Skidmore, D. (1981) *Caring for the Mentally Ill.* London: Croom Helm.

Byng-Hall, J. (1980) 'Symptom bearer as marital distance regulator: clinical implications.' *Family Process 19*, 355–365.

Callahan, J. (1996) 'A specific therapeutic approach to suicide risk in borderline clients.' *Clinical Social Work Journal 24*, 443–459.

Cantor, C. and Sheehan, P. (1996) 'Violence and media reports – a connection with Hungerford?' *Archives of Suicide Research 2*, 255–266.

Carlsten, A., Allebeck, P. and Brandt, L. (1996) 'Are suicide rates in Sweden associated with changes in prescribing medicines?' *Acta Psychiatrica Scandinavica 94*, 94–100.

Caudill, W., Redlich, F., Gilmore, H. and Brody, G. (1952) 'Special structure and interaction processes on a psychiatric ward.' *American Journal of Ortho-psychiatry 22*, 314–334.

Chesler, P. (1971) 'Women as psychiatric and psychotherapeutic patients.' *Journal of Marriage and the Family 33*, 746–759.

Chesler, P. (1972) *Women and Madness.* London: Allen Lane.

Cheung, P. (1992) 'Suicide precautions for psychiatric inpatients. A review.' *Australian and New Zealand Journal of Psychiatry 26*, 592–598.

Chuang, H. and Huang, W. (1996a) 'A reexamination of "sociological and economic theories of suicide: A comparison of the USA and Taiwan".' *Social Science and Medicine 43*, 3, 421–423.

Chuang, H. and Huang, W. (1996b) 'A reexamination of "sociological and economic theories of suicide: A comparison of the USA and Taiwan".' *Social Science and Medicine 43*, 3, 421–423.

Cohen, S. and Young, J. (1973) *The Manufacture of News, Deviance, Social Problems and the Media.* London: Constable.

Coser, L. (1962) 'Some functions of deviant behaviour and normal flexibility.' *American Journal of Sociology 68*, 172–181.

Crocker, L. (1952) 'The discussion of suicide in the eighteenth century.' *Journal of the History of Ideas 13*, 47–72.

Croog, S., Lipson, A. and Levine, S. (1972) 'Help patterns in severe illness: the roles of kin network, non-family resources and institutions.' *Journal of Marriage and the Family 34*, 32–41.

Cushman, D. and Whiting, G. (1972) 'An approach to communication theory: toward con census on rules.' *The Journal of Communication 22*, 217–238.

Dallos, R. and Aldridge, D. (1987) 'Handing it on: family constructs, symptoms and choice.' *Journal of Family Therapy 9*, 39–58.

Davies, M., Rose, C. and Cross, K. (1983) 'Life events, social interaction and psychiatric symptoms in general practice: a pilot study.' *Psychological Medicine 13*, 159–163.

Davies, R. (1994) *The Kenneth Williams Diaries.* Glasgow: HarperCollins.

De Moore, G. and Robertson, A. (1996) 'Suicide in the 18 years after deliberate self-harm.' *British Journal of Psychiatry 169*, 489–494.

de Shazer, S. (1982) *Patterns of Brief Therapy: An Ecosystemic Approach.* New York: The Guilford Press.

Dean, P. and Range, L. (1996) 'The escape theory of suicide and perfectionism in college students.' *Death Studies 20*, 4, 415–424.

Debats, D., Drost, J. and Hansen, P. (1995) 'Experiences of meaning in life: A combined qualitative and quantitative approach.' *British Journal of Psychology 86*, Part 3, 359–375.

Decatanzaro, D. (1995) 'Reproductive status, family interactions, and suicidal ideation: Surveys of the general public and high-risk groups.' *Ethology and Sociobiology 16*, 5, 385–394.

Dell, P. (1980) 'Researching the family theories of schizophrenia: an exercise in epistemological confusion.' *Family Process 19*, 321–335.

Dell, P. (1982) 'Beyond homeostasis: toward a concept of coherence.' *Family Process 21*, 21–41.

Dentler, R. and Erikson, K. (1959) 'The function of deviance in groups.' *Social Problems 7*, 98–107.

Denzin, N. (1970) *The Research Act: A Theoretical Introduction to Sociological Methods.* Chicago: Aldine.

Diekstra, R. (1989) 'Suicidal behavior and depressive disorders in adolescents and young adults.' *Neuropsychobiology 22*, 4, 194–207.

Diekstra, R. (1992) 'The prevention of suicidal behavior – evidence for the efficacy of clinical and community-based programs.' *International Journal of Mental Health 21*, 3, 69–87.

Diekstra, R. (1993) 'The epidemiology of suicide and parasuicide.' *Acta Psychiatrica Scandinavica 87*, Suppl. 371, 9–20.

Diekstra, R. (1996) 'The epidemiology of suicide and parasuicide.' *Archives of Suicide Research 2*, 1–29.

Diekstra, R. and Garnefski, N. (1995) 'On the nature, magnitude, and causality of suicidal behaviors: an international perspective.' *Suicide and Life – Threatening Behavior 25*, 1, 36–57.

Dohrenwend, B. and Dohrenwend, B. (1974) *Stressful Life Events: Their Nature and Effects.* New York: John Wiley & Sons.

Dooley, D., Catalano, R., Rook, K. and Serxner, S. (1989) 'Economic stress and suicide: multilevel analyses. Part 1: Aggregate time-series analyses of economic stress and suicide.' *Suicide and Life-Threatening Behavior 19*, 4, 321–36.

Dooley, D., Fielding, J. and Levi, L. (1996) 'Health and unemployment.' *Annual Review of Public Health 17*, 449–465.

Douglas, J. (1967) *The Social Meanings of Suicide.* Princeton, NJ: Princton University Press.

Draper, B. (1996) 'Attempted suicide in old age.' *International Journal of Geriatric Psychiatry 11*, 7, 577–587.

Duck, S. and Spencer, C. (1972) 'Personal constructs and friendship formation.' *Journal of Personality and Social Psychology 23*, 40–45.

Durkheim, E. (1951) *Suicide.* New York: Macmillan.

Durkheim, E. (1958) *The Rules of Sociological Method.* Translated by S.A. Soloray and J.H. Mueller. New York: The Free Press.

Eckstein, H. (1996) 'Culture as a foundation concept for the social sciences.' *Journal of Theoretical Politics 8*, 4, 471–497.

Eggert, L., Thompson, E. and Herting, J. (1994) 'A measure of adolescent potential for suicide (MAPS): Development and preliminary findings.' *Suicide and Life – Threatening Behavior 24*, 4, 359–381.

Eggert, L., Thompson, E., Herting, J. and Nicholas, L. (1995) 'Reducing suicide potential among high-risk youth: Tests of a school-based prevention program.' *Suicide and Life – Threatening Behavior 25*, 2, 276–296.

Erikson, K. (1962) 'Notes on the sociology of deviance.' *Social Problems 9*, 307–314.

Erikson, K. (1966) *Wayward Puritans.* New York: John Wiley and Sons.

Evans, J. (1967) 'Deliberate self poisoning in the Oxford area.' *British Journal of Preventive Medicine 21*, 97–107.

Fagerhaugh, S. and Strauss, A. (1977) *The Politics of Pain Management.* Chicago: Addison Wellesley Publishing Co.

Fagin, L. (1978) *Unemployment and Health in Families.* London: Department of Health and Social Security.

Farmer, R. and Hirsch, S. (1980) *The Suicide Syndrome.* London: Croom Helm.

Favazza, A. and Rosenthal, R. (1993) 'Diagnostic issues in self-mutilation.' *Hospital and Community Psychiatry 44*, 2, 134–140.

Fawcett, J. (1969) 'Suicide: clues from interpersonal communication.' *Archives of General Psychiatry 21*, 129–137.

Fernandez, J. (1974) 'The mission of metaphor in expressive culture.' *Current Anthropology 15*, 119–145.

Ferreira, A. (1968) 'Information exchange and silence in normal and abnormal families.' *Family Process 7*, 251–276.

Finlay-Jones, R. and Brown, G. (1981) 'Types of stressful life events and the onset of anxiety and depressive disorders.' *Psychological Medicine 11*, 7303–815.

Fisch, R., Weakland, J. and Segal, L. (1982) *The Tactics of Change: Doing Therapy Briefly.* San Francisco: Jossey Bass Publishers.

Fishbain, D. (1995) 'Chronic pain and suicide.' *Psychotherapy and Psychosomatics 63*, 1, 54.

Fisher, D. (1992) 'The suicide of a survivor – some intimate perceptions of Bettelheim's suicide.' *Psychoanalytic Review 79*, 4, 591–602.

Folkins, C. (1970) 'Temporal factors and the cognitive mediators of stress reaction.' *Journal of Personality and Social Psychology 14*, 173–184.

Frankel, B., Ferrence, R., Johnson, F. and Whitehead, P. (1976) 'Drinking and self-injury: towards untangling the dynamics.' *British Journal of Addiction 71*, 299–306.

Fransella, F. and Frost, K. (1977) *On Being a Woman: A Review of Research on How Women See Themselves.* London: Tavistock.

Freidson, E. (1975) *Profession of Medicine.* New York: Dodd Mead & Co. Inc.

Freud, S. (1925) *Mourning and Melancholia. Collected Papers, Vol.4.* London: Hogarth Press.

Fry, W. (1962) 'The marital context of an anxiety syndrome.' *Family Process 1*, 245–252.

Fullilove, M. (1996) 'Psychiatric implications of displacement: Contributions from the psychology of place.' *The American Journal of Psychiatry 153*, 12, 1516–1523.

Garfinkel, H. (1956) 'Conditions of successful degradation ceremonies.' *American Journal of Sociology 61*, 420–424.

Garfinkel, H. (1972) 'Common-sense knowledge of social structures: the documentary method of interpretation.' In J.G. and M.E. Marris (eds) *'Symbolic Interaction'. A Reader in Social Psychology*, p.356–378. Boston: Allyn and Bacon Inc.

Garland, A. and Zigler, E. (1993) 'Adolescent suicide prevention – current research and social policy implications.' *American Psychologist 48*, 2, 169–182.

Geertz, C. (1973) *The Interpretation of Cultures.* New York: Basic Books.

Gergen, K. (1991) *The Saturated Self: Dilemmas of Identity in Contemporary Life.* New York: Basic Books.

Ginsburg, G. (1971) 'Public conceptions about attitudes about suicide.' *Journal of Health and Social Behaviour 12*, 201–207.

Glanz, L., Haas, G. and Sweeney, J. (1995) 'Assessment of hopelessness in suicidal patients.' *Clinical Psychology Review 15*, 1, 49–64.

Glaser, B. and Strauss, A. (1965) *Awareness of Dying.* Chicago: Aldine Pub. Co.

Goffman, E. (1959) 'The moral career of the mental patient.' *Psychiatry 22*, 123–142.

Goffman, E. (1961) *Asylums.* New York: Anchor Books, Doubleday & Co.

Gould, M., Fisher, P., Parides, M., Flory, M. and Shaffer, D. (1996) 'Psychosocial risk factors of child and adolescent completed suicide.' *Archives of General Psychiatry 53*, 1155–1162.

Graber, J.A. and Brooksgunn, J. (1995) 'Models of development: Understanding risk in adolescence.' *Suicide and Life – Threatening Behavior 25*, Suppl., 18–25.

Gralnick, A. (1993) 'Suicide in the psychiatric hospital.' *Child Psychiatry and Human Development 24*, 1, 3–12.

Greenblatt, M., Becerra, R. and Serafetinides, E. (1982) 'Social networks and mental health: an overview.' *American Journal of Psychiatry 139*, 977–984.

Greer, S. (1979) 'Psychological enquiry: a contribution to cancer research.' *Psychological Medicine 9*, 81–89.

Gunnell, D. (1994) *The Potential for Preventing Suicide.* Bristol: Health Care Evaluation Unit, University of Bristol.

Gupta, K., Sivakumar, K. and Smeeton, N. (1995) 'Deliberate self-harm: A comparison of first-time cases and cases with a prior history.' *Irish Journal of Psychological Medicine 12*, 4, 131–134.

Gutierrez, P., King, C.A. and Ghaziuddin, N. (1996) 'Adolescent attitudes about death in relation to suicidality.' *Suicide and Life – Threatening Behavior 26*, 1, 8–18.

Haider, I. (1968) 'Suicidal attempts in children and adolescents.' *British Journal of Psychiatry 114*, 133–134.

Hair, H. (1996) 'Expanding the context of family therapy.' *The American Journal of Family Therapy 24*, 4, 291–304.

Haley, J. (1961) 'Control in brief psychotherapy.' *Archives of General Psychiatry 4*, 139–153.

Haley, J. (1976) *Problem Solving Therapy.* San Francisco: Jossey Bass.

Haley, J. (1980) *Leaving Home.* New York: McGraw Hill.

Hall, J. (1997) 'Dirty protests: a phenomenological assessment.' *Medical Science Law 37*, 1, 35–36.

Hansen, D. and Johnson, V. (1979) 'Rethinking family stress theory: Definitional aspects.' In W. Burr, R. Hill, F. Nye and D. Reiss (eds) *Contemporary Theories about the Family.* New York: The Free Press.

Harré, R. and Secord, P. (1973) *The Explanation of Social Behaviour.* Totowa, NJ: Littlefield Adams and Co.

Hawton, K. (1978) 'Deliberate self-poisoning and self-injury in the psychiatric hospital.' *British Journal of Medical Psychology 51*, 253–259.

Hawton, K. (1992) 'By their own hand.' *British Medical Journal 304*, 1000.

Hawton, K. and Catalan, J. (1982) *Attempted Suicide: A Practical Guide to its Nature and Management.* Oxford: Oxford University Press.

Hawton, K., Cole, D., O'Grady, J. and Osborn, M. (1982a) 'Motivational aspects of deliberate self-poisoning in adolescents.' *British Journal of Psychiatry 141*, 286–291.

Hawton, K. and Fagg, J. (1992) 'Deliberate self-poisoning and self-injury in adolescents – a study of characteristics and trends in Oxford, 1976–89.' *British Journal of Psychiatry 161*, 816–823.

Hawton, K., Fagg, J. and Hawkins, M. (1993) 'Factors associated with suicide after parasuicide in young people.' *British Medical Journal 306*, 1641–1644.

Hawton, K., Fagg, J. and Simkin, S. (1996a) 'Deliberate self-poisoning and self-injury in children and adolescents under 16 years of age in Oxford, 1976–1993.' *British Journal of Psychiatry 169*, 2, 202–208.

Hawton, K. and Goldacre, M. (1982) 'Hospital admissions for adverse effects of medicinal agents (mainly self-poisoning) among adolescents in the Oxford region.' *British Journal of Psychiatry 141*, 166–170.

Hawton, K., O'Grady, J., Osborn, M. and Cole, D. (1982b) 'Adolescents who take overdoses: their characteristics, problems and contacts with helping agencies.' *British Journal of Psychiatry 140*, 118–123.

Hawton, K., Ware, C., Mistry, H., Hewitt, J., Kingsbury, S., Roberts, D. and Weitzel, H. (1996b) 'Paracetamol self-poisoning – characteristics, prevention and harm reduction.' *British Journal of Psychiatry 168*, 1, 43–48.

Heather, N. (1979) 'The structure of delinquent values: a repertory grid investigation.' *British Journal of Clinical Psychology 18*, 263–275.

Hedge, B. and Sherr, L. (1995) 'Psychological needs and HIV/AIDS.' *Clinical Psychology and Psychotherapy 2*, 4, 203–209.

Heider, F. (1946) 'Attitudes and cognitive organisation.' *The Journal of Psychology 21*, 107–112.

Heidersohn, F. (1968) 'The deviance of women: a critique and an enquiry.' *British Journal of Sociology* 160–175.

Heikkinen, M., Isometsa, E., Marttunen, M., Aro, H. and Lonnqvist, J. (1995) 'Social factors in suicide.' *British Journal of Psychiatry 167*, 747–753.

Henry, A. and Short, J. (1954) *Suicide and Homicide.* Glencoe: The Free Press.

Henry, C., Stephenson, A., Hanson, M. and Hargett, W. (1993) 'Adolescent suicide and families: An ecological approach.' *Adolescence 28*, 110, 291–308.

Heyman, B. and Shaw, M. (1978) 'Construct of relationship.' *Journal of the Theory of Social Behaviour 8*, 231–262.

Hill, O. (1978) 'The psychological management of psychosomatic diseases.' *British Journal of Psychiatry 131*, 113–126.

Hjelmand, H. and Bjerke, T. (1995) 'Parasuicide in the county of Sor-Trondelag, Norway.' *Social Psychiatry and Psychiatric Epidemiology 31*, 272–283.

Hjelmeland, H. (1995) 'Verbally expressed intentions of parasuicide: 1. Characteristics of patients with various intentions.' *Crisis 16*, 4, 176–181.

Hoffman, L. (1981) *Foundations of Family Therapy: A Conceptual Framework of Systems Change.* New York: Basic Books.

Holding, T., Buglass, D., Duffy, C. and Kreitman, N. (1977) 'Parasuicide in Edinburgh – a seven year review, 1968–1974.' *British Journal of Psychiatry 130*, 534–543.

Holinger, P. and Ofler, D. (1981) 'Prediction of adolescent suicide: a population model.' *American Journal of Psychiatry 139*, 302–306.

Holmes, J. (1982) 'Phobia and counter phobia: family aspects of agoraphobia.' *Journal of Family Therapy 4*, 133–152.

Hopkins, P. (1959) 'Health and happiness and the family.' *British Journal of Clinical Practice 13*, 5, 311–313.

Horesh, N., Rolnick, T., Iancu, I., Dannon, P., Lepkifier, E., Apter, A. and Kotler, M. (1996) 'Coping styles and suicide risk.' *Acta Psychiatrica Scandinavica 93*, 6, 489–493.

Hunter, R. and McAlpine, I. (1963) *Three Hundred Years of Psychiatry.* Oxford: Oxford University Press.

Hurvitz, N. (1973) 'Psychotherapy as a means of social control.' *Journal of Consulting and Clinical Psychology 40*, 232–239.

Hydén, L.-C. (1996) 'Illness and narrative.' *Sociology of Health and Illness 19*, 1, 48–69.

Iga, M. (1996) 'Cultural aspects of suicide: The case of Japanese oyako shinju.' *Archives of Suicide Research 2*, 87–102.

Illich, I. (1977) *Disabling Professions.* London: Marion Boyars.

Inch, H., Rowlands, P. and Soliman, A. (1995) 'Deliberate self-harm in a young offenders' institution.' *Journal of Forensic Psychiatry 6*, 1, 161–171.

Isometsa, E., Heikkinen, M., Henriksson, M., Aro, H. and Lonnqvist, J. (1995a) 'Recent life events and completed suicide in bipolar affective disorder. A comparison with major depressive suicides.' *Journal of Affective Disorders 33*, 2, 99–106.

Isometsa, E., Heikkinen, M., Marttunen, M., Henriksson, M., Aro, H. and Lonnqvist, J. (1995b) 'The last appointment before suicide: Is suicide intent communicated?' *American Journal of Psychiatry 152*, 6, 919–922.

Jackson, D. (1957) 'The question of family homeostasis.' *Psychiatric Quarterly Supplement 31*, 79–90.

Jackson, D. (1965a) 'The study of the family.' *Family Process 4*, 1–20.

Jackson, D. (1965b) 'Family rules: marital quid pro quo.' *Archives of General Psychiatry 12*, 589–594.

Jadhav, S. (1996) 'The cultural origins of Western depression.' *International Journal of Social Psychiatry 42*, 4, 269–286.

Jeffrey, R. (1979) 'Deviant patients in casualty departments.' *Sociology of Health and Illness 1*, 90–108.

Jennings, C. and Barraclough, B. (1980) 'Legal and administrative influences an the English suicide rate since 1900.' *Psychological Medicine 10*, 407–418.

Jobes, D., Berman, A., O'Carroll, P., Eastgard, S. and Knickmeyer, S. (1996) 'The Kurt Cobain suicide crisis: Perspectives from research, public health and the news media.' *Suicide and Life-Threatening Behaviour 26*, 3, 260–271.

Johnson, F., Framkel, B., Harvis, G. and Whitehead, P. (1975) 'Self-injury in London, Canada: a prospective study.' *Canadian Journal of Public Health 66*, 307–316.

Jung, C. (1957) *Psychiatric Studies.* New York: Pantheon.

Kaplan, B., Cassel, J. and Gore, S. (1977) 'Social support and health.' *Medical Care 15*, 45–58.

Karst, T. and Groutt, J. (1977) 'Inside mystical heads: Shared and personal constructs in a commune with some implications for a Personal Construct Theory Social Psychology.' In D. Bannister (eds) *New Perspectives in Personal Construct Theory.* London: Academic Press.

Keeney, B. and Sprenkle, D. (1982) 'Ecosystemic epistemology: critical implications for the aesthetics and pragmatics of family therapy.' *Family Process 21*, 1–19.

Kelleher, M.J., Daly, M. and Kelleher, M.J.A. (1992) 'The influence of antidepressants in overdose on the increased suicide rate in Ireland between 1971 and 1988.' *British Journal of Psychiatry 161*, 625–628.

Kelly, G. (1955) *The Psychology of Personal Constructs*. New York: McGraw Hill.

Kelly, G. (1961) 'Suicide: the personal construct point of view.' In E. Shneidman and N.L. Farebrow (eds) *The Cry for Help*. New York: McGraw Hill.

Kerfoot, M., Dyer, E., Harrington, V., Woodham, A. and Harrington, R. (1996) 'Correlates and short-term course of self-poisoning in adolescents.' *British Journal of Psychiatry 168*, 1, 38–42.

Kessels, N. (1966) 'The respectability of self-poisoning and the fashion of survival.' *Journal of Psychosomatic Research 10*, 29–36.

Kienhorst, I., Dewilde, E., Diekstra, R. and Wolters, W. (1995) 'Adolescents' image of their suicide attempt.' *Journal of the American Academy of Child and Adolescent Psychiatry 34*, 5, 623–628.

King, C., Segal, H., Kaminski, K., Naylor, M., Ghaziuddin, N. and Radpour, L. (1995) 'A prospective study of adolescent suicidal behavior following hospitalization.' *Suicide and Life – Threatening Behavior 25*, 3, 327–338.

King, C., Segal, H., Naylor, M. and Evans, T. (1993) 'Family functioning and suicidal behaviour in adolescent inpatients with mood disorders.' *Journal of the American Academy of Child and Adolescent Psychiatry 32*, 6, 1198–1206.

Kirmayer, L. (1993) 'Healing and the invention of metaphor: The effectiveness of symbols revisited.' *Culture, Medicine and Psychiatry 17*, 161–195.

Koopmans, M. (1995) 'A case of family dysfunction and teenage suicide attempt: Applicability of a family systems paradigm.' *Adolescence 30*, 117, 87–94.

Korzybski, A. (1958) *Science and Sanity*. Connecticut: The Non-Aristotelian Library.

Kozak, D. (1994) 'Reifying the body through the medicalization of violent death.' *Human Organization 53*, 1, 48–54.

Kreitman, N. (1977) *Parasuicide*. Chichester: John Wiley.

Kreitman, N., Smith, P. and Eng-Seong, T. (1969) 'Attempted suicide in social networks.' *British Journal of Preventive Social Medicine 23*, 116–123.

Laing, R. and Esterson, A. (1964) *Sanity, Madness and the Family*. London: Tavistock Publications Ltd.

Latimer, P. (1979) 'Psychophysiologic disorders: a critical appraisal of concept and theory illustrated with reference to the irritable bowel syndrome (IBS).' *Psychological Medicine 9*, 71–80.

Lawless, S., Kippax, S. and Crawford, J. (1996) 'Dirty, diseased and undeserving. The positioning of HIV positive women.' *Social Science and Medicine 43*, 9, 1371–1377.

Lazarus, R. (1974) 'Psychological stress and coping in adaptation and illness.' *International Journal of Psychiatry in Medicine 5*, 321–333.

Lazarus, R. and Averill, J. (1972) *Anxiety: Current Trends in Theory and Research*. New York: Academic Press.

Leach, E. (1976) *Culture and Communication: The Logic by Which Symbols are Connected*. London: Cambridge University Press.

Leenaars, A. (1996) 'Suicide: A multidimensional malaise.' *Suicide and Life-Threatening Behaviour 26*, 3, 221–236.

Leenaars, A. and Lester, D. (1996) 'Testing the cohort size hypothesis of suicide and homicide rate in Canada and the United States.' *Archives for Suicide Research 2*, 43–54.

Leonard, P. (1996) 'Three discourse on practice: A postmodern re-appraisal.' *Journal of Sociology and Social Welfare XXIII*, 2, 7–26.

Lester, D. (1968) 'Attempted suicide as a hostile act.' *The Journal of Psychology 68*, 243–248.

Lester, D. (1969) 'Resentment and dependency in the suicidal individual.' *The Journal of General Psychology 81*, 137–145.

Lester, D. and Leenaars, A. (1996) 'The ethics of suicide and suicide prevention.' *Death Studies 20*, 2, 163–184.

Lester, G. and Lester, D. (1971) *Suicide: The Gamble with Death.* Englewood Cliffs, NJ: Prentice Hall.

Levine, R. and Reicher, S. (1996) 'Making sense of symptoms: Self-categorization and the meanings of illness and injury.' *British Journal of Social Psychology 35*, 245–256.

Levy, S., Jurkovic, G. and Spirito, A. (1995) 'A multisystems analysis of adolescent suicide attempters.' *Journal of Abnormal Child Psychology 23*, 2, 221–234.

Liazos, A. (1972) 'The poverty of the sociology of deviance: nuts, sluts and perverts.' *Social Problems 20*, 103–120.

Lindsay, J. (1973) 'Suicide in the Auckland area.' *The New Zealand Medical Journal 77*, 149–157.

Linn, M. and Lester, D. (1996) 'Content differences in suicide notes by gender and age: Serendipitous findings.' *Psychological Reports 78*, 2, 370.

Lish, J., Zimmerman, M., Farber, N., Lush, D., Kuzma, M. and Plescia, G. (1996) 'Suicide screening in a primary care setting at a veterans affairs medical center.' *Psychosomatics 37*, 5, 413–424.

Littlewood, R. (1996) 'Psychiatry's culture.' *International Journal of Social Psychiatry 42*, 4, 245–268.

Litwak, E. and Szeleny, I. (1969) 'Primary group structures and their functions: kin, neighbours and friends.' *American Sociological Review 34*, 465–481.

Livingston, R., Witt, A. and Smith, G. (1995) 'Families who somatize.' *Journal of Developmental and Behavioral Pediatrics 16*, 1, 42–46.

Lockridge, L. (1995) 'Least likely suicide: The search for my father, Ross Lockridge, Jr., author of Raintree County.' *Suicide and Life – Threatening Behavior 25*, 4, 429–436.

Lofland, J. (1969) *Deviance and Identity.* Englewood Cliffs, NJ: Prentice Hall Inc.

Lukianowicz, N. (1972) 'Suicidal behavior: an attempt to modify the environment.' *British Journal of Psychiatry 121*, 387–390.

Madanes, C. (1981) *Strategic Family Therapy.* San Francisco: Jossey Bass.

Maris, R. (1995) 'Suicide prevention in adults (age 30–65).' *Suicide and Life – Threatening Behavior 25*, 1, 171–179.

Maris, R. and Silverman, M. (1995) 'Suicide prevention: Toward the year 2000 – Postscript: Summary and synthesis.' *Suicide and Life – Threatening Behavior 25*, 1, 205–209.

Marks, J., Goldberg, D. and Hillier, V. (1979) 'Determinants of the ability of general practitioners to detect psychiatric illness.' *Psychological Medicine 9*, 337–353.

Markush, R. (1974) 'Mental epidemics – a review of the told to prepare for the new.' *Public Health Reviews 11*, 4, 353–442.

Martin, G. (1996) 'The influence of television suicide in a normal adolescent population.' *Archives of Suicide Research 2*, 103–117.

Martin, G., Rozanes, P., Pearce, C. and Allison, S. (1995) 'Adolescent suicide, depression and family dysfunction.' *Acta Psychiatrica Scandinavica 92*, 5, 336–344.

Mastekaasa, A. (1995) 'Age variations in the suicide rates and self-reported subjective well-being of married and never married persons.' *Journal of Community and Applied Social Psychology 5*, 1, 21–39.

Matschinger, H. and Angermeyer, M. (1996) 'Lay beliefs about the causes of mental disorders: a new methodological approach.' *Social Psychiatry and Psychiatric Epidemiology 31*, 309–315.

Maturana, U. and Varela, F. (1980) *Autopoiesis and Cognition: The Realization of the Living.* Dordrecht, Holland: Reidel.

Mauk, G. and Rodgers, P. (1994) 'Building bridges over troubled waters – school-based postvention with adolescent survivors of peer suicide.' *Crisis Intervention and Time – Limited Treatment 1*, 2, 103–123.

McClure, M. (1984) 'Trends in suicide rate for England and Wales 1975–1980.' *British Journal of Psychiatry 144*, 119–126.

McClure, M. (1994) 'Suicide in children and adolescents in England and Wales 1960–1990.' *British Journal of Psychiatry 165*, 510–514.

Mccrea, P.H. (1996) 'Trends in suicide in Northern Ireland: 1922–1992.' *Irish Journal of Psychological Medicine 13*, 1, 9–12.

McCulloch, J. and Philip, A. (1972) *Suicidal Behaviour.* Oxford: Pergamon Press.

McFarlane, A., Norman, G., Streiner, D. and Roy, R. (1983) 'The process of social stress: stable, reciprocating and mediating relationships.' *Journal of Health and Social Behaviour 24*, 160–173.

McGovern, J. (1996) 'Management of risk in psychiatric rehabilitation.' *The Psychologist* September, 405–408.

McLaughlin, J., Miller, P. and Warwick, H. (1996) 'Deliberate self harm in adolescents: hopelessness, depression, problems and problem-solving.' *Journal of Adolescence 19*, 523–532.

Mcloone, P. and Crombie, I. (1996) 'Hospitalisation for deliberate self-poisoning in Scotland from 1981 to 1993: Trends in rates and types of drugs used.' *British Journal of Psychiatry 169*, 1, 81–85.

McNeil, G. and Vance, S. (1978) *Cruel and Unusual.* Toronto: Deneau and Greenberg.

McPhail, C. (1972) 'Student walkout: a fortuitous examination of elementary collective behaviour.' In J. Manis and B. Meltzer (eds) *Symbolic Interaction.* Boston: Allyn and Bacon Inc.

Mead, G. (1925) 'The genesis of self and social control.' *International Journal of Ethics 35,* 251–273.

Mead, G. (1934) *Mind, Self and Society.* Chicago: Chicago University Press.

Mechanic, D. (1966a) 'Perception of parental responses to illness: a research note.' *Journal of Health and Human Behaviour 6,* 253–257.

Mechanic, D. (1966b) 'Response factors in illness: the study of illness behaviour.' *Social Psychiatry 1,* 11–20.

Mechanic, D. (1974) 'Social structure and personal adaptation: some neglected dimensions.' In G. Coelho, D. Hamburg and J. Adams (eds) *Coping and Adaptation.* New York: Basic Books.

Michel, K., Valach, L. and Waeber, V. (1994) 'Understanding deliberate self-harm: The patient's views.' *Crisis 15,* 4, 172–178.

Miller, F. and Bashkin, E. (1974) 'Depersonalisation and self-mutilation.' *Psychoanalytic Quarterly 43,* 638–649.

Miner, J.R. (1922) 'Suicide in relation to climatic and other factors.' *American Journal of Hygiene 2,* 111.

Minuchin, S. (1974) *Families and Family Therapy.* Cambridge, Mass: Harvard University Press.

Mireault, M. and De Man, A. (1996) 'Suicidal ideation among the elderly: Personal variables, stress and social support.' *Social Behavior and Personality 26,* 4, 385–392.

Mishler, E. and Waxler, N. (1965) 'Family interaction processes and schizophrenia: A review of current theories.' *Merril-Palmer Quarterly 11,* 269–315.

Morgan, H. (1979) *Death Wishes? The Understanding and Management of Deliberate Self Harm.* Chichester: John Wiley.

Morgan, H., Barton, J. and Pottle, S. (1976) 'Deliberate self-harm: a follow-up study of 179 patients.' *British Journal of Psychiatry 128,* 361–368.

Morrell, S., Taylor, R., Quine, S. and Kerr, C. (1993) 'Suicide and unemployment in Australia 1907–1990.' *Social Science and Medicine 36,* 6, 749–756.

Morrison, G. and Collier, J. (1969) 'Family treatment approaches to suicidal children and adolescents.' *Journal of American Academy of Child Psychiatry 8,* 140.

Moscicki, E. (1995) 'Epidemiology of suicidal behavior.' *Suicide and Life – Threatening Behavior 25,* 1, 22–35.

Mulder, R., Wells, J., Joyce, P. and Bushnell, J. (1994) 'Antisocial women.' *Journal of Personality Disorders 8,* 4, 279–287.

Murthy, V. (1969) 'Personality and the nature of suicide attempts.' *British Journal of Psychiatry 115,* 791–795.

Myers, J., Jacobs, J. and Pepper, M. (1972) 'Life events and mental status: a longitudinal study.' *Health and Social Behaviour 13,* 398–406.

Nisbett, R. (1973) 'Behaviour as seen by the actor and the observer.' *Journal of Personality and Social Psychology 27,* 154–164.

Nordentoft, M., Breum, L., Munck, L., Nordestgaard, A., Hunding, A. and Bjaeldager, A. (1993) 'High mortality by natural and unnatural causes: a 10 year follow-up study of patients admitted to a poisoning treatment centre after suicide attempts.' *British Medical Journal 306,* 1637–1641.

O'Brien, S. and Farmer, R. (1980) 'The role of life events in the aetiology of episodes of self-poisoning.' In R. Farmer and S. Hirsch (eds) *The Suicide Syndrome.* London: Croom Helm.

O'Connor, W. and Stachowiak, J. (1971) 'Patterns of interaction in families with low adjusted, high adjusted and mentally retarded members.' *Family Process 10,* 229–241.

Odonnell, C.R. (1995) 'Firearm deaths among children and youth.' *American Psychologist 50,* 9, 771–776.

Odonnell, I. and Farmer, R. (1995) 'The limitations of official suicide statistics.' *British Journal of Psychiatry 166,* 458–461.

Odonnell, I., Farmer, R. and Catalan, J. (1996) 'Explaining suicide: The views of survivors of serious suicide attempts.' *British Journal of Psychiatry 168,* 6, 780–786.

Ohberg, A., Lonnqvist, J., Sarna, S. and Vuori, E. (1996) 'Violent methods associated with high suicide mortality among the young.' *Journal of the American Academy of Child and Adolescent Psychiatry 35,* 2, 144–153.

Ovenstone, I. and Kreitman, N. (1974) 'Two syndromes of suicide.' *British Journal of Psychiatry 24,* 1, 336–345.

Pallis, D., Levewy, A., Jenkins, J. and Sainsbury, P. (1982) 'Estimating suicide risk among attempted suicides I. The development of new clinical scales.' *British Journal of Psychiatry 141,* 37–44.

Pang, A., Catalan, J. and Booth, J. (1996) 'Audit of a multi-disciplinary assessment unit for deliberate self-harm patients in a general hospital.' *Archives of Suicidal Research 2,* 207–212.

Parker, A. (1981) 'The meaning of attempted suicide to young parasuicides: a repertory grid study.' *British Journal of Psychology 139,* 306–312.

Parker, R. (1994) 'Ritualised self harm in traditional Aboriginal society.' *Australian and New Zealand Journal of Psychiatry 28,* 4, 696–697.

Parker, R. (1995) 'Conflicting constructions of Aboriginal suicide: reply.' *Australian and New Zealand Journal of Psychiatry 29,* 2, 337.

Parsons, T. (1951) *The Social System.* New York: Free Press.

Paykel, E. (1978) 'Contributing life events to causation of psychiatric illness.' *Psychological Medicine 8,* 245–253.

Paykel, E., Myers, J., Underthal, J. and Tanner, J. (1974) 'Suicidal feelings in the general population: a prevalence study.' *British Journal of Psychiatry 124,* 460–469.

Paykel, E., Prusoff, B. and Myers, J. (1975) 'Suicide attempts and recent life events: a controlled comparison.' *Archives of General Psychiatry 32,* 327–333.

Payne, B. and Range, L. (1996) 'Family environment, depression, attitudes toward life and death, and suicidality in young adults.' *Death Studies 20,* 3, 237–246.

Payne, B.J. and Range, L.M. (1995) 'Attitudes toward life and death and suicidality in young adults.' *Death Studies 19,* 6, 559–569.

Pearce, W. (1976) *The coordinated management of meaning: a rules based theory of personal communication*. San Francisco: Sage.

Pearce, W. and Cronen, V. (1980) *Communication, Action and Meaning*. New York: Praeger Scientific.

Pearce, W., Cronen, V. and Conklin, F. (1979) 'On what to look for when analysing communication: an hierarchical model of actors' meanings.' *Communication 4*, 195–220.

Pelz, E. (1965) *Some Factors in 'Group Decision'*. New York: Holt, Reinhart and Winston.

Penn, P. (1982) 'Circular questioning.' *Family Process 21*, 267–280.

Pfohl, S. (1977) 'The "discovery" of child abuse.' *Social Problems 24*, 310–323.

Pleasants, N. (1996) 'Nothing is concealed: De-centring tacit knowledge and rules from social theory.' *Journal for the Theory of Social Behaviour 26*, 3, 233–255.

Power, C. and Manor, O. (1992) 'Explaining social class differences in psychological health among young adults: a longitudunal perspective.' *Social Psychiatry and Psychiatric Epidemiology 27*, 284–291.

Powers, W. (1973) *Behaviour: The Control of Perception*. Chicago: Aldine.

Pritchard, C. (1996a) 'New patterns of suicide by age and gender in the United Kingdom and the Western World 1974–1992; An indicator of social change?' *Social Psychiatry and Psychiatric Epidemiology 31*, 3–4, 227–234.

Procter, H. 1981 'Family construct psychology.' In S. Walrond-Skinner (ed) *Family Therapy and Approaches*. London: Routledge and Kegan Paul.

Psathas, G. (1968) 'Ethnomethods and phenomenology.' *Social Research 35*, 3, 500–520.

Quarnatelli, E. (1960) 'A note on the protective function of the family in disasters.' *Marriage and Family Living 22*, 263–264.

Rank, O. (1969) *The Myth of the Birth of the Hero*. New York: Vintage Books.

Rapoport, R. (1965) 'Normal crises, family structure and mental health.' In H. Parad (ed) *Crisis Intervention*. New York: Family Service Association.

Reich, J., Newsom, J. and Zautra, A. (1996) 'Health downturns and predictors of suicidal ideation: An application of the Baumeister model.' *Suicide and Life-Threatening Behavior 26*, 3, 282–291.

Reiss, D. (1967) 'Individual thinking and family interaction. II. A study of pattern recognition and hypothesis testing in families of normals, character disorders and schizophrenics.' *Journal of Psychiatric Research 5*, 193–211.

Reiss, D. (1971) 'Varieties of consensual experience, 1. A theory of relating family interaction to individual thinking, 11. Dimensions of a family's experience of it's environment.' *Family Process 10*, 1–35.

Reiss, D. (1981) *The Family's Construction of Reality*. Cambridge, Mass: Harvard University Press.

Retterstol, N. (1993) 'Death due to overdose of antidepressants – experiences from Norway.' *Acta Psychiatrica Scandinavica 87*, Suppl. 371, 28–32.

Richman, J. (1978) 'Symbiosis, empathy, suicidal behaviour and the family.' *Suicide and Life-Threatening Behaviour 8*, 139–148.

Richman, J. (1979) 'The family therapy of attempted suicide.' *Family Process 18*, 131–142.

Richman, J. and Rosenbaum, M. (1970) 'A clinical study of the role of hostility and death wishes by the family and society in suicidal attempts.' *Israel Annals of Psychiatry and Related Disciplines 8*, 213–231.

Rihmer, Z. (1996) 'Strategies of suicide prevention: focus on health care.' *Journal of Affective Disorders 39*, 2, 83–91.

Rihmer, Z., Rutz, W. and Pihlgren, H. (1995) 'Depression and suicide on Gotland – An intensive study of all suicides before and after a depression-training programme for general practitioners.' *Journal of Affective Disorders 35*, 4, 147–152.

Rippere, V. (1981) 'Depression, common sense and psychosocial evolution.' *British Journal of Medical Psychology 54*, 379–387.

Roberts, J. and Hawton, K. (1980) 'Child abuse and attempted suicide.' *British Journal of Psychiatry 137*, 319–323.

Robinson, D. (1971) *The Process of Becoming Ill*. London: Routledge and Kegan Paul Ltd.

Rogers, C. (1951) *Client Centred Therapy*. Boston: Houghton Mifflin.

Rosen, G. (1971) 'History in the study of suicide.' *Psychological Medicine 1*, 267–285.

Rosenbaum, M. and Richman, J. (1970) 'Suicide: the role of hostility and death wishes from the family and significant others.' *American Journal of Psychiatry 126*, 1652–1654.

Rosenbaum, M. and Richman, J. (1972) 'Family dynamics and drug overdoses.' *Suicide and Life-Threatening Behaviour 2*, 19–25.

Rosenthal, R., Rinzler, C., Walsh, R. and Klausner, E. (1972) 'Wrist cutting syndrome: the meaning of a gesture.' *American Journal of Psychiatry 128*, 47–52.

Rosenwald, G. and Ochberg, R. (1992) *Storied Lives: The Cultural Politics of Self-understanding*. New Haven: Yale University Press.

Ross, R. and McKay, H. (1979) *Self Mutilation*. New York: Lexington Books.

Rotheram-Borus, M.J., Trautman, P.D., Dopkins, S.C. and Shrout, P.E. (1990) 'Cognitive style and pleasant activities among female adolescent suicide attempters.' *Journal of Consulting Clinical Psychology 58*, 5, 554–561.

Rotheram-Borus, M.J., Trautman, P.D., Dopkins, S.C. and Shrout, P.E. (1996) 'Enhancing treatment adherence with a specialized emergency room program for adolescent suicide attempters.' *Journal of the American Academy of Child and Adolescent Psychiatry 35*, 5, 654–663.

Rudd, M., Joiner, T. and Hasan Rajab, M. (1996) 'Relationships among suicide ideators, attempters and multiple attempters in a young adult sample.' *Journal of Abnormal Psychology 105*, 4, 541–550.

Runeson, B., Eklund, G. and Wasserman, D. (1996) 'Living conditions of suicide attempters: a case control study.' *Acta Psychiatrica Scandinavica 94*, 125–132.

Ryle, A. and Breen, D. (1972) 'A comparison of adjusted and maladjusted couples using the double dyed grid.' *British Journal of Medical Psychology 45*, 375–382.

Sadowski, C. and Kelley, M. (1993) 'Social problem-solving in suicidal adolescents.' *Journal of Consulting and Clinical Psychology 61*, 1, 121–127.

Sainsbury, P. and Jenkins, J. (1982) 'The accuracy of officially reported suicide statistics for purposes of epidemiological research.' *Journal of Epidemiology and Community Health 36*, 43–48.

Sale, I., Williams, C., Clark, J. and Mills, J. (1975) 'Suicide behavior: community attitudes and beliefs.' *Suicide 5*, 158–168.

Sands, R. (1996) 'The elusiveness of identity in social work practice with women: A postmodern feminist perspective.' *Clinical Social Work Journal 24*, 2, 167–186.

Sapir, E. (1949) *Selected Writings in Language Culture and Personality.* San Francisco: University California Press.

Sapsford, R. (1983) *Life Sentence Prisoners.* Milton Keynes: Open University Press.

Saunderson, T. and Langford, I. (1996) 'A study of the geographical distribution of suicide rates in England and Wales 1989–92 using empirical bayes estimates.' *Social Science and Medicine 43*, 4, 489–502.

Schachter, S. and Singer, S. (1962) 'Cognitive, social and psychological determinants of emotional state.' *Psychological Review 69*, 379–399.

Scheff, T. (1968) 'Negotiating reality: notes on power in the assessment of responsibility.' *Social Problems 16*, 3–17.

Schmidtke, A., Billebrahe, U., Deleo, D., Kerkof, A., Bjerke, T., Crepet, P., Haring, C., Hawton, K., Lonnqvist, J., Michel, K., Pommereau, X., Querejeta, I., Phillipe, I., Salanderrenberg, E., Temesvary, B., Wasserman, D., Fricke, S., Weinacker, B. and Sampaiofaria, J. (1996) 'Attempted suicide in Europe: Rates, trends and sociodemographic characteristics of suicide attempters during the period 1989–1992. Results of the WHO/EURO Multicentre Study on Parasuicide.' *Acta Psychiatrica Scandinavica 93*, 5, 327–338.

Schrut, A. (1968) 'Some typical patterns in the behavior and background of adolescent girls who attempt suicide.' *American Journal of Psychiatry 125*, 69–74.

Schuman, A. (1970) 'Power relations in emotionally disturbed and normal family triads.' *Journal of Abnormal Psychology 75*, 30–37.

Schwab, J. and Schwab, M. (1978) *Sociocultural Roots of Mental Illness.* New York: Plenum Medical Book Co.

Schwarz, S. (1996) 'Shrinking: a postmodern perspective on psychiatric case histories.' *South African Journal of Psychology 26*, 3, 150–156.

Searles, H. (1965) 'Schizophrenia and the inevitability of death.' *American Journal of Psychiatry 138*, 84–87.

Seguin, M., Lesage, A. and Kiely, M. (1995) 'Parental bereavement after suicide and accident: A comparative study.' *Suicide and Life – Threatening Behavior 25*, 4, 489–498.

Selvini-Palazzoli, M. (1983) 'The emergence of a comprehensive systems approach.' *Journal of Family Therapy 5*, 165–177.

Selvini-Palazzoli, M., Boscolo, L., Cecchin, G. and Prata, G. (1973) *Paradox and Counterparadox.* New York: Jason Aronson.

Selvini-Palazzoli, M., Boscolo, L., Cecchin, G. and Prata, G. (1980) 'Hypothesising-circularity-neutrality. Three guide-lines for the conductors of the session.' *Family Process 19*, 3–11.

Senay, E. and Redlich, F. (1968) 'Cultural and social factors in neuroses and psychosomatic illness.' *Social Psychiatry 3*, 89–97.

Shepherd, D. and Barraclough, B. (1980) 'Work and suicide: an empirical investigation.' *British Journal of Psychiatry 136*, 469–478.

Sherif, M. (1965) 'Foundations of social norms: the experimental paradigm.' In H. Proshansky and B. Seidenberg (eds) *Basic Studies in Social Psychology*. London: Holt Reinhart and Wilson.

Shibutani, T. (1962) 'Reference groups and social control.' In A. Rose (eds) *Human Behaviour and Social Processes*. London: Routledge and Kegan Paul.

Shneidman, E. (1993a) 'Commentary: suicide as psychache.' *Journal of Nervous and Mental Disease 181*, 3, 145–147.

Shneidman, E. (1993b) 'Some controversies in suicidology: towards a mentalistic discipline.' *Suicide and Life-Threatening Behavior 23*, 4, 292–298.

Siegal, L. and Fried, J. (1955) 'The threat of suicide.' *Diseases of the Nervous System 16*, 45.

Sifneos, P. (1966) 'Manipulative suicide.' *Psychiatric Quarterly 40*, 525–537.

Silverman, E., Range, L. and Overholser, J. (1995) 'Bereavement from suicide as compared to other forms of bereavement.' *Omega – Journal of Death and Dying 30*, 1, 41–51.

Silverman, M. and Maris (1995) 'The prevention of suicidal behaviors: an overview.' *Suicide and Life – Threatening Behavior 25*, 1, 10–21.

Silverman, M.M. and Felner, R.D. (1995) 'The place of suicide prevention in the spectrum of intervention: Definitions of critical terms and constructs.' *Suicide and Life – Threatening Behavior 25*, 1, 70–81.

Simkin, S., Hawton, K., Whitehead, L., Fagg, J. and Eagle, M. (1995) 'Media influence on parasuicide – A study of the effects of a television drama portrayal of paracetamol self-poisoning.' *British Journal of Psychiatry 167*, 754–759.

Singh, G.K. and Yu, S.M. (1996) 'US childhood mortality, 1950 through 1993: Trends and socioeconomic differentials.' *American Journal of Public Health 86*, 4, 505–512.

Sjoberg, L. (1969) 'Alcohol and gambling.' *Psychopharmacologia 14*, 284–298.

Skinner, B. (1953) *Science and Human Behaviour*. New York: Macmillan.

Sluzki, C. (1981) 'Process of symptom production and patterns of symptom maintenance.' *Journal of Marital Therapy 7*, 273–280.

Sluzki, C. and Veron, E. (1971) 'The double bind as a universal pathogenic situation.' *Family Process 18*, 397–410.

Soal, J. and Kottler, A. (1996) 'Damaged, deficient or determined? Deconstructing narratives in family therapy.' *South African Journal of Psychology 26*, 3, 123–134.

Sonneck, G. and Wagner, R. (1996) 'Suicide and burnout of physicians.' *Omega Journal of Death and Dying 33*, 3, 255–263.

Speck, R. and Attneave, C. (1973) *Family Networks: Retribalisation and Healing*. New York: Pantheon.

Speer, D. (1970) 'Family systems: morphostasis and morphogenesis or Is homeostasis enough?' *Family Process 9*, 3, 259–278.

Spickard, J. (1994) 'Body, nature and culture in spiritual healing.' In H. Johannessen, S. Olesen and J. Andersen (eds), *Studies in Alternative Therapy 2*. Odense: Odense University Press.

Stack, S. (1996) 'The impact of relative cohort size on national suicide trends, 1950–1980: A comparative analysis.' *Archive of Suicide Research 2*, 213–222.

Starrin, B., Larsson, G., Brenner, S., Levi, L. and Petterson, I. (1990) 'Structural changes, ill health, and mortality in Sweden, 1963–1983: a macroaggregated study.' *International Journal of Health Services 20*, 1, 27–42.

Stenager, E. and Jensen, K. (1994) 'Attempted suicide and contact with the primary health authorities.' *Acta Psychiatrica Scandinavica 90*, 109–113.

Stengel, E. (1958) *Attempted Suicide: Its Social Significance and Effects*. Oxford: Oxford University Press.

Stengel, E. (1962) 'Recent research into suicide and attempted suicide.' *American Journal of Psychiatry 118*, 726.

Stotland, N. (1997) 'Refusal of medical treatment: Psychiatric emergency.' *The American Journal of Psychiatry 154*, 1, 106–108.

Suh, E., Diener, E. and Fujita, F. (1996) 'Events and subjective well-being: Only recent events matter.' *Journal of Personality and Social psychology 70*, 5, 1091–1102.

Summers, A. (1992) *Goddess: The Secret Lives of Marilyn Monroe*. London: Vista.

Suominen, K., Henriksson, M., Suokas, J., Isometsa, E., Ostamo, A. and Lonnqvist, J. (1996) 'Mental disorders and comorbidity in attempted suicide.' *Acta Psychiatrica Scandinavica 94*, 234–240.

Szasz, T. (1986) 'The case against suicide prevention.' *American Psychologist 41*, 1, 806–812.

Tabachnick, N. (1961) 'Interpersonal relations in suicide attempts.' *Archives of General Psychiatry 4*, 42–47.

Tajfel, H. (1969) 'Social and cultural factors in perception.' In G.L. and E. Aronson (eds) *The Handbook of Social Psychology*. Reading, Mass: Addison-Wesley.

Tanney, B. (1995) 'Suicide prevention in Canada: A national perspective highlighting progress and problems.' *Suicide and Life – Threatening Behavior 25*, 1, 105–122.

Teicher, J. and Jacobs, J. (1966) 'Adolescents who attempt suicide.' *American Journal of Psychiatry 122*, 1248–1257.

Topp, D. (1979) 'Suicide in prison.' *British Journal of Psychiatry 134*, 24–27.

Toulmin, S. (1964) *The Uses of Argument*. London: Cambridge University Press.

Towl, G. (1996) 'Homicide and suicide:assessing risk in prisons.' *The Psychologist* September, 398–400.

Trovato, F. (1986) 'A time series analysis of international immigration and suicide mortality in Canada.' *International Journal of Social Psychiatry 32*, 2, 38–46.

Trovato, F. (1992) 'A Durkheimian analysis of youth suicide: Canada, 1971–1981.' *Suicide and Life-Threatening Behavior 22*, 4, 413–427.

Tschudi, F. (1977) 'Loaded and honest questions.' In D. Bannister (eds) *New Perspectives in Personal Construct Theory*. London: Academic Press.

Tuckman, J. and Connor, H. (1962) 'Attempted suicide in adolescents.' *American Journal of Psychiatry 119*, 228–232.

Tuckman, J. and Youngman, W. (1964) 'Attempted suicide and family organisation.' *Journal of Genetic Psychology 105*, 187–193.

Tuckman, J., Youngman, W. and Leifer, B. (1966) 'Suicide and family disorganisation.' *International Journal of Social Psychiatry 12*, 187–191.

van Geert, P. (1996) 'Commentary.' *Human Development 39*, 195–199.

Vanpoppel, F. and Day, L.H. (1996) 'A test of Durkheim's theory of suicide – Without committing the "ecological fallacy".' *American Sociological Review 61*, 3, 500–507.

Varela, F. and Johnson, D. (1976) 'On observing natural systems.' *Co-evolution Quarterly 10*, 26–31.

Viinamaki, H., Kontula, O., Niskanen, L. and Koskela, K. (1995) 'The association between economic and social factors and mental health in Finland.' *Acta Psychiatrica Scandinavica 92*, 3, 208–213.

Warde, A. (1994) 'Consumption, identity-formation and uncertainty.' *Sociology 28*, 4, 877–898.

Wassenaar, D. (1987) 'Brief strategic therapy and the management of adolescent Indian parasuicide patients in the general hospital setting.' *South African Journal of Psychology 17*, 93–98.

Wasserman, I. and Stack, S. (1993) 'The effect of religion on suicide: An analysis of cultural context.' *Omega – Journal of Death and Dying 27*, 4, 295–305.

Watt, J. (1996) 'The family, love, and suicide in early modern Geneva.' *Journal of Family History 21*, 1, 63–86.

Watzlawick, P. and Beavin, J. (1967) 'Some formal aspects of communication.' *American Behavioural Scientist 10*, 4–8.

Watzlawick, P., Beavin, J. and Jackson, D. (1967) *Pragmatics of Human Communication*. New York: W.W. Norton and Co.

Watzlawick, P. and Weakland, J. (1977) *The Interactional View*. New York: W.W. Norton.

Watzlawick, P., Weakland, J. and Fisch, R. (1974) *Change: Principles of Problem Formation and Problem Resolution*. New York: W.W. Norton & Co.

Waxler, N. (1975) 'The normality of deviance: an alternative explanation of schizophrenia in the family.' *Schizophrenia Bulletin I*, 38–47.

Weakland, J., Fisch, R., Watzlawick, P. and Bodin, A. (1974) 'Brief Therapy: focused problem resolution.' *Family Process 13*, 141–169.

Wells, N. (1981) *Suicide and Deliberate Self-Harm*. London: Office of Health Economics, No.69wx.

Wenzel, S. (1967) *The Sin of Sloth: Acedia in Medieval Thought and Literature*. Chapel Hill: University of North Carolina Press.

Wetzler, S., Asnis, G., Hyman, R., Virtue, C., Zimmerman, J. and Rathus, J. (1996) 'Characteristics of suicidality among adolescents.' *Suicide and Life – Threatening Behavior 26*, 1, 37–45.

Weyerer, S. and Wiedenmann, A. (1995) 'Economic factors and the rates of suicide in Germany between 1881 and 1989.' *Psychological Reports 76*, 3 Part 2, 1331–1341.

Whitaker, C. (1973) 'My philosophy of psychotherapy.' *Journal of Contemporary Psychotherapy 6*, 49–52.

Whitfield, W. and Southern, D. (1996) 'The prevention of suicide: some practical steps.' *Journal of the Royal Society of Health 116*, 5, 295–298.

Wiggins, J., Dill, F. and Schwartz, R. (1965) 'On "status liability".' *Sociometry 28*, 197–209.

Wilbraham, L. (1996) '"Few of us are potential Miss South Africas, but…": Psychological discourses about women's bodies in advice columns.' *South African Journal of Psychology 26*, 3, 162–171.

Wilde, E., Kienhorst, I., Diekstra, R. and Wolters, W. (1992) 'The relationship between adolescent suicidal behaviour and life events in childhood and adolescence.' *American Journal of Psychiatry 149*, 1, 45–51.

Wildes, K. (1996) 'Death: A persistent controversial state.' *Kennedy Institute of Ethics Journal 6*, 4, 378–381.

Wilkins, J. (1967) 'Suicidal behaviour.' *American Sociological Review 32*, 268–298.

Williams, C. and Lyons, C. (1976) 'Family interaction and adolescent suicidal behaviour: a preliminary investigation.' *Australian and New Zealand Journal of Psychiatry 10*, 243–252.

Winter, W., Ferreira, A. and Bowers, N. (1973) 'Decision-making in married and unrelated couples.' *Family Process 12*, 83–99.

Wright, K. (1976) 'Exploring the uniqueness of common complaints.' *British Journal of Medical Psychology 43*, 221–232.

Yang, B. and Clum, G.A. (1996) 'Effects of early negative life experiences on cognitive functioning and risk for suicide: A review.' *Clinical Psychology Review 16*, 3, 177–195.

Young, D. (1994) 'Behaviors and attributions – Family views of adolescent psychopathology.' *Journal of Adolescent Research 9*, 4, 427–441.

Young, T. and French, L. (1995) 'Status integration and suicide among Native American women.' *Social Behavior and Personality 23*, 2, 155–158.

Zborowski, M. (1952) 'Cultural components in responses to pain.' *Journal of Social Issues 4*, 16–30.

Zhang, J. (1996) 'Suicides in Beijing, China, 1992–1993.' *Suicide and Life – Threatening Behavior 26*, 2, 175–180.

Zola, I. (1966) 'Culture and symptoms: an analysis of patients presenting complaints.' *American Sociological Review 31*, 615–629.

Zola, I. (1972) 'Medicine as an institution of social control.' *Sociological Review 20*, 487–504.

Subject Index

Author Index